CCAR Journal
The Reform Jewish Quarterly

Spiritual and Mental Wellness

Contents

FROM THE GUEST EDITORS
At the Gates — בשערים 1
Lisa Sari Bellows and Sue Levi Elwell

ARTICLES
SELF-CARE IN TIMES OF TRAUMA
When the Rabbi Feels Trauma 4
Paul Kipnes

Unconsumed: Emotional Resilience through Fiery Times 15
Stephanie Kramer

**Timeline of a Trigger: A Personal Journey Toward
    Healing Complex PTSD** 24
Paul Jacobson

Healing from Pain 37
Stephen Robbins

Thoughts on a Living God 43
Richard Agler

SPIRITUAL PRACTICES AND LIFELONG WELLNESS
**Embodied Spiritual Practices: Cultivating Sense
    Perceptions as Gateways to Holiness** 52
Myriam Klotz

**Receiving and Giving Love: A Meditation on the *Sh'ma*
    and Its Blessings** 64
Sheila Peltz Weinberg

CONTENTS

A Jewish Cleric's Meditation for Self-Care and *A Jewish Cleric's Meditation at a Moment of Challenge* 71
Alden Solovy

Talmud Torah as Spiritual Practice 73
Jonathan P. Slater

Chevruta as Spiritual Practice............................. 84
Beth Huppin

Slumbering at Sinai: Sleep as a Spiritual Practice 88
Jo Hirschmann

Divorce: A Different Story 93
Lisa J. Grushcow

Embracing Reality: Spiritual Preparation for Living with Dementia.. 102
Dayle A. Friedman

When the Rabbi Is Also the Caregiver 110
Eva Robbins

The Professional Pursuit of Spiritual and Mental Health

Minding Our Behavioral Health for the Sake of Spiritual Fulfillment................................... 118
Laura Stein

Creating a Somatic Psychospiritual Practice 128
Karen Lee Erlichman

Watering the Earthly Garden with Sacred Flow: Tending to the Mental Health of Our Jewish Communities 138
Nancy E. Epstein and Elisa Goldberg

Addiction and Recovery

Addiction Is a Spiritual Malady and Judaism Is a Spiritual Solution 155
Mark Borovitz

Addiction and Recovery in the Minds of the Rabbis 164
Annie Belford

Married to a Sex Addict................................. 175
Anonymous

A Daily Reprieve: Addiction, Recovery, and Finding God... 179
Michael Richker

CONTENTS

Lost in TV Land 183
Monique Mayer

With the Blink of an Eye, I Finally Saw the Light 188
Edwin Goldberg

Maayanot (Primary Sources)
T'filah Zakah: **A Yom Kippur Eve Self-Evaluation from Head to Toe** 193
Audrey R. Korotkin

Book Reviews
And God Created Recovery: Jewish Wisdom to Help You Break Free from Your Addiction, Heal Your Wounds, and Unleash Your Inner Faith 207
Ilan Glazer
Reviewed by Laurie E. Green

Recovery, the 12 Steps and Jewish Spirituality: Reclaiming Hope, Courage and Wholeness. 210
Paul Steinberg
Reviewed by Michael Shefrin

The Talmud of Relationships 213
Amy Scheinerman
Reviewed by Paul Golomb

Mourning and Mitzvah: A Guided Journey for Walking the Mourner's Path through Grief to Healing, **revised and expanded 25th anniversary edition** 215
Anne Brener
Reviewed by William (Bill) Cutter

Poetry
Ben Zoma Asks, "Who Is a Hero?" 220
Daniel Polish

On Studying Sacred Texts 221
Judith Offer

Elon Musk, I Trusted You with My Bionic Heart 223
Matthue Roth

CONTENTS

The Day God Destroys Sodom and Gomorrah 224
The Ox 224
*Passed Out under His Daughters' Hands, Lot Dreams
   of His Wife* 225
Deborah Bacharach

Pregnant with the Dead 226
First Graduate School Reception, September 227
A Poem for Mr. Raphael Siv at the Irish Jewish Museum 228
Susan Rich

Variations on a Horizon (Autumn 2018) 230
Marc Nieson

Psalm 51: Variations 231
Ken Seide

Tzaddik 232
Jack M. Freedman

Join the Conversation!

Subscribe Now.

Engage with ideas about Judaism and Jewish life through essays, poetry, and book reviews by leading scholars, rabbis, and thinkers.

A Journal for All Jews
The *CCAR Journal: The Reform Jewish Quarterly*
$150 for one-year subscription
$199 for two-year subscription

For more information and to order, go to
www.ccarpress.org or call 212-972-3636 x241
CCAR | 355 Lexington Avenue | New York, NY 10017

At the Gates — בשערים

If I am not for myself, who will be for me?
If I am only for myself, who am I?
And if not now, when?

—*Pirkei Avot 1:14*

We are busy people. We dedicate our lives to serving others, and we value the importance of nourishing our personal lives. Striving to be the best we might be in our professional and personal lives often means that we have no time left for taking care of ourselves: our mind, body, soul, and spirit. We often share our woes, challenges, concerns, successes, and joys, but it is a rare and blessed opportunity to sit with one another and share our experience, strength, and hope. This issue is a testament to holy work: The work of self-care, of *t'shuvah*—returning to our highest self.

The articles, *Maayanot*, book reviews, and poetry reflect the strength, openness, and vulnerability of our collective hearts and minds. We are immensely grateful for the insights, ideas, and generosity of all our contributors. We particularly thank Laurie Green, who provided the spark for this issue by suggesting a call for papers on Addiction and Recovery.

This issue, which is devoted to Spiritual and Mental Wellness, begins with poignant articles on *Self-Care in Times of Trauma*. The

---

RABBI LISA SARI BELLOWS (C98) is senior rabbi of Congregation Beth Am, Buffalo Grove, Illinois, and a Rabbi Without Borders fellow. She is a graduate of Yoga and Jewish Spirituality Teacher Training and the Institute for Jewish Spirituality's Rabbinic Leadership Program and Jewish Mindfulness Meditation Teacher Training. She is a RYT-200 yoga teacher and a certified Relax and Renew Restorative yoga teacher. She is happy to serve on the *CCAR Journal* Editorial Board and is grateful to be an ongoing student of mindfulness practice.

RABBI SUE LEVI ELWELL, Ph.D. (C86) serves as a spiritual director at HUC-JIR/NY and is blessed to accompany additional souls on portions of their sacred journeys. A Senior Hartman Fellow, she completed the Institute for Jewish Spirituality's Rabbinic Leadership Program and Mindfulness Meditation Teacher Training. She is nourished by love, *chevruta* study, yoga, and strengthening community by bringing together her passions for prayer, song, and justice work in Philadelphia.

honest and courageous voices in this section remind us that no one is exempt from trauma. Engaging in the hard work of healing involves effort, faith, community, and self-compassion. The section on *Spiritual Practice and Lifelong Wellness* describes the tools we might use as we pursue ongoing self-care, each tool grounded in the traditions and teachings of our people. The next section, *The Professional Pursuit of Spiritual and Mental Health*, guides us towards awareness of how self-care and the work we do within the community are related and inform each other.

The *Addiction and Recovery* articles offer insight into the pain of addiction and how Torah and tradition might help in the recovery process. Finally, the *Maayanot* article and translation provides a sacred resource towards self-evaluation—and thus self-care—during Yom Kippur.

Our book reviews and poetry further reflect our theme of Spiritual and Mental Wellness. We are proud to lift up outstanding classic and new studies on recovery, interpersonal relationships, and mourning—books that not only examine these important subjects with sensitivity and expertise, but that guide us through sacred texts and values as we wrestle with their challenges. And once again, this issue blesses us with talented poets whose unique voices enable, inspire, and even dare us to explore new and compelling facets of spiritual and mental wellness.

Several of these topics, such as addiction and recovery, have been explored in previous issues of our *Journal*. We hope that our conversations on self-care and spiritual and mental wellness will continue, and that future *CCAR Journal* issues will address vital topics such as spiritual direction, counseling, and chaplaincy.

Preparing this issue has been a privilege and a delight. We first met when we participated in the fourth cohort of the Institute for Jewish Spirituality's Rabbinic Leadership Program; and over the last decade, each of us has continued to deepen our own journeys. Sharing the honor of editing this issue has been a pleasure. We are indebted to Elaine Rose Glickman, our brilliant Editor, who guided and accompanied us at every step of this project. Her skill, intellect, generosity, organizational expertise, and unfailing good humor are a gift to us, to this issue, and to our Conference.

This special issue of the *Journal* is a Chodesh Heshvan present. We hope that you will find something in these pages to open your eyes, touch your heart, provide a window into your own life, and support your personal growth, healing, and happiness.

With gratitude to the Holy One, we share the teachings, truth, and love from our colleagues, teachers, and friends.

Lisa Sari Bellows
Sue Levi Elwell

Self-Care in Times of Trauma

When the Rabbi Feels Trauma

Paul Kipnes

A mass shooting in a Pittsburgh synagogue.
A mass shooting in the local dance bar.
A raging fire, forcing the evacuation of the synagogue and 75 percent of our congregation.

These three crises, all happening in eleven days, utilized skills honed over almost three decades as a rabbi, enabling me to engage in nonstop pastoral care, support the evacuees, and help organize the Jewish community. I was proud of our work we were doing. Well, until one morning when I found myself sobbing in bed. Then I knew that I had hit a wall, and that I needed significant help to put myself back together.

When the Rabbi Feels Trauma

This is a story about how the fallout from those events almost broke me. Me, a rabbi, trained in crisis counseling and pastoral care, who knew what to expect and yet succumbed to trauma anyway.

I share these reflections, written in the midst of the trauma, to help me reflect for my own edification and also to illuminate the journey for other colleagues who might find themselves facing their own crises. I am consciously pulling back the curtain because we rabbis need to do so. Only by honestly sharing our experiences

---

RABBI PAUL KIPNES (NY92) is spiritual leader of Congregation Or Ami (Calabasas, California) and author, with his wife Michelle November, of *Jewish Spiritual Parenting: Wisdom, Activities, Rituals and Prayers for Raising Children with Spiritual Balance and Emotional Wholeness*. A former NFTY regional advisor and currently dean of faculty of URJ Camp Newman, Rabbi Kipnes also leads a two-year Federation-funded mental health and wellness project to realign the synagogue's reality with its vision to be a safe space for teens. His current project is MidrashicMonologues.com, where with Rabbi Rachel Bearman, he restore the voices of biblical women and men who have not been given the opportunity to speak.

will we break through the isolation and loneliness to gain the help we so desperately need.

What I share here has ceased to be (as) raw, though it is still very real. While editing this, I am still fully engaged in my own healing process and am not using the writing to deflect or skirt the feelings and challenges.

Seeking Advice to Understand How to Respond

Like all Jewish communities, Congregation Or Ami (Calabasas, California)—its congregants and clergy—were already reeling from the mass shooting at Pittsburgh's Tree of Life Synagogue. Ten days later, a gunman murdered many in the nearby Borderline Bar and Grill, a country-western dance bar frequented by our high school and college students. In fact, one of our congregants narrowly escaped the carnage. The next day, even before we had a chance to process the shooting, the Woodley fires began, destroying hundreds of homes and forcing nearly 75 percent of our congregation to face mandatory evacuations. The fires, which came within thirty feet of our synagogue's front door, caused significant smoke damage and pushed us out of the building for a month.

It never occurred to me that I wouldn't be able to handle the overflowing anxiety, worry, and fear surrounding me, because the fires were far from my home, because over the years I have had additional training in pastoral counseling, and because I thought I fully understood the cycle of trauma. In addition, after the mass shootings and as the fires began to rage, my partner Rabbi Julia Weisz and I proactively contacted our rabbinic colleagues who had previously faced communal crises to learn from them: in Santa Rosa, California, which was decimated by fires a year before; Houston, Texas, which endured horrible floods; and Parkland, Florida, which faced a murderous mass shooter in the high school. We knew we needed to know what to expect and how we might help heal our community. We failed to consider our own experience with and response to these crises.

Those rabbis—Stephanie Kramer, Oren Hayon, and Marci Bloch—cautioned that the traumatic experience would not end when our community returned to their homes, found new homes, or when the dead were buried. They wisely explained that the process of healing would be long and arduous. We also would need to come to terms with the new normal, namely that these fires—and increased mass shootings—are now the new normal. Fires and shooting are just going to happen again and again, getting worse before they get better. So the repair of our broken hearts and broken world would take time.

Our rabbinic colleagues told us that those who survived, those who evacuated returning to their houses now aware of how close the fires came to their backyards, and those who saw their friends' homes burnt down, would experience trauma. Meaning, most of us. We needed to face our trauma.

As the Tears Began to Flow . . . And Not Stop

My story began one evening, as I was recounting with my kids our communal response to the fires. I was at home because I had to take a day off; because after dealing with these events for a week, I hit the wall. Sitting in my home, far enough away from the fires to be assuredly safe, I shared our work organizing the community. The tears began to fall. I figured I was just exhausted.

But then I woke in the middle of the night. While streaming a TV show in an attempt to fall back asleep, all of a sudden I found myself bawling again. It was 4:30 in the morning and I couldn't stop. I knew I had a problem. Later that morning, while participating in an early CCAR conference call, I had to break away numerous times because I kept shedding tears. I committed to getting myself some help.

Calling My Therapist

I called my therapist. He opened up an appointment for me at 5:00 P.M. I then texted Sally Weber, a social worker and friend from Jewish Family Services, who earlier in the week "kidnapped me" from the relief work to encourage me to begin to process. She could talk at 2:30 pm.

Then I contacted Rabbi Rex Perlmeter, the CCAR's crisis counselor, who said he would call me in twenty minutes.

Rex and I talked for an hour. Sally and I spoke for an hour. My therapist and I spent an hour together. And you know what I discovered in those three hours of therapy? That although I thought I was not directly touched by any of this, all that had happened actually traumatized me. It was partly exhaustion, but not just that.

Shaken Up by the Shootings

I discovered how deeply the mass shootings had shaken me. I was experiencing the double shootings as deeply personal attacks. First "they came after us" at a synagogue. (I'm Jewish. I work in a synagogue. It could easily have been my synagogue.) Then, over at the Borderline Bar, that country-western dance bar, a twenty-three-year-old congregant who had been in there dancing fled for his life. I'm glad that he is physically unharmed. Yet just five days earlier I had been counseling him through his emotional turmoil over the synagogue shooting and all those shootings at churches, schools, concerts, malls, and elsewhere. I cautioned him that as terrible as it was, it was going to get worse before it gets better. Nonetheless, I assured him, the chances of him getting shot at was about as likely as him stepping off the curb and getting hit by a bus (I buried someone from that only once, very early in my rabbinate). Five days later, that young man was almost killed in the Borderline Bar shooting.

In my three counseling sessions, I realized that I no longer believed I could keep my kids safe, or my congregant kids safe, or my congregation safe, or the school safe. From the shootings. Or from the fires. I discovered that I was frustrated and so sad. I realized that I couldn't sit back anymore.

Survivor's Guilt

The therapists explained that I also had a form of survivor's guilt. I was feeling guilty that while many were evacuated, most escaped with only smoke damage to their homes. Although the fires raged all the way up to people's homes, workplaces, and backyards, I and most of our congregants were safe.

As we dug deeper, the counselors helped me discover the intensity of the repetitious nature of these fires. What had endangered people I cared about in the Woodley fires had also happened in nearby Ventura, California, a year ago, and to a lesser degree, two years before that in our Calabasas neighborhoods. In fact, back then, I rescued our two Torah scrolls from the approaching fires, carrying them across the freeway bridge to safety.

Personal Sense of Loss

Amidst my tears, I also remembered I had deep connections with the three Jewish camps destroyed by the Woolsey fire. I had been a camp director of Camp Hess Kramer and Gindling Hilltop Camp for four years. It was so long ago, I had forgotten. Camp JCA Shalom hosted our NFTY regional retreats, where I had visited our temple teens multiple times a year. And just one year ago, our Camp Newman in Santa Rosa, where my family spent every summer for twenty years, had burned down. My therapy team helped me realize that I had trauma on top of trauma—compound trauma, they called it.

I became aware of the self-growth I needed to undertake: if I really wanted to do something to stop these annual fires and to stop these constant mass shootings, I had to stand up. I had to become a leader in a different way than I had been before. That was intense and a little bit scary, too.

Recognizing that I needed to remain on track toward health, I quickly released control to my wife, Michelle. I agreed I would eat whatever she told me to eat (and I would stay away from all the donated baked goods). I would go to sleep whenever she told me to go to bed. Additionally, I arranged with trusted friends who knew me well to check in regularly. I immediately scheduled additional counseling appointments.

I thought I had my response to the trauma under control. On some level, I believed that I was over the worst of it.

Why Did I Sometimes Still Feel Drained and Despondent?

Soon enough the fire was extinguished and most of our evacuated congregants were back in their homes. The fire spared the synagogue, but because the fire came within thirty feet of our front door, we endured a few weeks out of the building while the remediation company cleaned the shul. Appropriately, we held a *chanukat habayit* (rededication ceremony) on Shabbat Chanukah. The local news cycle moved onto the next tragedy.

Weeks later, in the midst of our Pop-Up Teen retreat, I stepped aside with our community social worker, a longtime friend, for a preplanned session to explore the nuances of the continuing trauma. She attended the teen retreat as part of a corps of social workers invited to support the teens. Focusing on *Where is the blessing?*, the retreat was intentionally designed as both an escape from, and a processing opportunity about, the past weeks of devastation. Unexpectedly yet importantly, most of the social workers found themselves supporting the staff as much as the teens.

We sat under a tree in Simi Valley's Camp Alonim; she patiently waited for my sharing. I began quietly, controlled, well aware of my inner stuff. Soon enough, warm tears again were running down my cheeks.

I said that I felt we were not doing enough. Although my congregants were for the most part back in their homes, many were not. And I worried about them all. Our congregants and their neighbors were:

Fighting with insurance companies.
Dealing with the trauma of evacuation.
Dealing with the trauma of the mass shootings.
Worrying about mudslides down the denuded hillsides.
Realizing that although their houses survived, the damage was severe.
Discovering upon return home that the mix of smoke and toxic soot has caused in some homes the walls to dangerously pucker, and elsewhere, piping melted causing internal flooding.
Struggling still to get things back together, even feeling guilty that their homes survived while neighbors' homes did not.

Even those who made it through the fires ostensibly unscathed were struggling. This child was wearing oversized socks that turn out to be the father's because everything still needed to be cleaned. That child shed tears as she confessed she felt she looked foolish in donated clothes. That mom was overwhelmed by the sheer volume of calls to banks, credit card companies, and insurance companies. This dad was frustrated that the road ahead is so long and arduous.

In truth, even after the multiple calls the previous week to the whole congregation, I could not assemble a true picture of the needs of my flock. After weeks of trying to be there for them, after partnering to organize the Jewish community, after raising money and gift cards to help them, and trying to be out there as a calming and hopeful presence, I felt unable to get a handle on the situation.

I Confessed That I Felt Like an Impostor

I said that if one more person called me a hero, I just might have lost it because I felt less like a hero and more like an impostor. I imagined myself then like a former star quarterback, standing on the sidelines unable to figure out how to move the team forward.

I confessed how I relished a day last week—finally a blessedly normal day—spent helping a young bat mitzvah student see her *parashah* in a new light, counseling an older woman through challenging life changes, and walking a couple toward the end stages as the cancer ravaged his body.

My social worker friend smiled at my statement, understanding how ironic it was that sitting with someone with cancer would feel like a "blessedly normal day." She asked me, "What are your expectations for yourself?" I looked at her incredulously and said, "Well, of course, to seek out my congregants and others, to ascertain their needs—immediate and longer term—and to help fulfill them. After all, I have gift cards, volunteers who want to help, and I have . . . myself. My expectations are to do the work we started."

"And what might be a slightly more realistic expectation," she asked.

I stuttered, struggling to fully comprehend the question, "M-m-maybe to have others call and triage the needs for us, and then for me to respond to those."

"And slightly more realistic?"

I just looked at her with incredulity. "Lower my expectations of what we need to accomplish? How can I do that? People are in need. In crisis. I am a caregiver. How can I stop?"

She told me about her decades' long work with rabbis and congregations, about how when people talked about how their rabbis were there for them, it was rarely about the rabbi providing a specific thing. It was not a car payment or new clothes or a new way to solve an insurance problem. There were other organizations, leaders, and professionals who do that, and do it a lot better. People who talked about their rabbis being there for them, she said, most often talked about the comfort and solace the rabbi offered, a spiritual support unique to the rabbinic role and persona.

They relished the knowledge that their rabbis were there when they needed them. As a listening ear. With a supportive shoulder. As someone to turn to when they feel lost and alone.

She said, "After all the amazing work you and your team did, being there 24/7 during the crises, maybe it's okay to slow down and breathe for a bit. Maybe you might entertain a more appropriate (or realistic) expectation: to let people know you are here and available, and to respond to the needs that arise."

I try to sit with that.

The Challenge of Ratcheting Down the Level of "Being There"

It violated my sense of what the biblical *heneini* ("here I am") demands. And yet my body (exhausted), my heart (aching and spent), and my mind (well aware of the dangers of continuing at this pace) all were asking me to agree with her.

Yes, I was (at times) spent. I was (at times) lost amidst the overwhelming needs that keep arising. My inbox was (still is) backed up. My programmatic responsibilities were about to resume. And (at the time of this meeting) we were not even back in our building.

She asked how things were with my family. I confessed that my wife and I had an argument, which became something much bigger than the issue deserved. We had to figure out this issue, but in no way did it require the intensity I brought to it. We talked about other family concerns that needed my attention. She reminded me that after weeks of outward focus, it was okay to turn inward for a bit.

Tears rolled down my cheeks some more. I wanted to be the hero for those who need one. I am constitutionally wired that way, to help others. But I was worn down.

I talked about the list I carry around in my head—of all the people I should call, text, or check in on. For them. For their families. For the good of the congregation. That list haunted me. It weighed me down. Because I just couldn't get to them all.

I recalled that my colleagues who have faced crises before me shared how they too felt this way, that they just try to keep slogging through.

My social worker friend reminded me of our work years ago teaching pastoral counseling together at the rabbinic school:

When we taught about the need for the rabbi to set boundaries. About the importance of taking time to rejuvenate. About the limits of our effectiveness in the face of burnout. I smiled knowingly. How ironic! I delivered those lessons to our rabbinic students many, many times. Could I listen to them now for myself?

She pushed forward, like only a trusted confidant can:

Could I find a way to do something for myself?
Could I get away—for a few hours, for a day—for some fun?
Could I stop for a moment with all the social media?
Could I cease for a moment answering my phone and texts?

I laughed, thinking she was asking me to cease being me. Yet I knew she was right.

That night my wife took me out to the movie *A Star Is Born*, about an aging rock star who finds love, nurtures another, yet becomes spent and self-destructive. I loved the music and the love story. I identified with the sense of exhaustion. My wife worried that the ending might upset me. I was not bothered by it, as I was just glad to have turned off my phone, to enjoy a night out holding my wife's hand.

The next night my wife took me to *Come from Away*, a play about the heroic efforts of the Newfoundlanders, who cared for 7,000+ "plane people" who were forced to land when 9/11 closed U.S. airspace. I identified with the Islanders' sense of responsibility for others. My heart was warmed by their organizing acumen and their overflowing sense of compassionate action. My heart broke a little as some of the joy was tempered by sadness. I too felt the letdown when the crisis ended and things began to return to normal (whatever that is). My wife and I both saw ourselves in those Newfoundlanders.

As we walked back to our cars, I remarked at how wonderful it was to smile and laugh. It had been weeks.

How Am I Taking Care of Myself Since?

1. I participated in training about caring in times of crisis to listen to and learn from the wisdom of professionals from Pittsburgh, Parkland, and the Israel Trauma Coalition.

2. I meet for spiritual direction by phone with the CCAR's Rex Perlmeter to continue to mine these weeks for lessons of transcendent holiness.
3. I meet with my rabbinic coach, Diana Ho, who guides my partner rabbi and me toward self-care and setting manageable realistic expectations.
4. I talk with a crisis therapist, and my social worker friend.
5. I regularly consult with rabbinic colleagues who had been through crises ahead of me, who kindly dropped everything to listen to and teach me. They probably had little idea how much our conversations carried me through a particularly difficult moment. Nonetheless I am grateful.
6. I try to eat well, sleep a lot, walk daily, and attended to the forgotten parts of my life.
7. And I write. Because writing helps me consolidate and clarify the thoughts and prayers and emotions running unchecked through my brain and heart.

If It Could Happen to Me, Could It Happen to You?

In the weeks and months since the fires and shootings, I learned that not only are we rabbis prone to stress and burnout, but we are subject to suffering trauma along with those we counsel and support. Although I was trained to handle this and I trained interns every year about just these types of situations, I still succumbed. If it could happen to me, why couldn't it happen to you?

The key question for me, and the challenge I try to share with my colleagues and interns, is how each of us is now—before the crises strike—developing the tools to carry us through. Because when we experience crisis, it's good to already have the tools to help deal with the trauma. Because in the aftermath of crisis, this new normal is insidious and can easily overwhelm. So I invite you to set up your crisis toolbox now.

Months have passed and we continue to care for those who lost homes, providing replacement seder plates for some and gift cards to purchase spring clothing as needed. We are supporting counseling for those struggling in the aftermath of the shooting and the fires, and we reach out to the staff at local Jewish institutions who are still out of their organizational homes. And I am and will be okay because I was and am doing what I must to ensure that I am okay. And so I bless:

Baruch atah Adonai, Eloheinu Melech haolam, hagomel l'chayavim tovim sheg'malani kol tuv.

Blessed are You, Eternal our God, Guide of the universe, Who nurtures within the undeserving goodness, and Who—through blessedly caring souls—continues to remind me of my goodness within.

Amen.

Unconsumed: Emotional Resilience through Fiery Times

Stephanie Kramer

Nothing could have prepared me for Sukkot 5778. My family had just had a wonderful evening reveling in a friend's sukkah; the perfect beginning of what was going to be a week filled with celebratory meals shared with *ushpizin*. We drove home happy, tired, and full.

The sukkah in our backyard was already decorated; adorned with lights, tables, and chairs prepared for the fiesta fundraiser we were hosting the following evening.

My husband, Adam, and I tucked our kids into bed, first singing the *Sh'ma* with Noa, our three-year-old daughter, and then to Micah, age seven. After the children, we kissed our mothers who were in town for the *chagim* and turned in early for bed.

I did not sleep soundly that night, tossing and turning as the wind picked up outside, rattling our windows and shaking the trees. Finally, at 2 AM, after fighting the urge to wake up from the noise, I was worried enough to check on the sukkah. The wind was so strong I feared the entire structure would fly through my bathroom window or our redwood tree would collapse on the house.

I stumbled out of bed and through the sliding glass door into my backyard. I immediately smelled smoke. I lifted my hand up in front of my face and realized that I couldn't even see my hand. I went back inside to discover we had no electricity; suddenly the sound of sirens blaring all around came into focus. After quickly checking Facebook, I learned there were dangerous fires all over the city, roads were already congested, and no one knew where to go or what to do.

RABBI STEPHANIE KRAMER (LA11) serves as associate rabbi at Congregation Shomrei Torah in Santa Rosa, California. She is a senior rabbinic fellow of the Shalom Hartman Institute and a current fellow of the Clergy Leadership Institute.

With my heart pounding and fear pumping through my veins, I frantically woke up my family.

We quickly collected some irreplaceable photo albums, a few toys, and a couple of baby blankets. Once in the car we drove south through thick smoke and pitch blackness. Searching on FB for information, we took refuge in a congregant's home in the next town over.

Once safely inside, my family quickly went back to sleep. Instead of joining them, I continued to text everyone I knew—either alerting people to the danger outside their doors or ensuring they were on their way to safety. I woke up my youth director who lives right by one of the deadliest fires, and I spoke with my evacuated clergy partner about opening the temple as soon as possible to be used as an evacuation center. I learned from a congregant that Camp Newman, my second home, had already been destroyed. My congregants and friends were evacuating in droves. There was no way to go back to sleep, no way to peel my eyes away from the phone screen, and really no way I would ever enjoy the sense of security I lost only moments ago.

It was surreal to think that sitting on coffee tables in evacuated homes or turning to ash in burning homes was our congregational newsletter. In that October newsletter was an article I had written about sukkot. The article was titled "This, too, shall pass. Gam zeh ya'avor." Having just gone home to witness the devastation of Hurricane Harvey in Houston, I wrote about the ultimate temporary nature of even our seemingly permanent homes. "We take a week out of every year to remember that we are beyond grateful for the shelter and security we have. Yet we are reminded that everything is temporary, and, therefore, we should be grateful and happy as we delight in the bounty of the season." Year after year our Jewish tradition teaches these timeless lessons, lessons that clearly no one is exempt from, as the accuracy of this particular lesson couldn't be more frightfully relevant.

As the sun began to rise, it was clear that my community was in total chaos. No one knew where the fires were or which way the wind was blowing. There were large power outages, and spotty Wi-Fi. The news had not yet caught up with the fires so accurate information was a thing of the past. We live in an age of social media and instantaneous information, so when it's spotty—or nearly nonexistent—we panic.

I learned months after the fires in group therapy with interfaith clergy that there are different types of people and therefore different types of clergy. Some who see a disaster and freeze and those who see a disaster and run towards it. I became a marathon runner. With more and more details coming in, my blood only pumped stronger and I gained energy. This reaction of course came with its own set of challenges.

Having grown up in Houston, Texas, I had closely followed the congregations and their responses to Hurricane Harvey only months before. I watched FB as many of my friends lost their first homes, their childhood homes, and their spiritual homes to flood damage.

Learning from their example, I knew we needed to check on everyone's welfare and also provide a place of refuge for displaced children and adults. From the thickness of the smoke and the reports of zero containment, it was clear schools would be closed for weeks.

However, I couldn't even focus to write an e-mail or decide on details. I had energy, but not clarity as yet. I wore out the floors in my congregant's home as I paced and paced while making phone call after phone call.

That is where colleagues become heroes. A neighbor rabbi with Rodeph Shalom in San Rafael, about forty minutes south of our temple, delivered hot lunch on Tuesday as our congregation opened its doors to anyone in the community. Hundreds without power, evacuated from their homes, terrified, and exhausted pored through our doors. It was during this lunch that IsraAid stepped up to help us open a day camp that would service our community for the next three weeks.

With IsraAid's arrival came much needed resources. They came with therapists who specialized in trauma; set up an entire resource area with toiletries, cots, blankets, and masks. They brought in air purifiers, art supplies, and probably a laundry list of things I will never know about.

It was clear that everyone who came through our doors needed to talk, needed to cry, and needed the comfort of community. Many who came to the temple with the intention to volunteer unconsciously sought conversation and solace. Everyone had their personal story to tell. For the next six months rarely a conversation happened that didn't include an exchange of evacuation stories.

The stories of chilling escape would haunt me for months. Having heard story after story firsthand with intimate details of sounds, smells, and fears, I would relive these stories down to these minutest details in moments of quiet.

But during those first few weeks, there were rarely moments of quiet. Throughout that time, I would arrive early at the synagogue and hit the ground running; directing the day camp, volunteers, food deliveries, meeting one on one with people in need while giving media interviews—sometimes all at the same time.

My family, along with hundreds of others, ate breakfast and lunch at the temple and left only in time to grab dinner on the way home to try and put the kids to sleep. I remember lying in bed either the fourth or fifth night reading article after article, watching video after video, about houses and lives lost, muffling my tears, trying not to wake my husband next to me. It was at this moment that the enormity of the situation started to sink in. It was then that I realized how much our community had changed overnight.

I muffled a lot of tears over those first few weeks. I had a hard time going to sleep. I tried to implement a coping mechanism that worked years ago after my husband was diagnosed with a brain tumor. I would lie in bed, and sing *Hashkeiveinu,* think about God's sheltering wings, and try to sleep. Even though this worked years ago, it had little effect now.

It's hard to pinpoint when I realized that I needed professional help. There was not one incident that clearly indicated a need for therapy, as the smoke figuratively and literally blurred every detail of that first month. It probably wasn't until the smoke cleared and the fires were contained twenty-three days later that I started to focus on my needs in addition to the needs of the community.

Although I never hit an actual breaking point, I think that once I was out of the initial trauma phase I began to see patterns throughout the marathon that initiated me to seek therapy: unexpected moments of clarity followed by surprising breakdowns and fears.

As soon as the fires broke out, rabbis from near and far filled my voicemail with messages of love and support and wanted to know how they could help. Listening was the best form of assistance. So many of my colleagues simply listened to me cry, vent, or strategize. This was the biggest gift.

So many rabbis offered assistance, I joked with these colleagues to bring drugs and alcohol. A rabbi did show up with a half a Xanax and instructed me to take it before bed. I secretly kept it wrapped up in protective tissue, carrying it around in my purse for weeks. I had never taken anything like it before, and I was nervous to even try it. After promising a rabbi I would do something for myself, I drove up to a spa for a massage. I was taken right away, and after finishing the foot part I kindly got up, apologized, paid, and left. My favorite activity brought me zero pleasure. I couldn't calm the thoughts enough to even enjoy sixty minutes of oily bliss.

That night I had a nightmare that I had shown up to work with a distorted face and my entire board of directors knew I had taken a nonprescribed Xanax. I woke up in a sweat at 2 AM, although waking up at 2 AM panicked and making sure there wasn't any fire danger had frankly become my only constant. That was when I knew I needed to try the Xanax.

I did try it, and honestly it felt good, almost too good. For the first time I can remember my head was clear, there were no thoughts racing through my brain. I wasn't constantly interrupting one thought with another; instead there was a calm, a euphoria that lasted blissfully throughout the night.

After I described this ecstasy to my doctor, she decided I should never take Xanax again, but rather Buspirone, a much lighter nonaddictive medication. I happily accepted the RX, filled it, and started to take it as necessary. Needless to say, I am a much calmer flier now!

The nonstop day camp filled with trauma circuses, continuous movies, sanctuary bounce houses, seaweed facial masks, and pickling cucumbers took its toll on my kids. My family, like many others, were evacuated and living with friends, so we spent every day at the temple. It should have been like a vacation, but the smell of smoke permeated every moment of the days. My typically independent and gregarious three-year-old daughter was permanently attached to my hip, and her tears flowed for the duration of a day, soaking through my only shirt. It was impossible for me to look after others like this, and I grew increasingly concerned about the reasons behind this sudden shift in behavior. I sought out a children's psychologist who was at the temple looking after kids. She sat with us, tried to speak to Noa, and then let me know that Noa's thumb and my shoulder were probably the best forms of comfort. The thumb sucking I had been trying to crack down on was now a necessary comfort. How could I blame her for throwing a temper tantrum? I was only jealous that at my age it's socially unacceptable to throw such a fit.

I knew instinctively it was no longer an emotionally safe environment for my family. I needed to be a rabbi for people who had lost their homes, and I could not at that moment also be the mother I strive to be. Like with most assertive children, my husband could not fill in if I was still in sight. With a heavy heart I made one of the hardest decisions I have ever made.

And that was sending my family away. More often than not when I leave the kids for travel or work, something is said that stings. It stings if my absence is under-noticed, and conversely it stings if I am missed too much. My Jewish guilt riddles me with working parent dilemmas of balance. This decision was even worse. The world was in chaos, and I felt driven to send my family to the safety of someone else's arms. I chose work over my family.

Once my mind was made up, I called my in-laws in LA and convinced my reluctant husband to drive down, while simultaneously packing the car and telling the kids they would get a surprise trip to their grandparent's house. The scheme worked beautifully, and before I knew it my kids were being doted over and well taken care of. The stress of the fire did not dissipate as quickly as the thick, smoky air did on their drive to Southern California blue skies, but in hindsight this was the best possible decision for my family. I only hope, in the years to come, they agree.

Without my family in town, I was able to focus on the needs of the community and staff at hand. Our amazing and dedicated staff showed up to work day after day, many of them crying throughout the day but refusing to leave. It was hard to be anywhere, but they felt like they would rather be at Congregation Shomrei Torah, their second home.

There were days filled with anxiety over missing congregants, there were huge hurdles while finding everyone adequate accessible sleeping arrangements. It's hard to image that it took nearly a month for the containment of the fires, reopening of schools and any sense of normality to return. But the month was jam packed with caring for immediate needs, Jewish needs, and spiritual breakdowns. In the midst of disaster there are some essential functions we could not overlook. We kept the synagogue open for all services through the fires, but in a sense the synagogue was transformed, as we retooled priorities to focus on helping families who lost their homes as well as providing mental health services to an entire community suffering from loss, grief, and PTSD.

We had two *b'nei mitzvah* services that happened during the fire. A bat mitzvah who was missing a lot of out of town guests that could not make it to the city, and whose caterer came even though she lost her home. And a bar mitzvah of a boy who had just lost his home, his pets, and the venue for his celebration. Both of these services were heart wrenching and breathtaking all at the same time.

Terribly, Marnie Schwartz, a past president of the congregation, a Legacy Member, and a beloved member of our community was not able to make it past her front door and died in the fire. Mourning Marnie was excruciating for our community. The loss of life during the first night of the fire are exacerbated as details continue to surface of the emergency system failures. With each new piece of information, it became hard to have any sense of security left.

Mourning the sense of security is probably the hardest part for me. I used to think that if there was a problem, calling 911 would ultimately solve it, yet I now know just how quickly a city can be ravished by fire and just as quickly, its systems can break down. No system is perfect, and we are ultimately not in control. That is where, for me, professional help came in. As I was coaching everyone in the community to seek therapy and specialized PTSD services. I too needed to take my own advice. I have since participated in several different forms of professional therapy. Through a recommendation from a congregant I went to a therapist who specializes in trauma therapy, and I joined several interfaith group therapy sessions.

I needed to reset and refocus so I could continue to serve. I was absolutely depleted. Through sessions of EMDR (Eye Movement Desensitization Reprocessing), I was able to lessen the effects of PTSD. That's not to say that every time there is a very foggy morning, or a strong-smelling BBQ or I see news reels of fire ravaging another part of California I am un-phased, but rather I am now more attuned to the triggers that spark anxiety and am better equipped to cope. This form of therapy, which seemed a little "hippie" to me at first is a proven method for reducing PTSD. It was through sessions I recalled the terror of our evacuation story, as well as others' stories, and learned to pull forward images of heroes, safety, and calm. EMDR, which I didn't even like carving out time for, was an important step in the process.

Another therapeutic resource were the inter-faith clergy sessions organized and executed by a psychologist from IsraAID who has worked all over the world with trauma victims. It was eye opening to hear about the recovery phases we would likely be facing. It was relieving to learn about the similarities amongst our struggles.

The clergy were eager at first for the idea of therapy opportunities. I think we all understood how in-need we were, yet they were hard to prioritize and hard to sit through. It's uncomfortable to talk about the disaster in a room full of clergy who reacted so differently. It's hard to hear how judgmental some clergy and congregants were to decisions made by others. After separating the participants into two distinct groups, bonds started to form. The clergy was separated into groups based on their level of participating in the initial weeks of the fire. I have always been a workaholic, and the fire proved no different. Through these sessions, I gained a greater sense of empathy for those clergy members who did not work in the manic sense that I did. Some clergy really stepped back and took time for themselves and their family before showing up for the broader community. Everyone reacted in different manners, and therefore everyone's post-traumatic struggles and healing look very different. While we are also working to serve our communities' needs, we still serve these needs in very distinct manners. There is no one correct way to help everyone.

Nearly two years later, many members of our community are just now seeking professional help for depression, PTSD, and anxiety. I hope that being open and honest about my personal struggles helps to bring awareness to and de-stigmatize mental health.

Even though the most frightening part of trauma is realizing ones lack of control, there were so many stories of everyday heroes saving lives and lending help to complete strangers. I will never forget the man who shattered his neighbor's sliding glass door and carried the frozen-in-shock ninety-year-old out in her bathrobe, then drove her to safety. I will never forget my dear friend who helped lift a neighbor's garage doors, allowing them to escape. The acts of kindness that the community showed were echoing through the streets—streets with no stories of looting or vandalism. Streets we could really be proud of.

If I'm being honest, despite these beautiful stories of everyday heroes, it's really hard for me to look back and find any silver lining. The days were dark, and the loss is still so raw and evident.

And yet, Brandon and Lauren, driven by their Jewish values, instinctively showed up to our congregation to volunteer during the fires. Brandon, a full-time middle school music teacher, had worked for our congregation for years, and Lauren, a Jewish girl from Fresno, California, had recently moved to our area, taking a job as a public school psychologist. The two of them met in our sanctuary where they were tasked with setting up the counseling corner and playing board games with kids. They returned day after day helping the kids with counseling, art therapy, board games, and meals. They began dating, and soon Lauren joined Brandon as a teacher in our religious school. Only weeks ago, they joyfully announced their engagement. *"Yet when two souls are destined to be together their light shines brighter in unison."*

.

Timeline of a Trigger: A Personal Journey Toward Healing Complex PTSD

Paul Jacobson

I.

"I want to tell you what a flashback is like. It is as if time is folded or warped, so that the past and present merge, as if I were physically transported into the past."[1]

Saturday, October 6, 2018—9:15 AM

I am preparing to teach Torah Study at my congregation. Having gone for a run and eaten breakfast, I am planning on teaching midrash related to the opening chapter of the Book of Genesis. Nearly ten months into my journey to heal personal trauma related to the surfacing of abusive childhood memories, I have, of late, been sleeping better, dissociating less, and when triggered, have managed to maintain control and bring my mind back to the present in a number of minutes. Being able to clear a trigger and settle myself in minutes is a true blessing, as throughout most of 2018, I have had triggers persist for days and even weeks at a time. This has indeed been the most fraught year of my life.

Checking in with my congregants, it becomes clear that the vote to confirm Judge Brett Kavanaugh's seat on the Supreme Court is on their minds. I feel tension in the room, a sense that my congregants are on edge and need a space to reflect on current events. Today will not be a day to discuss midrash.

I am well aware that the words and actions of others may trigger me. Given my responsibility as a rabbi to speak in defense of and

---

RABBI PAUL JACOBSON (C06) recently completed thirteen years as a congregational rabbi. He lives with his family in Sydney, Australia, and is currently pursuing professional interests beyond the congregational rabbinate.

in support of others, I am cognizant that my own comments may cause uncomfortable traumatic memories to return. Regardless of the impositions on my own life, I am becoming accustomed to those moments when it may be necessary to trigger myself so that I can fulfill what I believe to be my professional obligations. Two days earlier, I wrote a message on the Kavanaugh hearings to my congregation, and a few months ago, I delivered a sermon about the child sex abuse scandal in the Catholic Church.

This morning; however, I am not expecting to be triggered in Torah Study. Nonetheless, a series of comments by congregants on the Kavanaugh hearings and Dr. Christine Blasey Ford's courageous testimony literally feel like claws digging themselves into my liver. The claws aren't meant for me; people are upset by the news and are angry with their politicians and the state of our country. Fear and disgust fill their words, rightfully so. I feel my throat begin to close and the backs of my hands begin to sweat. My face becomes heated and I have the awful taste of bile in my mouth. The images begin to flash.

Uh oh. We are only twenty minutes into class; I still need to finish teaching and lead Shabbat services. I have found that the best way to manage a flashback is to address it in the very moment that it happens, to sit with the feelings that are surfacing, but amidst my professional responsibilities, I don't have such a luxury. I could say to my congregants, "I need to go to the bathroom," or "I need a breath of fresh air," but I don't want to draw attention to myself. My journey through trauma has often made me feel like I am a two-headed beast. I appear fine on the outside, but no one else can see the horror behind my eyes.

The pictures are terrible. I see my younger self, whom I call paul, getting sick in our third grade classroom. Taken to the examination room in the rear of the nurse's office, he lies fetal-curled on a padded table, in the very room where weeks earlier, he was assaulted. Simultaneously, I am hit by a barrage of other memories from childhood, each a separate episode of illness. I watch as my mother leaves paul with Grandma and Pop. I see paul resting beneath a peach-colored wool blanket on the dark-orange, floral-patterned couch in my grandparents' den. On the outside, I am merely sweating, possibly a bit flushed, carrying an adult conversation about Genesis 1 and 2, but inside, paul is so unwell.

You're triggered. Just stay calm. You don't need to react right now. You've been triggered enough to know that you can get through this and that the feelings will pass. The images are only feelings and memories. They won't kill you, even though they are real. None of these experiences killed you the first time. You survived. Keep your mind focused on the present. Just keep bringing your focus back to where you are now. You can do this.

II.

"So you face, and you face, and you face, and you continue to face each aspect of yourself. You have to remember and claim each individual experience. Acknowledge that it happened. Acknowledge that it is real."[2]

10:30 am

Torah Study concludes and I meander to my office, take a few sips of water, and contemplate eating a banana before starting Shabbat services. Thank God there isn't a bar or bat mitzvah celebration this morning, just a small *minyan* service held in our synagogue library. The water doesn't go down smoothly and I feel a burning inside that robs me of my breath. Forget the banana.

I take a few deep breaths, steel myself, walk into the library, and decide to lead part of the service sitting down because I don't have the strength to stand. Thankfully, no one notices that I am not standing. It often amazes me that the expectations I place on myself are easily forgiven or generally unnoticed by other people.

I would rather sit on the floor. While "grounding" during a flashback often refers to those efforts to keep a person focused on the present rather than what is taking place in their mind,[3] I take the concept of "grounding" literally. Positioning myself firmly on the floor is the safest place for me until my feelings subside.

I know, as my wife, close friends, and colleagues have taught me, that the only recipe for addressing my pain, is *addressing the pain*. Name it. Acknowledge that it is real. Sit with it until it subsides, however long it takes. As one female survivor remarks, "You have to accept yourself as the awakener, as the victim, as not wanting to be the victim, and then as the survivor."[4]

I am thankful that this particular flashback has not led to an increase in suicidal ideation, a condition with which I have wrestled since my teenaged years. But as I begin to lead my congregants in singing *Mah Tovu*, I wish I had the luxury of stopping the service long enough to sit myself in a corner of the room, curl into a ball, and cry. As psychologist Mike Lew has written, "Crying is not grief; it is a way to get over your grief . . . Crying is a valuable and necessary aspect of recovery."[5] Allowing myself to cry for the small boy lost inside me who I've only recently rediscovered has been a vital part of my healing.

I am blessed to serve a congregation that truly cares about me, not only as their spiritual leader but also as a human being. Yet I don't feel comfortable explaining to my congregants what I'm really feeling inside. I continue pushing through.

III.

"It might be useful to let people around you know about the flashbacks and how they can work, so that you can receive support. Friends can help you to slow your breathing, to talk to you, to get you a warm drink. The purpose is to help reconnect with the present in a safe and supportive way."[6]

11:45 AM

I walk home from the temple, a short stroll of eleven minutes, hoping that the fresh air will help to settle me. It doesn't. I enter the house and see my daughters Hannah and Emily, doing arts and crafts and chatting happily. It is approximately two hours into my triggered state, and I have no control over the raging images. As I enter the kitchen, my wife Lisa takes one look at me and recognizing the glazed look in my eyes, she sends me upstairs with the hope that I will be able to settle myself.

By this stage, since I didn't manage the trigger when it began, I am feeling exhausted and my body is shaking. I crawl into bed beneath my charcoal-colored, weighted therapeutic blanket. When I am triggered, I cannot be touched, but I crave the feeling of being held. The weighted blanket provides comfort during surges of anxiety by wrapping me in a safe hug. I am out as my head hits the pillow.

12:20 PM

My alarm has been going off for five minutes and as I am so deeply asleep, I only hear it now. Hyper-arousal[7] is a common symptom of PTSD, and I know that if I sleep any longer than thirty minutes, I will not sleep come nighttime. I am still feeling sick; the images are still flashing. It is such a disconcerting feeling to notice my younger self get sick, over and over again. I seat myself on the floor for about eight minutes, try to focus on my surroundings in our bedroom, look at the light streaming in through the shutters of the windows, run my fingers through the softness of the carpet, and remind myself over and over that "I am here and I am now," reciting a mantra to convince my brain that I am present, even though I am suffering pain and illness from more than thirty years ago. None of my strategies work, so I give up and go downstairs. I hope that a change of scenery will calm my nerves.

"Any better?" Lisa asks, chopping vegetables for lunch.

"I'm having a hard time beating this one."

Lisa asks me to describe the flashback. Putting the memories into words, naming and concretizing the feelings associated with the images, often help tremendously. Lisa encourages me to eat something light, to help my body carry through. I follow her advice, eat some toast with peanut butter, and feel a little bit better.

"Are you good to go out or do you need to stay home?" Lisa asks, referencing our original plan to take Hannah and Emily apple picking. Knowing that I have an option is comforting. I don't have to pretend to be fine. In fact, we don't even use the word "fine" anymore to describe how we are feeling. If I'm feeling lousy, all I have to say is, "I'm feeling lousy." Honesty during a flashback is critical.

"Let's go out. I think I can push through this."

IV.

"For real change to take place, the body needs to learn that the danger has passed and to live in the reality of the present."[8]

2:20 PM

The parking lot at the apple orchards is full so we have to park offsite and take a yellow school bus back to the farm. The smell of the bus triggers me further. More memories surface, of my time on the school bus as a child. I hear the playful banter of my classmates. I see their faces. I remember the words that we shared. I feel every bump on the bus. But all of this happened decades ago.

Stay focused on the present, Paul.

I look out the window and stand up to open it, allowing fresh air to enter the stifling bus. I glance across the aisle as Hannah and Emily act like goofballs making silly faces toward one another, just like children should.

Direct your attention to them, Paul. Just enjoy being with your wife and children on this ordinary Saturday afternoon.

But remaining present while being buffeted by memories is just not that easy. And instead of accepting myself and treating myself compassionately, I minimize what I am going through by saying to myself, "You know, it could be worse." I would do better to follow the advice of one female survivor who writes:

> When really strong feelings came up, I was able to say to myself, "I'm going through this now, but this isn't who I am. This is going to pass. In twenty minutes or an hour, I'm not going to be sobbing anymore." And because of that, I experienced much less turmoil. I was able to calm down afterwards in a way I had never calmed down before. And I learned to ease my own suffering by not adding on to what I was going through by being judgmental, harsh or critical of myself. I began to have more compassion for myself.[9]

I know I should be kinder toward myself. But I am having trouble accepting the truth of my past and the depth of the abuse that I endured. I was screamed at, humiliated countless times, and for four years in high school, my sexual orientation was questioned every single day. Chairs were pulled out from under me. My head was smashed into lockers and the asphalt of the playground. I was turned upside down, held by my ankles and dropped twice, by a relative. On a family outing I became locked underground in a cellar, and when the doors were opened and I was discovered, my feelings of fear and terror were silenced, I was told, "only wimpy boys cry," and a family member simply walked away, leaving me alone and in shock. I also suffered two forms of sexual assault *before I turned nine*.

I recognize that my journey through trauma is individual, unique, and should not be minimized in the slightest. I realize that none of these painful childhood experiences need to define me now, that I survived, and that my beautiful adult life requires no pity whatsoever. Still, I wish that somebody would shine a light on me, give me a map, and show me the path through this mental and emotional hell.

3:00 pm

After the bus arrives at the farm, we ride on the back of a tractor to access the apple orchards. The bumpy hayride only heightens my already nauseated state.

But relief is in sight. Being able to walk around outside unencumbered, breathing fresh air, I feel as if I am coming back into a state of control. The boy in me feels calmer and the sense of relief is palpable. We wander through the orchards noting the different varieties of apples and the rotten fruit scattered all over the ground.

Lisa climbs a couple of trees to pick some apples, reliving happy memories from her own childhood. I marvel at her empowered sense of embodiment. One method for conquering childhood trauma involves addressing the parts of the body where trauma is being held. Our bodies remember the abuse that we have suffered, storing the memory until we are ready to address the long-held pain.[10] My running, other exercise, and grounding practices have certainly helped me on my pathway to healing, but God how I wish I had the strength to just let myself give in and go climb a tree. Thirty years after the worst abuse, any sense of leaving the ground, even just to jump three feet off a diving board into the pool, leaves me fear-stricken.

Nonetheless, I realize that for the first time in five and a half hours, I am not noticing my traumatic memories at all. I am grateful to be feeling better. Returning from the orchards to the market, we sample some fresh cinnamon donuts and Lisa purchases some sweet-and-salty popcorn for the kids as a treat. I keep drinking water, nibble on the popcorn, chat with our kids, and I keep breathing as deeply as I can.

5:00 pm

Freedom from my memories is short-lived and once we are back in the car, I am beset once more by flashbacks. The nausea slaps me upside the face again and I feel like someone wants to pull my innards out. I am frustrated to no end. Cranky. Agitated. Fed up. A gentle dinner of grilled chicken and steamed rice is really all I can muster. As I am eating, truly unable to focus on any semblance of conversation with Lisa or our daughters, I wonder how much longer it will be until I feel better. At this point, I am ready to give up on feeling whole or healed. I just want to feel *better*, to experience some sense of lasting *relief*. For a trigger to last this long is becoming quite disturbing.

V.

"He's a grown man. He has to heal from the inside out."[11]

6:30 PM

Hannah and Emily are sitting on the couch watching television with Lisa. I fix myself a cup of peppermint tea and go upstairs to watch Cleveland play Houston in Game 2 of the American League Division Series, hoping that a bit of distraction might help my addled state. In our bedroom, resting beneath the weighted blanket, I watch the ballgame, but I am not focused on what is happening. I begin to lose track of time and drift off. But I am not asleep.

In my mind, I am standing inside my childhood bedroom. The white door is closed. I look at the white bookshelves, matching desk and dresser, the rainbow-striped wallpaper, the door to the closet, and the wall poster with the flags of the United Nations. My childhood bedroom was a refuge for me, a silent place where I could close and lock the door from the bullies in my life. I would write fantasy stories, watch television on a five-inch black-and-white screen or listen to music. In this room, only I could open the door and decide who could come in.

Ironically, once I was grown, I never wanted to come back here. On one visit back to New Jersey, I confessed to Lisa that I thought that ghosts haunted this room and house. There were ghosts—they were my own unresolved nightmares.

Over the course of this year, I have stood next to my childhood bed watching paul and trying to connect with him. When I first began suffering from flashbacks, I couldn't touch or go near paul. I could hear him crying. I could see him shaking beneath a green blanket decorated with the helmets of every NFL team. Sometimes, paul would peek out from underneath the blanket, red-faced and with tear-streaked eyes, and he would tell me, "You wouldn't understand." paul wasn't accustomed to trusting anyone, so how would he be able to trust me?

Early in my healing journey, a smattering of people said, "Just give that boy inside of you a hug and tell him he turns out okay." If only things were that easy. Befriending myself, overcoming years of self-hatred, conquering a lifetime of never feeling *good enough*, is the most difficult challenge I have ever undertaken.

I began running away from New Jersey at the end of high school, never thinking I would need to look back on the earliest years of my life. I fled to St. Louis for university, studied abroad in Madrid, and during my first year of rabbinical school in Jerusalem, I even started going by my Hebrew name *m'nachem*. But the only person I couldn't seem to comfort was myself, and after my mother died during my last year of rabbinical school, I sought a pulpit in Australia and began my life anew, as far away from reality as possible.

As long as I could travel the world, enjoy adventures, and embrace new destinations, I appeared happy. Working between sixty and eighty hours each week caring for other people, relying on numbing behaviors, such as exercise and developing an addiction to empathy, suppressed my pain just enough for me to fill the void of my life with an outpouring of affection and validation from countless others.

Yet my body was beginning to break apart from the inside out. I had the physical endurance to run and complete half-marathons, and weightlift at the gym, but from 2011 onward, I would become sick regularly with crushing chest pain, swollen ankles, and severe achiness throughout my body. Lisa and I thought that I was suffering from a mitral valve prolapse with pronounced symptoms. But a series of emotional breakdowns throughout 2018 led to the surfacing of terrible childhood memories, and a tenuous battle with complex post-traumatic stress disorder.[12] I didn't have a heart condition. I was holding a heartbroken, abandoned child deep within me. I had *left paul behind*.

Reconnecting with my childhood wounds has been critical for healing my trauma—an odyssey[13] from victim, to survivor, to one who is living actively in the present, as a fully integrated adult. I needed to learn that befriending requires only a paucity of words. For what could the adult wordsmith actually say to the shattered, violated boy deep inside him? Over many months, I found that more than talking to paul, I needed to start listening to what he was saying. Sometimes, I would sit with him, kneeling beside the bed, and I would imagine myself placing a hand on his shoulder. He shuddered at first, just as I often do when someone's touch is unwanted. I said nothing, and would withdraw my hand, letting him have his space. I asked paul to tell me about his experiences only when he was ready to. I stayed with him and rather than react to his emotions, I developed more skill in noticing his feelings, becoming, in a sense, an attentive, supportive parent toward my inner child.

In the height of my trauma, I would regularly endure night terror, with fits of crying and shaking, often between 2:00 and 4:00 AM. I reminded myself that if Hannah or Emily were suffering from a similar reaction in the middle of the night, I wouldn't yell at them or disregard them. I would hold them until they reached a place of deeper calm. The same practice held true with paul. Getting angry at myself for being unable to sleep was counterproductive. I needed to learn to hold paul.

Over many months, paul and I started to bond. He showed me everything—even the damning, hurtful, and soul-crushing memories that I did not want to see, confront, or accept about my early life. Suffering from flashbacks required me to endure surges of anxiety, sadness, anger, terror, and dread, like never before.

At times, when I was triggered, past and present events became horrifyingly indistinguishable. On occasion, I acted shamefully and impulsively toward other people. Reflecting on my behavior months later, I know that I cannot retrace my steps. I must live, like everyone else, in the shadowy depths of my own imperfect humanity while also sensitively embracing and accepting others in their own lesser moments.

Ultimately, facing images of such cruelty in my childhood has led me to reconsider my own penchant for snide and cynical comments, as well as the seemingly bottomless depth of my own rage. I truly have no excuse to be anything other than kind, and compassionate toward other people, and when I miss the mark, the pain and shame of my hurtful missteps do not easily dissipate.

At some stage, as my eyes are closed and I am daydreaming about my childhood bedroom, I feel Lisa climb into bed next to me. Her left hand reaches for my right and our fingers lock together in the simplest of comforting gestures. Lisa has walked every step of this journey with me and knows how hard I am fighting to push through, to be a better husband, a less reactive father, and not let my own past continue to weigh me down. She embraces my fingers lovingly; her gentle presence is all that I need.

Back in my mind, I look at paul. Fetal-curled, his head is resting on a Mickey Mouse pillowcase beneath the green blanket. I see the floppy black ears of his Mickey Mouse stuffed animal peeking out from the blanket and I know that he is clutching Mickey for dear life. My heart breaks for him.

Up to this stage on my healing journey, I have looked at paul eye-to-eye, and I have sat with him on the bed when he has let me. Right now, however, he is fast asleep from a full day of feeling sick. And so I prepare to do something that I have never done.

I climb into my childhood bed, imagining that the soft mattress sinks and the box-spring creaks under my adult weight. I lie down next to paul, placing my arm over him. For the first time in nearly ten months of trauma, I find myself holding paul as he rests quietly. Tears begin to stream down my face with what has become, in nearly every episode, a signal that my flashback is finally coming to an end. It is the first time all day that I have been able to cry, the salty wetness a necessary emotional release.

Lisa notices my tears and holds my hand more tightly. I wipe my tears with my free hand, leaving my eyes closed. I have always wanted someone to take away the pain, to help me to feel better, to listen to me, and to validate my feelings, but the truth is what our Rabbis teach, that those who visit us in our time of suffering only take away one-sixtieth of our pain.[14] I never thought that I would simply have the strength to hold myself, without words or affirmation—nothing, just presence, just the gift of holding my own small boy in my adult embrace, knowing that he was perfectly, truly, safe.

Hannah and Emily come running into our bedroom.

"Can Daddy come and play with us?" one of them asks.

"Daddy is just resting," I hear Lisa say.

"Awww . . ." An expression of their disappointment.

"Just give me a few minutes girls, and I'll come to you. I just have my eyes closed."

God, please, just a few more minutes with paul. I have worked so hard to get here. I just want to savor this moment, this beauty, for a little while longer.

Today has been a difficult day. I cannot know what tomorrow will bring. But in the present, I am ready to take myself out of my memory. I open my eyes, smile at Lisa, and climb out of bed to go and play with Hannah and Emily. In the back of my mind, I have a new, special, younger friend, who I am coming to learn is a smart, sweet, sensitive boy who *survived*, became a good man, and now, is healing deep wounds and thriving as an adult.

TIMELINE OF A TRIGGER

* * * * *

Author's Note—Summer 2019

Medication and ongoing therapy, coupled with a greater adeptness in navigating my triggers, further assisted in lessening the intensity of my memories, enabling me to find considerable relief. As of the beginning of August 2019, having chosen to leave the congregational rabbinate and return to Australia with my family, I am pleased to report that I no longer require medication. I am experiencing only minimal flashbacks. Night terror is no longer a cause for concern and for the first time since I was a teenager, I am not plagued by suicidal ideation. With each passing day, I feel much more present and secure in myself, and the joy with which I am approaching my life is palpable.

Notes

1. Bessel van der Kolk, *The Body Keeps the Score: Brain, Mind and Body in the Healing of Trauma.* (New York: Penguin Books, 2015), Kindle Locations 3736–88.
2. Ellen Bass, *The Courage to Heal: A Guide for Women Survivors of Child Sexual Abuse,* 4th ed. (Collins Living, 2008; 1st. ed. 1998), Kindle Locations 12417–19.
3. https://www.verywellmind.com/grounding-techniques-for-ptsd-2797300.
4. Bass, *Courage to Heal,* Kindle Location 12461.
5. Mike Lew, *Victims No Longer: The Classic Guide for Men Recovering from Sexual Child Abuse,* 2nd ed. (Boston: Small Wonders Books, 2004), Kindle Locations 1365–78.
6. https://www.livingwell.org.au/managing-difficulties/dealing-with-flashbacks/.
7. https://www.verywellmind.com/hyperarousal-2797362.
8. van der Kolk, *Body Keeps the Score,* Kindle Location 564.
9. Bass, *Courage to Heal,* Kindle Locations 13468–73.
10. van der Kolk, *Body Keeps the Score,* Kindle Locations 558–560.
11. From *Creed II,* motion picture (2018), said by Mary Anne Creed, played by Phylicia Rashad to Bianca, played by Tessa Thompson.
12. https://www.medicalnewstoday.com/articles/322886.php. The diagnosis of c-PTSD may be issued in circumstances where the individual has suffered repeated or prolonged abuse. Classified as an anxiety disorder with implications arising from confused or insecure attachments in childhood, c-PTSD is best addressed by

helping the individual to achieve a stronger sense of self, firmly grounded in present activities.

13. The term "odyssey" to describe a healing journey is used by Mike Lew in *Victims No Longer*, Kindle Locations 441–47. Lew writes, "The first time I used the term "odyssey" to describe the recovery process, my editor, Peter Nevraumont, responded, "I think this word is a key one . . . the word has many pertinent, positive connotations. Odyssey meaning voyage of discovery of a problem that has been hidden and discovery by the victims that they are not alone. Odyssey meaning heroic journey in (to the psyche) requires as much if not more bravery than a journey out (to the external unknown). Odyssey meaning journey of considerable length; the odyssey you are proposing is not like a trip to the corner for a quart of milk. The odyssey you are proposing requires strength of character, curiosity, a sense of adventure, and a willingness to stick with it."

14. BT *N'darim* 39b.

Healing from Pain

Stephen Robbins

I am well acquainted with traumatic illness, near death experience, long periods of pain, and enforced recovery. Beginning with the trauma of being born dead in 1944 and revived by the doctor, I entered the world setting a major theme for my life. A chronology of my illness and recovery: traumatic eye operations at age 2–3; near fatal hepatitis; rupture of two discs and immobility for months; influenza, which destroyed the lining of my lungs with recurring lung collapses; and long hospitalizations when I was rabbi at Temple Emanuel, Beverly Hills, and the resulting massive shingles infection destroying extensive nerves on the right side of my body, leaving me in level 10 pain for the past fourteen years. Even more astounding, throughout I experienced NDEs (near death experiences), which culminated in new focus and direction for my work as rabbi.

Each of these illnesses provided its own unique impact on my inner life, spiritual development, and direction.

My critical and chronic respiratory illnesses in 1987 and 1991 led to a shift in my view of Judaism and personal spiritual practice as a Jew and service to my congregation. It was shortly thereafter that I left Temple Emanuel and cofounded with my wife, Eva, Congregation N'vay Shalom, based on psycho-spiritual and kabbalistic wisdom as a means for serving the needs of individual Jews. From 1993 to 2005 my wife and I shared a fulfilling work partnership leading our congregation, my wife as cantor and me as teacher and guide. I was also teaching in the continuing education department at the then University of Judaism, teaching introductory

---

RABBI STEPHEN ROBBINS (C72) received his Psy.D. from Ryokan College, Los Angeles. He was Hillel Director at the University of Cincinnati and University of Berkeley, 1970–1978. In 1978 he became rabbi of Temple Emanuel of Beverly Hills, California, and in 1993 he cofounded with Rabbi Eva Robbins N'vay Shalom, followed by cofounding the Academy for Jewish Religion, California in 2000, and is presently on the faculty. He is also in private practice using kabbalistic principles and techniques.

and advanced classes in Kabbalah and Jewish meditation for over twelve years, when our lives imploded. Consumed with a pain that I had never experienced before in my life, I was given pain medication, none of which worked. My wife reluctantly agreed to take me home and so began a journey of tests and challenges that have brought me, and my wife, to where we are today.

Professionally I was devastated. As president of the AJRCA (Academy for Jewish Religion, California), of which I was a co-founder, teaching a number of classes, I realized that I had to withdraw, and life was going to take a devastating turn. I was heavily sedated by a protocol of fentanyl, methadone, and Norco, and it quickly became clear that I had to get off these dangerous drugs or be a zombie the rest of my life. The spiritual practice I had taught to others was something I drew from during these tumultuous times.

My rich professional life came to a crashing end. There was no way that I was mentally coherent and physically dependable, and it was my wife who stepped into the breach and began her own odyssey of transformation. We faced a total reversal of roles. This was a challenge for me as I was always the one who spoke, stood in front, and led the way.

Having lived a rich professional life with a profound sense of gratitude and accomplishment, I wondered whether this was a message that I was to stop and begin a whole new path of serving as rabbi. I experienced not only the inner loss of the work I loved, but many of our congregants left because I could no longer fulfill their needs. Over the years our congregation became an empty vessel with only a limited number of devoted supporters.

I found great strength in profound memories with my grandmother, Dorah Luria. She had come to America at sixteen in the 1890s sent by my great-grandfather Avraham Joseph Luria from Kasrolov in Bellarus. My grandmother has since passed, but in remembering her loving touch and understanding, I was able to face the coming traumas and illnesses with a sense of purpose rather than the feeling of being a victim.

All of my life and work as a rabbi has been oriented toward serving people. My work focused more intently on the spiritual and psychological experience of Judaism. After devastating hepatitis during my years at HUC-JIR/Los Angeles, which resulted in my withdrawal from the school for one year, I began to practice more regularly my own spiritual rituals including wearing tallit and *t'fillin*, nighttime prayers and ceremonies, and the focusing of my inner experience of the spiritual challenges that I had met and overcome. I needed to connect all Jews on this level of the personal, psychological, and spiritual journey. Very soon after my recovery I was hired by several synagogues and other institutions to begin teaching this integrative approach of confluent education, based both on intellectual and experiential models, what today we refer to as psycho-spiritual.

In 1978, we made the big move, as I became the assistant rabbi at Temple Emanuel in Beverly Hills, California. In my first full-time synagogue pulpit, I immediately began applying the approach that had been developing all these years. Teaching and preaching this psycho-spiritual healing message, I began the early years of doing *kavanot* before certain prayers, helping the congregation find their own personal connection to the Holy One. The congregation responded so positively to my teaching that I was encouraged to apply it in other venues. Our synagogue also became a central place for those seeking conversion, of which I became a primary teacher. I also became active in awakening the Jewish community to the dangers of cults and missionary programs. This work enabled me to further develop the pathways of Jewish wisdom and spiritual practice, awakening those who were controlled of mind, body, and spirit.

My first devastating flu, in 1985, began a series of three bouts with collapsed lungs, NDEs, and long-term recoveries. The NDEs made me aware that my life could be turned upside down in a second. This was particularly challenging as our family had grown now to three children. The impact of this original flu was traumatic for the whole family, particularly because I became inordinately sensitive to environmental influences and was on high doses of medications with very negative side effects both physically and on my behavior. I didn't have the tools to cope well with the resulting impact, and it was by my family's patience and the grace of God that I managed to come through more whole and insightful than I had ever been.

I returned to work determined to make a commitment to my life and my family—but in late December 1990 I once again faced another lung collapse and near-death moment accompanied by another extensive stay at the hospital. After my release, I discovered alternative forms of medicine from two brilliant practitioners who opened in me the capacity to experience my illness and its psycho-spiritual messages. Their tutelage taught me new approaches to healing, which I then incorporated into my own personal life and professional teaching and practice. This led me to embark on the next stage of my spiritual growth, founding, with Eva, N'vay Shalom, a synagogue especially committed to spiritual practice and awareness.

So here we are, living with the perpetual searing pain that has forced me to look deeply into my mind and my soul for ways to cope with what I face. What I've learned and developed falls into multiple categories: western medicine, naturopathic medicine, meditation, hands-on healing, psychoneuroimmunology of trauma, and the application of kabbalistic wisdom. Everything I have learned was in preparation for this moment, particularly, the spiritual path of *kavanah* (spiritual intention and focus) and *d'veikut* (bonding and attachment to the Holy One). I am inspired by the Book of Job; the prophecies of Ezekiel; the narrative of Elijah; the transformative moments for Moses, Abraham, Jacob; and the rabbis from the fall of Jerusalem to the collapse of the *Bar Kochba* revolution; along with kabbalistic texts of *Sefer Yetzirah*, *Bahir*, and the *Zohar*; as well as the wisdom of my ancestor, the Ari, and my great-grandfather Avraham Joseph Luria. All of them have taught me, and continue to teach me, as my life unfolds from abject suffering to the capacity to work, study, and teach, when my attention and strength allow it.

I have learned that to have human contact is one of the most healing resources that aids me in my capacity to heal myself. The most important is my wonderful wife, Eva, who has accompanied me through every moment of this agonizing journey. Her touch eases pain and helps me find *shalom uv'racha*. When she sings, her voice is like wings of the *Shechinah*, who lifts me up and flies me above raging disorder.

It says in *Maavor Yavok* (Crossing the Yabok River) Chapter 6, that whoever visits a sick person becomes their healer. For me the few loyal friends, students, congregants, and colleagues, who have expressed their love and their gratitude have kept me from withdrawing into my tortured existence and enabled me to rediscover joy.

My use of meditation helps silence the pain and helps me transcend it. The medications I take lower the pain from 10 to about 7, which means I need to use my own resources to bring it down even lower. I focus on my breath, what I call *n'ran* breathing (*nefesh, ruach, and n'shamah*), which I developed years ago to still the mind and provide the source for consciousness to overcome physical condition. Drawing on the experience of being revived in my birth, and the image of Genesis 2:7, where God blows into the nostrils of Adam, I created this image and three-step process I call Divine CPR. As I breathe in through my nose slowly, I am inspired to live, and as I exhale, I am returning the gift of breath back to the One who gave it to me. Last is a pause which represents *n'shamah*, the presence of the Holy One. This triangular breath reconnects me to my soul and the spark of God's Presence that is always within.

God's name has helped sustain me and led me to know that suffering is a state of mind and pain a state of the body. Most of the time I live in this separation and the pain is irrelevant. There are times when the pain breaks through and I lose my focus, falling into the pain and all of the consequences. I reach out and receive, again, that precious name that is given to us, *yod-hei-vav-hei* (*YHVH*) in its vertical calligraphy that is the shape of the human body. In *The Anatomy of the Soul*, Rebbe Nachman makes the point that the most holy part of the human body is the physical skeleton, which itself contains that holy name. I have learned to focus on this name to reawaken my bonding with it when pain makes me lose touch. In addition, I have learned to apply the form of the kabbalistic *Eitz Chayim* and the Four Worlds to the specific places where the pain, emotional, cognitive, and spiritual dimensions are most present and active. In doing this, the pain and the dysfunction is ameliorated, and I find joy and a sense of gratitude.

Despite not having had a full night's sleep over these fourteen years, I still find myself reciting *Modeh Ani*, which reminds me that my pure soul is returned to me and I have another day to live. Following, there are certain *t'filot* that are fundamental to my healing. In the prayers and meditations before donning the tallit, there is the spiritual focus on its meaning; the unfinished nature of the edges, which represent the incomplete universe in which we live; and the *tzitzit*, whose five knots represent the five dimensions of the soul: *y'chidah, chayah, n'shamah, ruach,* and lastly *nefesh*; and the four spaces of the letters of The Name. The four tzitzit represent the Four Worlds, *assiyah, yetzirah, briah,* and *atzilut*. When I prepare to put on the tallit, I focus on the weaving of the fabric and the weaving of my being. Holding the tzitzit in my hands, I meditate on the meaning of the knots and spaces that lifts me above physical reality and psychological dysfunction, so I can live in gratitude, joy, and love. Then I read the *Barchi Nafshi*, which has come to mean for me that I am wrapped in light, like a garment, and I find my place in this existence. Then I take my *t'fillin* and meditate on *l'shem yichud* and the deep meaning of *yichud* between the Holy One and *Shechinah* and how it brings me a sense of wholeness and repair of my body.

Along with this practice I find two prayers essential for my healing: The first is the *Sh'ma*, and the second is the *G'vurot*. There is a particularly unique way I have constructed the meditating of the *Sh'ma*. I break it down into five in and five out breaths with four pauses. This has given me the experience of transcending this world. In addition, it draws the presence of the Holy One into this world, into me, and out through me to those who are in my life.

The *G'vurot* is for me the most profound of healing prayers in that the phrase *m'chayei hameitim* is used as a verb instead of a noun, meaning reviving "the dying" and not "the dead" since all the verbs in this prayer are in *kal*; they are each a gerund. What this does is reinforce this experience of the Holy Presence as continuing healing of the shattering and reforming of this world every day.

Focusing on my spiritual practice has brought continued healing. I have a very specific sense of purpose that has been redirected as a result of these past fourteen years. I have discovered a new community for myself, as a result of the NDEs. I haven't found any of my colleagues, as yet, who have experienced NDEs; perhaps this writing will encourage them to share. I have found a new home where I can share my personal knowledge as well as the Judaic approach to illness, dying, death, and return. It is fulfilling to find a new community to share the richness of my tradition in the hopes that it will help others in their healing.

I am grateful for a forum within my own tradition to share what I have experienced and learned in the hopes that it can support you, or someone in your community, to find hope and ways to manage pain which afflicts so many of us. Lastly, let me share a prayer I use for myself and with those in need of healing:

> May it be Your will, Hashem, my God, that this medicine/treatment should bring me healing,
> for You send healing as a free gift. Blessed is the Healer of the Sick.
>
> *Y'hi ratzon milfanecha, Adonai Elohai, she'yehai aisek*
> *Zeh li lir'fuah ki rofeh chinam Atah. Baruch Rofeh Cholim.*
> (*B'rachot* 60a, *Shulchan Aruch* 230:4)

Thoughts on a Living God

Richard Agler

A God about whom we dare not think is a God a thinking mind cannot worship.

— E. S. Brightman[1]

Writing my book *The Tragedy Test: Making Sense of Life-Changing Loss—A Rabbi's Journey*, required a healthy quotient of God-thinking. The book looks at questions such as, Where is God in tragedy? What kind of God-understanding can help us through it? and What kind of God-understanding fails us when we most need it?

Bringing the book to life was not merely an academic exercise. These questions, familiar to clergy of all faiths, became burning issues for me after my wife Mindy and I experienced the sudden, accidental, and tragic death of our twenty-six-year-old daughter Talia in 2012.

We know that such questions are at least as old as the Book of Job. Most often, rabbis face them in the wake of serious loss. Most often, we take our cue from Harold Kushner's *When Bad Things Happen to Good People* (1981). We acknowledge that there are things we cannot explain, that there are questions we cannot answer—and we hug. If we think it will be comforting, we might also add words about *olam haba* (a life after this one).

It is a decent response insofar as it goes, and it is what my family experienced after Tali's death. In the near-term, we were cared for, extraordinarily, by colleagues, family, friends, and loved ones. I've said that no one should ever have to go through something like this; but anyone who does should only be taken care of by people

---

RABBI RICHARD AGLER (NY78) is the founding rabbi, now rabbi emeritus, of Congregation B'nai Israel in Boca Raton, Florida. He currently serves as co-director of the Tali Fund, Inc., and as resident scholar at the Keys Jewish Community Center in Tavernier, Florida. *The Tragedy Test—Making Sense of Life-Changing Loss* is his first book.

of the caliber who cared for us. We were grateful beyond words for every bit of it.

But when the dust settled, it was clear that we were only at the beginning. In addition to the continuing heartbreak, and even in the presence of the redemptive *tzedakah* projects we had undertaken in Tali's name, there were too many questions that I needed to answer but couldn't. If this was true for me, an arguably mature rabbi, what did that say for everyone else?

So I sat down to write. For the most part, to come to terms with one essential question: What, in the name of God, had just happened to us?

Things like this are not supposed to happen. She was too good. We had done everything right. Not perfectly, of course, but right. It was catastrophically unfair.

And where was God? The Righteous Judge of our tradition, who asks devotion, service, and decency from us in exchange for blessing, and we are told, protection, in return? Where was that God—the God of our sacred texts, books, and legends? That God was nowhere to be found, at least not by me, at least not then.

Again, these questions are not new. Like all of us, I knew many ways to answer them. But now, when I needed them most, those answers were not good enough.

The God Questions

Rabbis typically become rabbis for love of some combination of God, Torah, and Israel. For me it started with God. I believed there was a God. I believed I had experienced God. As a young adult, with sky above and mother earth below, I felt a powerful sense of what I took to be God's presence. No drugs were involved. I later learned it could be described as a mystical experience, such as have been recorded in every age and culture since time immemorial.

I had also experienced what I took to be God's presence on countless occasions since—in my rabbinate, as a husband, father, friend, and while journeying through life in general. Now, in addition to the shock on the emotional, family, and every other level, my spiritual-religious life was upended, too. Where was the God I had been serving? Where was the God I thought I knew?

We've all had to answer questions like these. What about the Holocaust? That one, of course, is relatively easy theologically because we can blame human evil, free will, and standing idly by. Other times it's not so easy. Why did my child die of cancer? Why would God do this to me? How can I believe in a God who acts in such a way?

Some rabbis, echoing voices from within the tradition, say things like, God has a master plan and while it may be hidden from us, we need to have faith that it exists. Or, Her work on earth was done and God took her to be in heaven. Or, It's not that God didn't answer our prayers, it was that God said no—for our own good, of course. And, Even when we don't comprehend them, God has God's own reasons. We heard some of that too. Generally not from colleagues (with the exception of a Chabad-nik or two), but from everyday people. I was forgiving. People were simply trying their best to be comforting.

Most of us, I'm guessing, don't say things like that. As graduates of the School of Kushner, we plead ignorance and act pastorally. Again, that's probably wise. There are things we don't understand, and it's better to admit it than to pretend otherwise.

Yet as a rule, we do not quote Elisha ben Abuya, "*Leit din v'leit dayan*" (there is no justice and there is no judge)—either. Nor do we customarily offer counsel based on Shakespeare's Macbeth, "Life's but . . . a tale told by an idiot, full of sound and fury, signifying nothing."[2]

We don't quote them, even if we have moments when we strongly suspect they are right, or at the very least, onto something. Who among us has not thought that there's an awful lot of *hefkerut* out there? And that the evidence that a responsible adult—much less a *Dayan Emet* (Righteous Judge)—is in charge is, at best, insufficient.

Neither of these alternatives appealed to me. The first, that God had some unfathomable reason, might be acceptable in some *batei midrash*, but to the grieving parent of an innocent child, or at least of a child who had not committed a capital offense, it is basically obscene. No God who is supposed to be just, to say nothing of loving, can act this way.

If the terms of the relationship are that I need to love and serve God with all my heart and then God is free to rip my heart out for no comprehensible reason, we might well describe the relationship in psychological terms as abusive. I had no interest in being a party to any such relationship.

Living in Aher's or Macbeth's world of no justice and no Judge, of sound and fury signifying nothing, did not appeal to me, either.

And Kushner's prescription likewise fell short. I was hugged. I felt the love. It was beautiful. Now what?

I needed something more. A life without a living God seemed as unpalatable to me as a life with a God who deliberately took Talia. Where was the faith that made sense, was coherent and supportive? I made it my business to look for it.

Progressive Jews, nonprogressive Jews, nonaffiliated Jews, so-called secular Jews, and for that matter non-Jews—all suffer life-changing loss, and all ask these same questions. People want to know what faith, theirs or any other, has to say in response.

We want to know how faith is going to help us get through. Not just for the shivah and *sh'loshim,* but for the rest of our lives. These questions go to the very heart of what faith is for—and they cannot be dismissed. When we take on the rituals, pray the words, and support the institutions to the extent that we do, we expect faith to be there for us when we need it.

There's an analogy to soldiers, police officers, and first responders, whose jobs, some say, are ninety-nine percent boredom and one percent terror; yet it's their ability to help us during those moments of one percent terror that we collectively appreciate and pay them for.

Religion's equivalent is loss, especially grievous loss. What is faith going to do for us during that one percent of the time when everything is on the line, when we are desperate for understanding, when it really matters?

We Need to Answer Them

Before I address this religiously and spiritually, I'd like to look at how it may be affecting us institutionally.

We know that we are living in a period of diminished religious affiliation. We have all heard numerous explanations for it. But there is one explanation we haven't heard very often—at least I haven't. It is that people keep their distance from established houses of worship because they are not especially impressed with the God they meet when they are there.

Those who claim to be "spiritual but not religious," and those who, when asked for religious affiliation, answer "none," meet a God in synagogues, churches, mosques, etc., who may not make as much sense as they wish God would—or need God to. Not to put too fine a point on it, the God of "organized religion," the God of many of our sacred scriptures and legends, is a God who offers too many answers that are inconsistent with people's life experiences and understanding.

I suspect that we, who are deeply invested in the whole enterprise, and are relatively sophisticated about it, may be willing to cut our texts and traditions a certain amount of slack. Those who are not may be less inclined to do so.

Rasha v'tov lo and *tzaddik v'ra lo* (the wicked who prosper and the righteous who suffer) are ancient conundrums. But they may matter to moderns and postmoderns more than we realize. And rabbis, priests, ministers, and imams who try to square the circle of a just and powerful God who allows (or even orchestrates) unjust outcomes may not be helping.

While historically, people may not have always liked the answers they heard (e.g., that God has God's own reasons; that it's a mystery; that she's in heaven; that God said no; that God is doing this because he loves us), they didn't always have anywhere else to turn. Today, they do. They are free to walk out the door with little, if any, social or cultural price to be paid.

Perhaps we should consider that people are disaffiliating because the God they meet in established houses of worship is not credibly, or adequately, addressing questions they are asking and consider important—those one percent questions that really matter.

When Tali died, that God was not credibly or adequately addressing them for me, either.

I needed a God that didn't ask me to believe in propositions that were, at best, holdovers from ancient times or at worst, upon further review, cruel and abusive. I needed an understanding of God that provided, to the greatest extent possible, believable answers to those one percent questions that really mattered.

The God of Law and Spirit

I may have found one. I hasten to add that this God does not give me everything I want, or even need. It may not give you everything you want or need, either.

Of course there are people who say that a God who doesn't give us everything we need is not much of a God to begin with. After all, we turn to God because there are gaps in our understanding, and in our lives. We turn to God to help us explain the inexplicable. We turn to God because we want wholeness, completeness (*sh'leimut*).

But as thinkers have pointed out for generations, if God really is, and does, everything, then the responsibility for the world's innumerable horrors rests on God's hands and shoulders. We are, at best, uncomfortable with this.

My former understanding of God finessed these issues and was perhaps too quick to plead ignorance in the face of them. In exchange, God provided me with comfort and reassurance.

My new understanding offers, I believe, greater understanding but, alas, less reassurance and comfort. No wonder that I, and many others, do not choose this path, or make this trade, unless we feel there is no other choice.

All this has led me to the God I call the "God of Law and Spirit." It is not complicated. The "Law" is derived, in varying degrees, from the understandings of Maimonides, Spinoza, Einstein, and others. In short, there is no getting around the fact that there are Laws in the universe that rule us all. They are invariable and immutable. The laws of physics and nature pervade everything, everywhere, from the most distant cosmos to the subatomic particles within us and around us. We either live in accordance with them or we do not live at all. I understand God as being one with these laws.

In addition to Law, there is Spirit, the qualities we all recognize as essential for religious life, for spiritual life, and even for life itself: love, kindness, compassion; the pursuits of wisdom, justice, holiness, and sacred experience.

Critically, and sadly, this God of Law and Spirit is limited. This God cannot and does not overturn the laws of nature in order to bring about desired outcomes on behalf of any person, people, or nation. And it is fruitless to try, and wrong to say, "It could happen so you might as well ask." Because making such requests only lays the foundation for a future sense of disappointment, resentment, anger, or even betrayal when God fails to act in what we perceive to be a just fashion.

Lest we think that this is radical or heretical, it's pretty clear that our Rabbis understood this dynamic as well. We can see it in their descriptions of *t'filat shav*, the so-called vain prayers that ask God that the fire we see in the distance be at someone else's house or the sex of our unborn child be one or the other.[3] The outcome of these events have already been determined and it is vain, empty, foolish, and wrong to ask God to change them.

It may be helpful to ask how many of our own prayers, by whatever name, formal or informal, official, published or not, are, in reality, *t'filat shav*, requests to change the laws of nature or events whose outcome has already been determined. In other words, how many of them are prayers addressed to a God who is not there?

Accepting this perspective means accepting that God is limited. It means accepting that God cannot, and certainly does not, do anywhere near the number of things we would wish, want, or need God to do. But while God does not implement justice in this world—God being far too limited to do so on her own—God's Spirit can inspire us to do so.

We can be strong in that Spirit—and we need to be. Spirit can change outcomes. But it does not prevail anywhere near as often as we would like. In the age-old struggle between Law and Spirit, in case of a tie, the Law wins.

There are certainly times when we would prefer it the other way. But the God who is Law and the God who is Spirit, this God who is limited, is a God who makes sense.

The answer to the question, "Why did this tragedy happen?" may well be that the Laws of the universe required it to. When my one-hundred-pound daughter was hit by a three-ton motor vehicle moving at speed, the Law instantly determined what the outcome would be. *Fini.*

But not quite *Fini*. Even after death and tragedy, Spirit lives on. And again, while it cannot do everything, it can do a great deal. Spirit enables us to heal from tragedy and trauma—in part by teaching us to honor, and build upon, legacy. Spirit enables us to feel, and recognize, *k'dushah*—that which is most holy. Spirit can bond us together, healing in community.

Reconnection

The God of Law and Spirit may well be worthy of our devotion, service, commitment, and aspiration. Because it is neither wrong nor foolish to believe that:

1. The laws of physics and nature are all-encompassing, universal, and determinative.

2. These laws, God's Laws, if you will, can create tragic outcomes—for no higher purpose or reason.
3. God does not intervene in our lives to prevent such tragedies—or to inflict them.
4. God nevertheless lives in Spirit. Through the sacred values of goodness, love, wisdom, compassion, justice, and more.

I daresay that this describes the God that many, if not most of us, believe in. But it is not the God that we have taught to our people, certainly not in any clear, much less systematic, way. It is not the God who is reflected in many of our most popular sacred texts, liturgies, and holidays. We've signed on to too much mythological narrative and not enough reality. And in tragedy, much of that mythology fails—and fails spectacularly.

Again, it took a tragedy for me to work through all of this. I was willing to do it because I was committed to and invested in a living Jewish faith. That faith had done much for me and when I needed it to do more, happy day, it could. Differently to be sure, but my living faith survived.

The God of Law and Spirit may not be all the God that we, or for that matter I, want. This God does not provide soothing answers to life's real horrors. But it is a God who provides honest ones. I've come to think of the God of Law and Spirit as a God for grownups.

This has been my journey. Even in retrospect, it has been a blessed one. I'm going forward with my learning, with my service, and with my faith in God, Torah, and Israel.

I am teaching, I am doing charitable work, I am perpetuating my daughter's legacy, and I hope, through the publication of *The Tragedy Test*, to be sharing these ideas with others.

But I remain deeply wounded. And no God in whom I can believe, at least at the present time, can erase that.

Epilogue

The words of the Twenty-Third Psalm are as famous as any in the Bible. After Talia's death, one of the words, and subsequently the Psalm as a whole, took on new meaning for me.

The well-known final verse reads, "Surely goodness and mercy will follow me all the days of my life, and I shall dwell in the house of God forever."

The first word of the verse is almost universally translated into English as "surely." But the original Hebrew, *ach*,[4] may not mean "surely" at all. According to the Rabbis, *ach* is a particle of speech indicating limitation or diminution.[5] Employing this definition, we can render the beginning of the verse as: "*A lesser sense of* goodness and mercy will follow me all the days of my life. . . ."

If we have, in fact, walked through the valley of the shadow of death, we know full well the diminished sense of God's goodness and mercy that now accompanies us. We can extend this understanding and read the psalm's conclusion as: "*Nevertheless*, I will dwell in the house of God forever."

Having been under the cast of death's shadow, we are not the same people we were before. There is no sense pretending otherwise. Nevertheless, walking along the paths that lead to righteousness give us some sense of being, still, in the presence of the Holy One who is Most High.

Notes

1. E. S. Brightman, The Finding of God (New York: The Abingdon Press, 1931), 26.
2. Shakespeare, Macbeth, act 5, scene 5.
3. Mishnah B'rachot 9:3.
4. אך.
5. JT B'rachot 9:14b, אכין ורקין מעוטין.

*Spiritual Practice and
Lifelong Wellness*

Embodied Spiritual Practices: Cultivating Sense Perceptions as Gateways to Holiness

Myriam Klotz

Though one day each of us will take leave of our bodies, while we are alive, all that we think, say, and do comes through the portal of this physical aliveness. We are housed in some square footage of skin, our largest organ, and moment by moment the continuing pulsations of breath and blood gift us with our ever-fluctuating capacities of vitality and strength in the body.

We have a unique capacity as humans to bring awareness to the fact that we are actually now alive, that our bodies are mortal physical forms of undying yet evolving and perhaps eternal consciousness itself. Therefore, does it matter how we choose to relate to this physical aliveness? What purpose might the cultivation of our sensory awareness or our capacities for placing our attention on the sensations or actions of the body serve, beyond the maintenance of living itself?

We could say that our body is like a rental car, a vehicle for getting from place to place and enabling us to live our lives and do all that we do in realms sacred and secular. Some may feel that we simply have to bear these unreliable, unpredictable bodies as they support the life of the mind, spirit, and heart, which are of primary

---

RABBI MYRIAM KLOTZ was the founding director of the Spirituality Initiative at HUC-JIR from 2009 to 2017, where she currently oversees Spiritual Direction programming and is the director of the Bekhol Levavkha Jewish Spiritual Direction Training Program. She has served on the faculty of the Institute for Jewish Spirituality since 2003 teaching yoga and embodied practice and has co-created and directed the Yoga and Jewish Spirituality Teacher Training at Isabella Freedman Jewish Retreat Center.

importance, meaning, and value. In this stance, the imperative is that we should get on with the important things rather than pause to feel a breath moving in the body, or to see the dew drop on the tip of a leaf, to hear the sound of wind whistling through tall grass, or to feel the soft warmth of skin as we place the palms of our hands against one another.

By contrast to this modern and postmodern worldview, in which faster is better and information moves at lightning speeds, Jewish wisdom teaches us that there is inherent value in the pause—that it is worthwhile to notice the change of light to darkness as day slides into evening and then into night. Jewish liturgy instructs us to quiet our busy minds to observe stars in the sky and the waxing and waning of the moon. It guides us to listen for the first sounds of the rooster, and to behold those first bands of light in the dawning new morning.

Jewish practices exist to help us attune not only our minds, hearts, and spirits to these sacred rhythms, but also our bodies. If not for our somatic, or bodily, capacity for sense perception, in fact, how could we see the dawn or twilight, the twinkle of the three stars marking the end of Shabbat, or hear the rooster crowing? Jewish wisdom guides us to cultivate sensory awareness so that we might live in a holy way. Jewish teachings guide us to touch, taste, smell, and see this world deeply and with awareness. Our bodies enable our existence to co-create a pathway of holy living. As yoga master BKS Iyengar writes, "If you say you are your body, you are wrong. If you say you are not your body, you are also wrong."[1] This paradox is not to be solved, but rather, perhaps clears a pathway of practice requiring plenty of patience, persistence, forgiveness, and humor over the course of a life.

For many of us who have chosen to become rabbis, we incline towards Jewish values and ways of living as we seek to sync our ancient inheritance with our present zeitgeist and create new possibilities for an evolving future. While it may not seem necessary to dedicate time towards contemplation of the realms of sensory experience and somatic intelligence that enliven us, it is as Jews and human beings wise, healing, and sane, to do so. The challenge for us, I believe, is that while we may know this to be true, it is a lot easier thought and said than done.

Because we cannot escape the moment in which we collectively live, the dissonance that may exist between what we think, what we profess, and what we actually do can be quite insidious. For example, we may sense that "taking" time to be aware of what our bodies are telling us, such as the need to slow down and simply be, is a very Jewish way of being in the world, an embodiment of Shabbat as practice and concept. We may even preach about taking a long slow deep breath and releasing it fully on Friday night in synagogue. However, it may be harder to actually live in a rhythm of doing and being, of pausing physically long enough to let rest find us and shift our blood pressure, our breathing, the tense places we carry stress as we rush from task to task.

How often, for example, have we thought, "I should take the time to do this one thing now and actually pay attention to what I'm doing. But since I only have a few minutes now, and so much needs to get done, I'm going to multitask and get it all done efficiently! Then, later, when I'm not rushed, I'll slow down and be where I am and do that thing slowly, fully, finishing it first and THEN turning my attention to the next thing"?

It may seem obvious that both Jewish tradition and our own life experience point to the importance of living in alignment with the wisdom and intelligence of our own bodies. We likely have studied that in biblical Hebrew, *nefesh* refers to a soul embodied in an inextricable way that is simple and a given. In other words, in the biblical period, there was no separation between the soul and the physical body, so long as body and soul were knit together in the form of a living human being. Yet, it may be far less obvious how we actually go about living our lives each day as if we really believed that we (and each human being) were a *nefesh*, a mortal embodiment of divine spirit housed in our every cell. Rather, in this sense we live in a kind of *galut*, like Mr. Duffy in James Joyce's *Dubliners*, who "lived a short distance from his body." It takes patience, perseverance, forgiveness, and humor to notice when we've traveled that short distance from our bodies, living as it were outside of ourselves, and to welcome ourselves home once again.

We may seek to live as rabbinic leaders teaching about living an integrated and healthy life of meaning, but if we live a short distance from our own body, we might find it hard to overcome the very forces that undermine such wholeness. In some cases, we can even become vulnerable to making an intellectual or spiritual "bypass" that separates rather than integrates the spiritual and the emotional, somatic realms within us.[2]

If we have experienced acute or chronic trauma, for example, we may not be able to process the painful events consciously. We may think we forget about them, but the memories lives inside our bodies, which do not forget. There is a cellular, bodily memory of suffering that has not had a safe way yet to be addressed. Traumas can be subtle, daily assaults on our beings we cannot identify but which we feel. In some instances, we can become vulnerable to manifestations of PTSD and habituated maladaptive coping mechanisms such as addictions, physical and mental illness, and of driving ourselves very hard in our lives in attempts to override and suppress the messages our bodies are giving us.

Trauma can be experienced collectively as well as individually. I believe that it is not a coincidence that Jews have been labeled as "the people of the book." Intellectually and spiritually rich, Jews have also been physically traumatized and displaced over centuries of *galut*.[3] Even if we did not directly experience traumas that our grandparents, parents, or other ancestors did, they live in us as they are literally passed down through our very DNA.[4] Some Jews, such as Jews of color, LGBTQI Jews, or those with physical or intellectual disabilities, have likely experienced traumas directly and indirectly, as they have received messages that it is not safe to be both in their bodies and in the Jewish community. We may not be aware of the stress responses that rule our constant choices about how we navigate through a day, or a life, but that doesn't mean that they aren't operative somatically and powerfully.

T'shuvah can be understood as returning to the state of innocent wholeness in which we are born, as the submerged somatic intelligence experiences redemption, ingathering, and integration.[5] To echo Audre Lorde's wisdom, cultivating a truthful and attentive relationship to one's own somatic aliveness is not a frivolous nor unimportant practice. It is "a vital necessity of our existence."[6] Through the process of coming home to, and experiencing, the authentic nature of our bodies' awareness, we can begin to heal the traumas and restore a sense of safety, wholeness, and well-being somatically. We could say that this is the resurrection or healing of the *nefesh*, the body-soul integration of being, that we are.

Because the societal and more intimate bodies of experience we carry within us and within which we function are conditioned so heavily towards rushing over, pushing down, and otherwise splitting ourselves from the nonbinary, sacred somatic consciousness that informs us, it is essential to wake up to the divine blessing of living in these bodies we inhabit. Through practicing ways to stay awake to the changing nature of our sensory worlds, we can live more deeply connected to the streams of sacred intelligence pulsing constantly through and towards us. In a "sense," we are training ourselves to receive and become a vessel for the *bat kol,* the divine voice streaming incessantly if only we could attune our ears to hear, to listen to what we hear, and to let those reverberations quiver in our souls and in our cells.

Embodied Spiritual Practice: A Healing Journey

For fifty-five years, I have been on a journey of coming home to my own embodiment. Today, I know that I am, through my uniquely embodied self, a sacred part of all that is alive in this universe, along with you and every one of us. This knowing saturates my cells. But I did not always know. I have struggled with the effects of addiction, internalized anti-semitism, and homophobia in my family of origin. As a young adult, I wrestled with gender expression, sexuality, and finding a place in a Jewish community where I could embody a serious spiritual practice while honoring the truths my body knew about how I loved. I still remember the nausea I felt in my body when I asked a traditional rabbi in Jerusalem how I could live my life openly as a lesbian and a practicing Jew, and I was told to marry, have children, and to have a lover "on the side." We were, after all, he said, living after the Holocaust and we needed to repopulate the Jewish people. While I wanted more than anything to be part of a tribal community in which I could live an embodied spiritual life, I could not surrender myself to a community in which traumas had calcified into attitudes that split people like me at the root.

For some time, a part of me was frozen in trauma from what I heard from that rabbi and others in the Orthodox world. It felt like a violent tug of war between what seemed to be starkly binary and clashing, reductionist extremes. It was a few years later, living in New York City and having left the Orthodox community, that I took my first yoga class. It only took a few minutes to feel something flood through my body. The warm and peaceful sensations seemed to whisper, "I am home. I am safe. I am in a sacred practice, and at peace with, not at war with, my body."

Since that first experience with yoga thirty years ago, I knew that it was possible to engage spiritual practices that happened through my body and honored my experience as sacred. Through hatha yoga practice I was opened to what I now understand as *nefesh*-consciousness. I began to heal. I moved to San Francisco, and I became a yoga teacher, a massage therapist, and a yoga therapist. And, in a fateful moment, I learned that there was an opening at a local progressive synagogue to teach *kitah alef* beginning Hebrew. I took the position, and as I taught a handful of young boys *alef* and *bet*, I remembered how deeply connected I felt to my Jewish roots through the physicality of those letters. From the innocence of those young boys, and the simple, beautiful shapes and sounds of Hebrew letters, I received the gift of clarity that I could have an authentic and whole place within Judaism. I set an intention to go to rabbinical school and in my studies, to find the teachings and practices that could affirm an authentic, whole-bodied Judaism.

I did become a rabbi, and have been teaching Torah Yoga and embodied spiritual practices to rabbis, cantors, and lay leaders for some time now. I continue to evolve my understanding of how best to live my embodied Jewish life, but what is constant is my deepening trust in this sacred somatic intelligence speaking through me every moment. For me, *Shechinah* Herself speaks through the language of breath, pulse, skin, movement, and the deep quiet knowing in my belly.

Avodah B'Gashmiut: Embodied Spiritual Practice

The bud
stands for all things,
even for those things that don't flower,
for everything flowers, from within, of self-blessing;
though sometimes it is necessary
to reteach a thing its loveliness
 —Galway Kinnell, from "Saint Francis and the Sow"[7]

We humans intrinsically know how to live fully embodied lives. We will, as Kinnell writes, "flower, from within, of self-blessing." Yet, sometimes "it is necessary to reteach a thing its loveliness." Sometimes, we need help to flower again into our wellness.

Many of us need to be retaught that our capacities for authentic movement, for expressing and consciously experiencing aliveness in and through our bodies, is inherent in our beings. It is not in spite of, but by way of, our sensory and other faculties that we come to know and embody spiritual and mental wellness. Just as I had to relearn the *alef-bet* one letter at a time to remember the depth of my connection to Jewish spiritual practice, sometimes we need to see afresh basic components of the lovely and sacred language of our bodies, letter by letter.

Avodah b'gashmiut is a Chasidic concept that means worshiping God through physical activities such as eating, dancing, and singing. The human body, beyond being a reflection of the Divine Being, becomes, in itself, a means of knowing and embodying the Divine. I prefer to translate *avodah b'gashmiut* as "embodied spiritual practice." I apply this way of seeing to my study of Torah, to prayer, to yoga, and to my life of Jewish spiritual practice. I have taught this approach with the Institute for Jewish Spirituality for over twenty years and have been moved again and again by what I have learned from participants' engagement of their somatic lives in these contexts.

In the following paragraphs, I'll share with you examples of what I have learned and of what I teach. I hope you find it inspiring, and that you will explore through your own body how practicing *avodah b'gashmiut* impacts your life and your relationship to Jewish teachings and actions.

Torah Yoga

When I returned to Jewish practice after becoming a yoga teacher and therapist, I wanted to uncover ways of cultivating Jewish spiritual life through somatic practices. I also wanted to find embodied practices in Jewish tradition and how these two wisdom paths could enhance and strengthen each other.

The practice of Torah Yoga[8] is one expression of this approach. I come to the Torah teaching—be it a spiritually focused Chasidic or Rabbinic text, a text from the written Torah, or liturgy. I study the text, and first try to understand what it is saying on its own terms. I then ask how it might instruct me if I were to read it in a hyper-literal way, and a hyper-embodied way. So, for example, there is a teaching in the Mishnah that says one ought not to come to pray if one is not *b'koved rosh*—in a state of appropriate respect and mindful awareness that one is preparing to engage the Holy One. First,

I would ask, what might the authors have intended to say here? Then, I look again at the phrase through the lens of somatic refraction. What might this phrase teach me if I take it as a very literal physical teaching? Literally, "heaviness of the head." What might this body-based postural instruction *koved rosh* (heaviness of the head) teach me about an appropriate way to prepare to pray? I know from hatha yoga that when one bows the head heavy towards the ground, in forward-bending poses, there often follows a quieting of the mind and a deeper inward focus. Ah! What practice might I physically do in order to embody this teaching?

I might then explore different ways of bending my head forward and being with those physical movements and breath long enough to feel the movements and shifts in my body. I might actually find that my body has quieted, that I might feel less fidgety, or less rushed and harried and less prone to multitasking. I might then move into liturgical or personal prayer and notice what opens from that physical and mental preparation.

The same approach can be applied to verses, phrases, or entire narratives in a Torah portion or to a spiritual teaching that otherwise might seem abstract, theoretical, or disembodied. For example, several years ago I developed a curriculum for studying *midot* from an embodied perspective. I wanted to explore what I could learn about my relationship to a *midah* if I came at it from my body, not only from intellectually focused teachings. So, for instance, take the quality or *midah* of *savlanut* (patience). To cultivate *savlanut*, and our self-understanding of what challenges our embodiment of being patient, the students and I studied traditional Musar teachings on this quality and discussed what situations we felt were challenging to us, when we might become impatient. The learning was interesting, but we were not experiencing impatience so it was in a sense, theoretical.

After clarifying our intentions, we took to our mats. I guided students through a yoga sequence designed to be challenging yet safe. I wanted to create somatic conditions that might arouse impatience so that we could learn what our bodies had to teach us about that quality and by contrast, how *savlanut* feels in the body.

Students reported a variety of different ways impatience arose in their bodies. For some, it was felt as great tension in the jaw or constriction in the belly. For others, it was experienced as a resistance to staying in a posture for very long. They felt "udgy" and wanted to move out of it and go onto the next posture. From seeing how their bodies spoke to them of their impatience, each person began to be able to put to language how they could imagine cultivating patience when they felt those body sensations and realized that they were feeling impatient. Their somatic awareness helped them internalize the *midot* work that they were to do, because they were more connected to their lived experience than if we had studied a text through discussion and thought alone. This process can be adapted for Torah study of many kinds and for any and all body types. It is not any more limited to "yogis" than traditional Torah study is limited to scholars and rabbis!

Sacred Dance

In my work with the Institute for Jewish Spirituality, we study the kabbalistic conception of the Divine as refracted through the energetic patterns of the *s'firot*. For some, the texts are accessible, yet for others, they appear abstract and opaque. After studying conceptual states of divine energy through texts and conversation, we practice learning how we experience these dynamic states in our bodies through movement. Not exactly dance, but authentic movements that spring from each person's feeling into the music played and exploring how the beat, tones, and flavors of the music move through them in ways that help them embody and move with the *s'firot* we are working with. Some of the most sacred and beautiful memories I have ever had include witnessing forty rabbis and cantors moving about a room in free-flowing innocence, flowering of self-blessing, as they explored how their own bodies could teach *Netzach* or *Hod* in a deeply penetrating language. Participants experienced themselves in their innocence, gentleness, and playfulness that felt sacred and holy, familiar even as it was brand new. These somatic learning processes danced with mystical Torah teachings to reveal fresh ways of grasping the subtlety of these divine emanations through the body.

Body Prayer

Another avenue for exploring *avodah b'gashmiut* is liturgical prayer. Where and how do we engage our bodies when praying? And how might listening to our bodies change how we pray? I explored such questions in a unit for the Prayer Project of the Institute for

Jewish Spirituality entitled "From My Flesh I See God: Embodying the *Amidah*."⁹

In this unit, we studied the weekday and Shabbat *Amidah*, through texts and traditional commentary as well as through experiential learning that included journaling and guided movements. As above, participants report that when we allow our bodies to teach us Torah, in conversation with the wisdom of teachings and practices in the written words and instructions before us, transformation can occur. It is often hiding in plain sight, and our practice opens our eyes so we can perceive what we are already seeing.

Preparing that unit, I thought about the choreographed action of lifting up to our tiptoes that we do during this prayer. The rabbis crafting this prayer and its choreography taught us something profound about the nature of our embodiment: even in this most intimate portion of the liturgy, even as the pray-er is invited into the most spiritual realm of connection with the Divine, we lift up our heels to approach the angels—yet we do not ever fully leave the ground, our ground of being on this earth.

We are yet on the ground, and we are yet standing. We engage the spiritual realms of divinity through the body, stretching open and receiving through a fully focused and given bodily stance. We do not transcend our bodies nor deny them even in spiritually focused moments. Now, when I lift up onto my toes during the *Amidah*, I hold this intention, that I may both stretch open my boundaries of self to receive Divine Presence, and to stay grounded and aware of the balls of my feet, the tips of my toes, finding strength and anchor on the earth. I am, we are, each a *nefesh*—a living embodiment of ineffable divinity. Adam: *Alef*, the metaphysical dimensions hidden in the invisible Mystery of Being. *Dalet-Mem*, blood. Flesh and blood, wet, earthy, mortal.

Conclusion

For rabbis and cantors, it is a common and conditioned response to push our own physical needs and selves away as we tend to the needs or expectations of others—and perhaps to our internalized voices of repression and bypass. Yet time spent in somatic practices is sacred and healing time. We are strengthening neurological synapses and creating healthier patterns of thinking and movement, for their own sake—not because they help us achieve any goals associated with the persona we assume when we are "on."

The most important transformations I have seen are not people's growing capacities to do a sun salutation or triangle pose. Rather, it is the inner shifts of consciousness when someone has deeply touched their inner beauty and aliveness and begins to trust the authority of that goodness. These moments signify a possible *t'shuvah*, a returning to the innocent resilience of being fully alive in spirit and body. One has come home to root safely in the body, holding mental and spiritual postures of integration with their somatic selves as well. When the experience of one's body awareness has come forth, that ingathering gains momentum and can transform even the most intractable of conditioned patterns in a life. To these moments, and transformations, I bow time and again. In these moments, I see *sh'lama raba min sh'maya* (great peace from the heavens), come home to land, one sacred body at a time, on this earth. And I remember that thing is very near to each and every one of us. The sacred sensory awareness we each have; the miraculous capacity for breathing that you possess; these are yours, mine, to claim and to practice *hidur chayim*, until our very last breath and movement leaves us.

Notes

1. B. K. S. Iyengar, Light on Life (Rodale, 2005), 26.
2. See Laurence Heller and Aline Lapierre, *Healing Developmental Trauma: How Early Trauma Affects Self-Regulation, Self-Image, and the Capacity for Relationship* (Berkeley, CA: North Atlantic Books, 2012).
3. See Tirzah Firestone, *Wounds into Wisdom: Healing Intergenerational Jewish Trauma* (Rhinebeck, NY: Adam Kadmon Books, 2019).
4. See Rachel Yehuda and Linda M. Bierer, "Transgenerational Transmission of Cortisol and PTSD Risk," *Progress in Brain Research* 167 (2008): 121–35, https://www.ncbi.nlm.nih.gov/pubmed/18037011.
5. Peter A. Levine and Ann Frederick, *Waking the Tiger: Healing Trauma* (Berkeley, CA: North Atlantic Books, 1997), and Bessel van der Kolk, *The Body Keeps the Score: Brain, Mind, and Body in the Healing of Trauma* (New York: Penguin Books, 2014), are two in a growing number of books reflecting research and clinical practice incorporating the somatic realm in the healing of trauma.

6. Audre Lorde, "Poetry Is Not a Luxury," in *Sister Outsider* (Berkeley, CA: Crossing Press, 1984), 36–39.
7. Galway Kinnell, "Saint Francis and the Sow," in *A New Selected Poems* (Boston and New York: Houghton Mifflin, 2000), 94.
8. I am grateful to my friend and colleague Diane Bloomfield for sharing the term "Torah Yoga" with me. Diane and I co-founded and co-directed the Yoga and Jewish Spirituality Teacher Training at Isabella Freedman Jewish Retreat Center for eight years. A Jerusalem resident, Diane teaches Torah Yoga classes in Israel and the United States.
9. https://www.jewishspirituality.org/go-deeper/prayer-project/.

Receiving and Giving Love: A Meditation on the *Sh'ma* and Its Blessings

Sheila Peltz Weinberg

The very center of the Jewish liturgy is love. Indeed, we might suggest that prayer itself is an act of love, designed to enhance the human capacity to love. The intention of our prayer is to liberate our innate loving capacities of care, tenderness, compassion, equanimity, and discernment.

The *Sh'ma* and its blessings are rooted in hearing God's love and God's oneness. Paying attention to the clarity of God's call brings us closer to healing of self and the world. In this paper I hope to share how these central prayers can be a practice for deeply receiving and extending love.

Ahavah Rabbah/Ahavat Olam

The prayer immediately preceding the *Sh'ma* in the morning liturgy is *Ahavah Rabbah* (great love). In the evening, the prayer is *Ahavat Olam* (eternal love). Why do these prayers precede the *Sh'ma*? How might we move beyond recitation of these prayers to actualizing the practice of receiving love and feeling loved? What are the obstacles and constraints that many of us face in receiving love from the Divine, human, or even nonhuman beings?

I have found the answer with a simple yet powerful set of meditations, known as Sustainable Compassion Practice (SCT), developed by John Makransky and an organization called Courage of

---

RABBI SHEILA PELTZ WEINBERG served as a congregational rabbi for seventeen years and was one of the founders of the Institute for Jewish Spirituality and the Jewish Mindfulness Meditation Teacher's Training. She is a spiritual director at HUC-JIR/New York and author of *Surprisingly Happy: An Atypical Religious Memoir* and *God Loves the Stranger: Stories, Poems and Prayers*. This paper is based on Rabbi Weinberg's course in the Institute for Jewish Spirituality's ongoing Prayer Project.

Care.[1] Inviting in the prayers surrounding the *Sh'ma* to become a practice of receiving, deepening, and extending love brings us towards compassionate action to ourselves and others, is healing, and ultimately allows us to cultivate more love for ourselves and the world.

Meditative Attention: A First Step

Before we can even imagine cultivating more love, we need to cover some basics. Cultivating meditative attention is how we train the mind and comprises two primary terms and activities. The first is *kavanah* (intention). It derives from the word "to direct" (*l'chavein*). We are encouraged to consider how we wish to direct our minds. In transposing Jewish prayer into a mediation practice, we become more receptive to love, recognize our deepest connection with life, and practice extending love in a variety of contexts. In order to prepare for the practice of cultivating love, we invite our attention to settle on something very accessible and present—namely our embodied presence in this moment. We are invited to gather our attention on a felt sense of pressure in the body, a sense of warmth or coolness, a feeling of tingling or tension. We can also practice with the felt sense of the breath as it enters and leaves our bodies.

As we practice, our attention will wander. Our thoughts will distract us. We will forget the *kavanah*, and our minds will begin to roam and settle into stories of past or future. This is completely natural. When we notice the trains of thought or pathways away from the initial *kavanah*, we have the opportunity for *t'shuvah*, a moment of wakefulness and return. Jewish tradition teaches that *t'shuvah* was created before the world itself, because it would not be possible to have a world unless there were pathways of return to intention. We would be completely lost. *T'shuvah* is an act of return, an act of love, an act of forgiveness. We do not judge these wanderings as wrong or bad. This is simply how the mind works, and we are training the mind to be more receptive to *kavanot* (wholesome intentions). In a sense, all spiritual practice depends on setting intentions, wandering away, and then returning. This is how we strengthen our bodies, hearts, and minds.

Anyone who has tried to sit in meditation for even ten or twenty minutes with the intention of cultivating awareness of our bodies knows that it is much more difficult than it sounds. Disturbances may arise even beyond the distractions of stories and memories surfacing in the mind. One might be overwhelmed with sleepiness. When this occurs, it is wise to open the eyes and even to stand in place. Sometimes annoying physical sensations arise—one might desire to shift in one's seat or get up and walk away. Sometimes the mind starts proliferating reasons why this might be a waste of time as there are so many pressing things to do.

It is very common to berate oneself for these distractions and to jump to conclusions, but we have an opportunity to meet our own minds with love. We are invited to soften around the judgments. Allow them to arise and pass. Remember to return, and return again, to the present felt sense of the body or breath in this moment. The more we return, the more the mind settles. The more the mind settles, the more power we have to orient ourselves toward the sacred, the whole, the loving and the wise. Similarly, the more settled the mind, the more we are able to resist the seductive, the delusional, and the self-serving tendencies that may have collected in the habits of our minds.

The practice of returning again and again to the present is a prayer in itself. We return to our awareness of being alive in this moment. We can feel this aliveness only in this moment. This aliveness is at once both individual and a part of the greater aliveness, the energy of life in this mysterious universe of which we are a manifestation.

Love

How are you at receiving love? Contrast that with how you are at receiving criticism, judgment, a sense of not measuring up to some standard somewhere, not getting enough accomplished, not being quite as good as you should be? I think a lot of us might answer that we are better at receiving criticism than we are at receiving love. In our highly individualistic and competitive culture this is not uncommon.

We get good at practicing not feeling quite good enough, and we also see others through the lens of limited ideas and impressions. As we wag the finger at ourselves, we also wag it at the other. They become the very limited impression of a this or a that, old or young, fat or thin, a person of color or a white person, etc. We miss their unlimited potential, the depth of their very being, the infinite potential that they are. We also miss seeing their suffering, their struggles, and their vulnerabilities.

We are often encouraged by our leaders to enhance their own power, to blame others rather than reach inside to our own potential for wise discernment and compassionate action. Our spiritual traditions, at their best and most transformational, encourage us to deeply receive love, sense our own potential for loving action, and see the other as a being of infinite complexity, dignity, and potential, just like ourselves. While there are other religious strands that separate us from the other, point the finger, and establish hierarchies, I wish to advocate for the more universal aspect, deeply interconnected teachings of each unique language of spirit.

Ahavah Rabbah translates as great love. The prayer begins "We are loved by a great love." Then it goes on to say that an exceedingly great compassion has been given us. How do we experience great love? What does that really mean to us? How do we receive that love in our bodies, hearts, and minds? We notice, too, that this prayer is formulated in the plural. Every one of us is included. Great love is our birthright.

I believe the prayer is inviting us into a practice. Just as we set a *kavanah* or intention when we are returning to bodily sensations or the felt sense of the breath, could we set a *kavanah* to strengthen our ability, in this very moment, to receive love?

Our ancient tradition is supported by recent research that has shown the great benefits of such a practice. Indeed "there are specific systems in our brain that respond to receiving love and kindness and to being loving toward others. Moreover, we see that our mental health; our immune system; the maturation of the frontal cortex; and our capacities for empathy, creativity, and lower stress—indeed, almost all facets of our being—function best under conditions of feeling love and being loving, in contrast to feeling unloved and feeling anxious or angry."[2]

One way to practice receiving love is by focusing on a caring moment. The first step is to think back on our life and choose a moment when we felt truly cared for, seen in our worthiness, our infinite potential and goodness, perhaps deeply known as *tzelem Elohim* (an image of the Divine). In this moment there were no conditions or limited ideas or impressions of who we were or who we were supposed to be.

This could be a recent moment when a kind stranger opened a door for us. It could be a memory from a long time ago with a beloved teacher, counselor, friend, or relative. It could be a moment with a beloved pet that had a capacity to exude a sense of care. It could be a place where you felt that sense of deep care, safety, and well-being. It is very important to avoid trying to find the perfect person who loved us "unconditionally." This will tangle us up in memories, judgments, and disappointments. We are looking for a simple caring moment, not a perfect person or relationship.

When we practice the meditation, we try to experience that moment in the present. This becomes our *kavanah* (our intention). You are invited to feel the feeling of being held in this quality of warmth, loving presence and care as if it were happening right now. You are invited to bring the experience into your senses, into your lived experience. Of course, after you set the intention, there will be forgetting, wandering of attention, analysis, argument, and judgment, etc. But there will also be remembering the intention, and the possibility of return (*t'shuvah*). This is the training of the mind that is the deep structure of our prayer practice: We become more and more awake, through prayer, of our capacities as human beings, children of the Source, to be fountains of goodness and love. Practicing receiving love is a basic step in this training.

Ahavah Rabbah immediately precedes the recitation of the *Sh'ma*. Just prior to the *Sh'ma*, it is a custom to gather the four sets of fringes from the corners of one's tallit in one hand and to cover one's eyes. These are meditative symbols of concentration. But upon what are we focusing so deeply?

Albert Einstein has written:

> A human being is a part of the whole, called by us "Universe," a part limited in time and space. He experiences himself, his thoughts and feelings as something separated from the rest, a kind of optical delusion of his consciousness. This delusion is a kind of prison for us, restricting us to our personal desires and to affection for a few persons nearest to us. Our task must be to free ourselves from this prison by widening our circle of compassion to embrace all living creatures and the whole of nature in its beauty. Nobody is able to achieve this completely, but the striving for such achievement is in itself a part of the liberation and a foundation for inner security.[3]

Arthur Green in his book *Ehyeh: A Kabbalah for Tomorrow*, frames Einstein's understanding as the basic teaching of Jewish mystics:

> God and the world are deep structure and surface of the same reality. This means that knowing God, knowing the world, and authentic self-knowledge are all aspects of the same search for truth. The same is true on the plane of emotion: love of God, love of all creatures, and proper self-love cannot be separated from one another. To worship God is to live with reverence, to treat all beings, including oneself (this is often the hardest part!) as embodiments of the single Being, called in Hebrew *alufo shel olam*, the cosmic *Aleph*, or the single One.[4]

The *Sh'ma* and its preceding prayer is an invitation to listen deeply to the oneness, which is present right here and right now. It is a deep acceptance of this moment without conditions, control, boundaries, or grasping on to ideas of who I am or how you are. In that sense of profound openness, the usual separateness dissolves, and we experience unity, which is love. In that unity, receiving and giving are also unified. We recognize that we are all made of the same stuff. Whatever *kavanah* I bring to myself I naturally will extend to you because on some fundamental level, neither you nor I exist as separate entities.

Of course we function with all our manifold uniqueness and preferences. This practice does not wish to eradicate authenticity and creativity. However, it emphasizes another element, which is part of consciousness, and this element can be profoundly soothing and healing. We experiment with setting a *kavanah* to settle into the present moment and allow whatever boundaries or fences exist to soften and release. This is letting be. Just letting be is less active and demanding than letting go. Just let it be. Let be in body. Let be in breath. Let be in the mind. We move toward a sense of wholeness, oneness, nonseparation, and loving presence as we practice the *Sh'ma* and its blessings.

As in all of our practices, we will become aware of restlessness and resistance. This is completely expected. We use the gift of *t'shuvah* to return, with kindness, again and again to the *kavanah*.

When we recognize and receive our own deep goodness and are able to rest in the present moment, we are filled up. There is necessarily a spilling over of this goodness. When we are isolated, hurting, angry, defensive, we transmit neither love nor goodness, but rather fear, distrust, and aversion. When we are in touch with the quality of care that resides in us and know that it resides in us all, we are able to behold beloved friends, strangers, and even those whom we might fear or shun with a kind and gracious view.

The practice of receiving and extending love calls upon us to touch our own worthiness and to trust the ultimate worthiness, or the spark of goodness, in the next person. Rather than label and dismiss the stranger, we are encouraged to realize that we are all a stranger to ourselves and each other. Jewish tradition invites us to protect the stranger, to care for the stranger because we are indeed all strangers. We are all limited beings; we experience the pains of human life, the illness, and the loss, the absence of control and then old age and death. We know, too, that we have the potential to see the heights, to create, to imagine, to aspire.

Immediately following the *Sh'ma* is the *V'ahavta*. I prefer the translation of *V'ahavta et Adonai* as "You shall love with *Adonai*" rather than "You shall love *Adonai*." Feeling deeply loved we become the ones who extend love, naturally. This is a flow of energy and acceptance from inside to outside. The *Sh'ma* has taught us that there is no real inside or outside. We are called to these heights by our spiritual traditions and our spiritual practices. It requires dedicated effort, teachers who have walked the path and communities of practice. The Sh'ma and the prayers of love and loving-kindness that surround the Sh'ma—which have survived three thousand years of history—call us forth. It is our task to listen and apply them to our own lives. Our passion for a just and peaceful world cannot be divided from the ongoing inner work of resting deeply in the love that flows through us and around us. This is a challenge, a practice, and a vision. May we be strong and strengthen one another in this sacred process at the heart of our tradition.

Notes

1. See John Makransky, *Awakening Through Love: Unveiling Your Deepest Goodness* (Somerville, MA: Wisdom Publications, 2007) and https://www.courageofcare.org.
2. Paul Gilbert and Choden, *Mindful Compassion* (Oakland, CA: New Harbinger Publications, 2014), 91.
3. Albert Einstein to Norman Salit, condolence letter, March 4, 1950. Copyright © The Hebrew University of Jerusalem.
4. Arthur Green, *Ehyeh: A Kabbalah for Tomorrow* (Woodstock, VT: Jewish Lights, 2004), 21.

A Jewish Cleric's Meditation for Self-Care

Alden Solovy

God of our mothers and fathers,
My life is dedicated to the Jewish people,
According to Your will,
To expand Torah and mitzvot in the world,
Keeping watch over this generation,
In service to Your Holy Name.

Source and Shelter,
Grant me the wisdom to care for myself
As I strive to do Your work,
Accounting for my own physical, emotional, and spiritual needs,
Day by day,
Which I can so easily neglect
In my zeal to fulfill this sacred calling.

Renewed, refreshed, and revitalized,
May I come back to this holy work
With a greater sense of wholeness
And a richer sense of peace,
Aware of the gifts You have bestowed upon me,
And the limitations of my strength and endurance.

Let my eyes sparkle with blessings.
Let my voice resound with truth.
Let my life reflect Your everlasting love.
Let me be a vital and worthy servant of Your Word.

ALDEN SOLOVY is a liturgist, poet, and educator whose writing challenges the boundaries between poetry, meditation, personal growth, and prayer. His work has appeared in six CCAR Press volumes, including *Mishkan HaNefesh: Machzor for the Days of Awe* and *Gates of Shabbat, Revised Edition*. Alden is the author of two solo anthologies from CCAR Press: *This Grateful Heart: Psalms and Prayers for a New Day* and *This Joyous Soul: A New Voice for Ancient Yearnings*. His writing also appears on RavBlog, Ritualwell.org, and ReformJudaism.org.

ALDEN SOLOVY

A Jewish Cleric's Meditation at a Moment of Challenge

Ancient One,
Source and Shelter,
Adonai, Eloheinu,
Shechinah, Yah.
What sorrow,
What fear,
What loss,
What profound helplessness and uncertainty
Your creation can face?
How many have I helped through the heart of these trials,
Walking along their paths of doubt or confusion,
Terror or grief?
Now I face my own distress,
My own human journey,
Profound in its power to challenge
My strength and endurance.

Eternal One,
Shine Your light upon me.
Grant me fortitude and faith,
Hope and healing.
Let Your grace flow from the storehouses of heaven
To me, my family, my congregation and all who suffer.

Even as I falter,
Even as I struggle,
I turn to You for blessings.

בָּרְכִי נַפְשִׁי אֶת־יהוה
Bless *Adonai*, O my soul . . .
Barchi nafshi et Adonai . . .

וְאַל־תִּשְׁכְּחִי כָּל־גְּמוּלָיו
. . . and don't forget all of God's blessings.
. . . V'al tishkechi kol g'mulav.

Talmud Torah as Spiritual Practice

Jonathan P. Slater

When we undertake any practice, we generally have a goal in mind. That is, we have answered for ourselves: Toward what end? When we engage in a Jewish practice, there are multiple possible answers to that question. A classical response is "because that is what Jews do": to keep the commandments, to connect to Jewish thought and tradition, to shape Jewish consciousness. Other possible answers could be to serve God, or to cultivate a felt sense of closeness to God, or to deepen a sense of love and reverence for God.

For the purposes of this essay, there is a different answer, perhaps ancillary, perhaps central: to maintain or nurture well-being and health. It should be a given that engaging in Jewish spiritual practice would include this goal, as living by Torah is for the sake of life.[1] Nonetheless, we are left to discern what constitutes well-being and health, and their foundations. And, even having clarified that, the question remains: How does this practice lead to those ends? What are we to do?

I'd like to suggest that the greatest impediment to our well-being, the greatest source of our ill-health, is the stress that comes from a divided heart. This inner division gives rise to the great dis-ease of our era: stress. While some degree of stress is valuable as motivation, as a spur to creativity, to attentiveness to our surroundings, most of us live with far more stress than that. We are torn in multiple directions; we are called by varied obligations and

---

RABBI JONATHAN P. SLATER is a senior program director of the Institute for Jewish Spirituality. He was ordained at the Jewish Theological Seminary of America and received a Doctor of Ministry degree from the Pacific School of Religion. He is the author of *A Partner in Holiness: Deepening Mindfulness, Practicing Compassion, and Enriching our Lives through the Wisdom of R. Levi Yitzhak of Berdichev's* Kedushat Levi and *Mindful Jewish Living: Compassionate Practice,* as well as many articles and book chapters.

responsibilities. We are also distracted by endless interruptions, all of which demand attention and immediate response.

This stress is felt by many, but it applies especially to clergy. They sense, perhaps most acutely, the tension between what they truly know their purpose to be—teachers of Torah and healers of souls—and the roles they are called to play.[2] To reduce their stress, to regain a degree of well-being, Parker Palmer suggests they must reconnect soul and role.[3] To do so they need some quiet to reconnect to their inner life, to listen deeply to their hearts, to know their true intentions. Feeling the passion that brought them to their chosen work and career once again, they may also then feel the pain of recognizing how different that work is now. It is first truly sitting in the awareness of the gap, of the pain of a divided heart, which is necessary to regain health and well-being.

Yes, but how? That is the charge of this essay. I suggest that mindfulness meditation is best suited to this purpose, as a foundational practice. Its goal is to bring us into an intimate relationship with our direct experience, learning to recognize the stories we tell about what is going on in any moment; our propensity for self-judgment; our own pain arising from the disconnect of role and soul. Having described this foundation or practice, I will offer a number of Chasidic texts on Talmud Torah that echo this practice and may help lead to this inner wholeness. It may be that in studying these texts themselves that some new awareness and inner wholeness might arise. Even more important, though, would be for them to spur a new orientation to our own practice of Torah study (and so, Torah teaching as well), for the sake of our souls and the souls of those with whom we work.

Mindfulness Meditation and Mindfulness Practice

Meditation is a tool that can be used to cultivate a non-judging, welcoming, moment-to-moment awareness. It is the practice of that awareness that is itself mindfulness. To be clear: to hold a non-judging orientation does not mean an abdication of values or nullification of concerns. Rather, it is the capacity to respond without judgment in a given moment, to a particular event or person, which frees us to discern precisely how our values and concerns should be enacted. Cultivating mindful awareness helps us to *respond* to the events in our lives, rather than *reacting*;

to choose wisely, rather than act out of habits of mind, heart, or body.

Mindfulness meditation encompasses a number of practices. One is concentration practice; one is open, non-discriminating practice. In the former we bring our attention to one particular phenomenon, returning the attention over and over as it is drawn away. To practice, we generally sit in a way that supports the body, allowing us to remain seated without discomfort for an extended period of time. Our orientation is to be both erect and at ease, attentive and relaxed. Most commonly, we bring our attention to the sensation of the breath in the body, wherever we feel it most prominently: at the nostrils, in the chest, in the belly. Connecting to sensation helps us to shift awareness from "thinking" to "feeling." Physical sensations happen only in the moment. In general, it is more difficult to recall or project a physical feeling than it is to feel it in the moment. By placing our attention in the sensation of the breath, we connect to what is occurring right now, providing us with an anchor for our attention. The breath can also provide a refuge from thought; a "place" to return to from memory, projections into the future, worry, or regret. As these thoughts arise and we are able to bring our attention back to the breath, we come to know directly these thoughts as thoughts, and not what is actually happening in the moment. The events they bring to mind are not happening now; this breath is happening now. In this manner we learn to distinguish between what is happening in this moment and what we think about it.

This practice of discernment is complemented by a non-judging attitude. As we sit with our attention in the sensation of the breath, thoughts and emotions may arise. They may distract us from our point of focus. Responding in a non-judging manner facilitates our return to the breath. First, we are relieved of the habit of self-judgment, for failing to stay with our intention. We can simply admit the truth—"I am thinking", "I am worrying"—and bring our attention back to the breath. Second, we need not judge whatever arises in the mind or heart: the content of our thought or feeling is not important. We can let that go to connect with our intention to sit, attending to the breath. Third, not giving our attention to assessing our success or failure frees us to ask the question, "What is true now?" We learn to discriminate between what appears to be happening and what is in fact happening. So often, we mistake our perception of an event for the event itself. Another's tone of voice, being startled, and experiencing pain can all induce a cascade of thoughts, conditioned by habits of mind and heart, that shape our perception of what is happening. When we can meet the moment without judgment and ask, "What is true now?" we are freed to remain connected to the immediate event itself, to discern more clearly what has in fact transpired. We are redeemed from the trap of habit to the freedom of awareness.

In open awareness practice we allow our attention to expand broadly. We allow whatever is arising to arise, without comment or judgment. Rather than bringing our attention back to a point of focus, however, we hold our attention open. The arising and passing away of thoughts, feelings, and sensations, occur as they do. We experience their evanescence, and so learn to give them their appropriate due, and no more. Attending to the impermanence of thoughts and feelings, we become less attached to them. We experience how they are not what constitute the "me" who is watching their comings and goings. There is an observer, awareness, a larger self, who knows them without being captured by them. As with concentration practice, holding a non-judging open awareness grants us freedom of choice, and a greater sense of self.

I would like to suggest that through these practices, through cultivating mindful awareness, we open to an awareness of God in our lives. God is intimately entwined in what is happening, and so present in our awareness, present in our hearts, unfolding moment by moment. This awareness *of* God is often obscured by our thoughts *about* God, by what we think we should be teaching about God, and by the hustle and bustle of daily life. Bringing our attention to our breath, calming or settling the body, gaining freedom moment-by-moment from the habits of mind and heart, we come into contact with Presence, the immediate, immanent *Shechinah*. Non-judging awareness allows us to meet this moment as experience, as it is, without the overlay of thought or prejudice.

Meeting God in this manner opens us, as well, to our souls. We relinquish the persona we wear as clergy, the face we have worn as teacher and preacher, as counselor and prophet. Turning inward, meeting this moment as it is, we connect with our true self. We re-member ourselves, perhaps painfully, connecting the person at synagogue with the one at home, the one in intimate relationships, the one alone in the darkness of night. This is what Palmer is pointing to: reconnecting role with soul. This is the work of spiritual practice, and the foundation for our health and well-being.

Talmud Torah as Spiritual Practice

Talmud Torah can be such a practice, as well, particularly if we engage with it as a mindfulness practice. All too often we find that our study is for the sake of preparing for a class, or some other ulterior purpose. We rarely engage in study for its own sake. And, even if we have a personal program of study, we often want to "get" something, to know that we have studied this or that text. For our study to help connect role and soul, we need a different orientation. R. Shmuel Shmelke of Nickolsburg (1726–1778, a student of the Great Maggid, R. Dov Baer of Mezritch) instructs us regarding the unification of intention and practice:

> 51. When you open a book to study from it, even in your youth you should recite this prayer: "I desire to study so that it will bring me to action and to embody good qualities (*middot tovot*), and to knowledge of the Torah. I do this for the sake of the unification of the blessed Holy One and the *Shekhinah*, unifying the Name *YHV"H* and the Name *ADN"Y* so that they might be united as *YAHDVNH"Y*,[4] by the power of the Hidden One, with fear and love, in complete unity, in the name of all Israel."

> 52. In the midst of studying you should stop regularly to say, "May the light in this [i.e., Torah] bring me back to the good" (cf. Lamentations Rabbah, Proem 2).[5]

In the first of these instructions, R. Shmuel Shmelke offers us a *kavanah* (a personal prayer to set an intention). The purpose of study is to know Torah, and for that knowledge to nurture inner qualities and dispositions (*midot*), which then will be manifest in action (performance of mitzvot; acts of kindness). It is possible that one could undertake this form of study and still fall into the sort of bifurcated life we eschew. Instead, however, this prayer frames the purpose of study in a very different manner: unification. Here it is expressed as the unification of the blessed Holy One and the *Shechinah*. There are many ways we can understand this. For our purposes, let's begin by suggesting that the blessed Holy One represents the God who is outside us, the idea we have about God, the One we teach and talk about. The *Shechinah* is what we know in our hearts. Our study is to bring them together, to bridge the gap between them (if there is one).

But, we can also suggest that the blessed Holy One is the truth of our experience, that which we touch when we pay close attention, without judgment, to what is happening. The *Shechinah* is the flow of experience, the comings and goings of life. We are instructed here to bring them into conversation, to unify them in our consciousness. The intimate merging of these two names suggests the inner transformation that takes place when study focuses our attention and allows us to know our hearts directly. We are then able to move back into the flow of life, into the world, with a unified heart.

As the second instruction suggests, this is not something that is accomplished simply by setting an intention. We need to return over and over again to our intention. Talmud Torah as spiritual practice is to bring us "back to the good," to change us. That change comes about when we connect with Torah, and our own hearts, and discover that the light in one is the light in the other. Just as we bring our attention back to the breath, over and over, we bring our attention back to our intention, to cultivate mindful inner unification.

The Heat of Torah Connects Heart to Head

The unification of mind and heart, of inner and outer, of role and soul, sounds good. Who would disagree that this is desirable?! But, it does not come easily, particularly for those who have been trained in the Western academy, studying Torah through the lens of *Wissenschaft*. The preference of mind over heart in that tradition is hard to overcome. Consider, then, the teaching of R. Tzadok Hakohen of Lublin (1823–1900, student and successor of R. Mordecai Yosef Lainer of Izbica):

> Words of Torah which pass through the heart, by which the heart feels and is affected, are called a "tree of life" and an "elixir of life."[6] For the heart is the source of vitality, as is written: "[More than all that you guard, guard your heart,] **for it is the source of life**" (Prov. 4:23). When we are aroused by the words of Torah, the root of our vitality is aroused, engendering vitality in us.
>
> This occurs when our fear of sin comes before our wisdom [i.e., Torah]. For fear of heaven is in the heart, as our Sages said on the

verse, "[What good is money in the hand of a fool,] **to acquire wisdom when there is no heart**" (Prov. 17:16; see BT *Yoma* 72b). Fear is feminine [i.e., embraces and contains that which flows to it]. The Torah of truth is masculine [i.e., flows forth to provide for recipients], bringing peace and joy in the heart, as it is written, "**The precepts of YHVH are right** (*y'sharim*), **rejoicing the heart**" (Ps. 19:9). After the fear, which engenders a broken heart and sadness, the words of Torah are absorbed and sustained in the heart.

For the heart is where the blood is heated. Through the force of desire and yearning for the sweetness of the words of Torah, the element of fire is strengthened, as the Rabbis said: "**The Torah boils in him**" (BT *Taanit* 4a). We know the power of boiling to cause absorption: that which is absorbed in this manner never escapes. This is not so with cool or cold elements, such as words of Torah which do not pass through the heart. We may be perfectly able to conceive wisdom in our mind and to perceive matters of divinity and Torah while our heart remains totally unaffected by it all. It will be as if we have studied some external wisdom, which has no relation to us. We lack the necessary prerequisite: the fear of sin, which causes us to reflect on our shortcomings and to feel a need for the words of Torah capable of perfecting us. Without this, our wisdom will not endure. This is akin to what is said regarding Doeg (BT *Sanhedrin* 106b): he forgot all his Torah learning because "**God** [*Rachmana*—the Compassionate One] **desires the heart**," namely, that one's Torah should leave a sensible imprint on one's heart. This is the principle: When our heart is actively inspired in our study of Torah, then it has vitality and is absorbed internally.[7]

While the gendered element of this teaching may be irritating and off-putting, the fundamental point still stands: Torah that does not pass through the heart will not be sustained. What arouses the heart? For R. Tzadok it is "fear": "the fear of sin, which causes us to reflect on our shortcomings." This surely does not seem nonjudgmental! Yet, he is pointing to the experience of mindfulness. So often we deny or repress our feelings of inadequacy, of failure, of doubt; or we wallow in them. This inner dynamic causes a great deal of stress; it is the source of sadness, anger, passivity, and dissatisfaction. To mend the inner chasm between our outward performance and inner experience, we bring mindfulness to bear. We allow for the inner stories to come to the surface, to hold them lightly, and ask, "Is this true?" In the moment, we recognize what is a story and what is true; we admit our failures and commit to making amends; or we correct our false self-assessment. Mindfulness supports our inner integration by helping us to move beyond the paralysis of blame or shame, to honesty and self-acceptance.

The "heat" that is brought to bear in the heart, then, is the light of awareness. It is our yearning for wholeness, our desire to be authentic. Rather than forcing ourselves to fit our persona, we accept that it exists, and that we live with it—and the sadness that may arise with that acknowledgment. At the same moment, in accepting this fact, we find release, expansiveness. Rather than living with the "idea" of who we are, we come into a more direct knowledge of our souls. This engenders a passion to live with greater wholeness, aligning role and soul. Instead of lethargy, or frustration, we find new resources in our own hearts. When we study—and teach—when connecting heart and mind, fear and love, inner and outer, we gain access to greater wisdom and insight. Our teaching comes from a deeper awareness in us and touches a deeper place in our students. We are more able and willing to invite our students to join us in this process of energizing the heart to access the mind (rather than vice versa). "God desires the heart": it is through compassion for ourselves that our hearts can open, and it is then that our hearts can more easily desire God, our own true wholeness.

Bringing Torah Fully Inside

In our presentation linking mindfulness practice and Chasidic spirituality, we are both grounding our awareness in our own direct experience and bringing God into this dimension. Torah, as well, moves from an "external wisdom" to an internal one. We do not create Torah, but we open to that Torah that is teaching us, and so, is revealed through us. In the following dramatic teaching of R. Naftali Tzvi Horowitz of Ropshitz (1760–1827, student of R. Elimkelekh of Lyzhansk) we learn how our mindful approach to Torah study links us internally to our own souls, to all other beings, and to God:

> There, at Sinai, a spark was aroused—the divine portion in all creation—with the arousal of the Source of all Sources, the Origin of all Origins, the Cause of all Causes to reveal Divinity in the world. Then the divine portion in all existence was aroused in response. This is as we read in the midrash (*Sh'mot Rabbah* 29:9):

Another explanation of "**I am *YHVH* your God**": It is written, "**The lion has roared, who will not fear? *YHVH* God has spoken; who can but prophesy?**" (Amos 3:8) . . . What is the meaning of, "***YHVH* God has spoken; who can but prophesy?**" R. Abbahu said in the name of R. Yohanan: When God gave the Torah no bird twittered, no fowl flew, no ox lowed, none of the Ophanim stirred a wing, the Seraphim did not say 'Holy, Holy,' the sea did not roar, the creatures spoke not, the whole world was hushed into breathless silence and a voice went forth saying *anochi* [i.e., "I am *YHVH* your God"].

What difference does it make that everything fell silent? Even if everything continued to make noise, "**the voice of *YHVH* is powerful**" (Ps. 29:4)? They surely would have heard [God's voice over any other sound]! Moreover, what would the Seraphim have done if they were not singing their song, as this is their sole divine service? Further, what does the midrash mean when it says, "a voice went forth saying: *anochi*"?

It appears to me, then, that this is the essence of the giving of the holy Torah: the divine portion in every [spiritual] world—*atzilut, beriah, yetzirah, asiyah*—and in all creation—inorganic, plant, animal and human—and in every element—fire, air, water and earth—was aroused. They all felt this; the divine power, the portion that emanated from God, was strengthened, as in the verse "**By the word of *YHVH* were the heavens created, by the spirit of His mouth their host**" (Ps. 33:6). This holy portion emerged from concealment to be revealed, particularly among us. We merited witnessing God's revelation; that which was hidden and concealed was revealed for us in the sweet pleasantness of our beloved saying "**I am *YHVH* your God**". Our souls were aroused in holiness and the cry emerged from our throats "**I am *YHVH* your God**". The part was drawn after the root.

This is how we can understand the verse "**He will kiss me with the kisses of His mouth**" (Song 1:2): God's speech kissed our mouths. The divinity in us was revealed, and our bodies followed its lead. That, then, is also the sense of the verse "***YHVH* God has spoken, who can but prophesy**": every portion and part of holiness spoke as one. God is unified with the whole, for all lives by virtue of God's portion in it. From all four directions they heard this voice, as the whole of creation depends on God's vital force for its existence, and in response it all cried out "**I am *YHVH* your God**". That is what the midrash signifies when it says, "a voice went forth saying: *anochi*": it went forth from the very being of all beings, from the divine portion in all existence.[8]

For R. Naftali, all of existence is animated by a portion of the Divine. The part is not separate from the whole. It resonates, in turn, responding to the inner movement of God in the world. The response of the part is to echo and enlarge the whole. Thus, at Sinai all creation held still to hear the divine voice. When God spoke *anochi*, the part—in every world and dimension—responded, speaking the same word; echoing and adumbrating the original. While creation is endowed with separate consciousness, it is not truly separate from God. In the end, it is all God. Thus, when God spoke, all existence spoke as well. God says to the world, "I am your God," and the world responds, "I am you, God."

What do we discover, then, when we study Torah as spiritual practice, with mindful awareness? As Judah Halevi muses,[9] when we move to find God—in Torah, in the world, in ourselves—we find that God is already there, moving to find us. Yet, so often we are too busy, too noisy, and too preoccupied with our selves, to notice. Parker Palmer captures this in a poignant image:

> The soul is also shy. Just like a wild animal, it seeks safety in the dense underbrush, especially when other people are around. If we want to see a wild animal, we know that the last thing we should do is go crashing through the woods yelling for it to come out. But if we will walk quietly into the woods, sit patiently at the base of a tree, breathe with the earth, and face into our surroundings, the wild creature we seek might put in an appearance.[10]

Mindfulness practice helps us to quiet down, to sit patiently, to listen carefully. Instead of asserting "I know" when studying, we can open to what is yet to be revealed. Instead of claiming ownership of Torah, we can allow ourselves to be part of it, a piece of a larger whole. In listening carefully to our own hearts and souls, without judgment, with compassion, we learn to hear that voice inside, echoing the Divine: "I am you, God." In this, a greater Torah is revealed than we can ever expect from head-learning alone. And, when we discover that we are not alone in this endeavor of life, that we are not solely in charge, our hearts can ease, we can become more whole.

This greater wholeness can unify our sense of self with the truth of each moment. This is where well-being rests. We may not be healthy always, but we will not be in an adversarial relationship with our illness. We will know: "This is true" and in this, find some ease. We will continue to teach others, but our goal will not be self-promotion. Rather, we will invite others to join us in our quest to know our souls more fully. We will continue to study on our own, or in *chavruta*, but without the desire to conquer a text, or "get" anywhere. Rather, we will invite the text to enter us, to help us live without self-judgment so that we will be better able to discern how to live wholeheartedly. In this we will slowly bring our roles into greater alignment with our souls. Our hearts will be one, and we will be whole.

Notes

1. BT *Taanit* 7a; BT *Sanhedrin* 74a.
2. I suspect that in the current climate of change in the medical field, this is felt among doctors, nurses, and others as well. In light of my reference to Parker Palmer, it has long been an issue for educators/teachers.
3. See Parker J. Palmer, *A Hidden Wholeness: The Journey Toward an Undivided Life* (San Francisco: Jossey-Bass, 2004), esp. 17–20.
4. This combination of holy names, in the mystical tradition, represents the emanation of God from the deepest recesses of infinite Being to this world. This is reflected in the first letter—*yod*—at the beginning (its tip representing Keter or Ayin, the first emergence of knowable divinity, about which we can say anything), and in the final letter—*hei*—representing *Shechinah*, immanent Presence.
5. *Sefer Hanhagot Tzaddikim: Hanhagot Tovot MiRabbi Shmuel Shmelke MiNickolsburg*, #51 and #52.
6. See again, BT *Taanit* 7a.
7. *Tzidkat Tzaddik*, #225
8. *Zera Kodesh*, pt. 2, 41a.
9. In his poem "Yah Ana Emtza'acha."
10. Palmer, *Hidden Wholeness*, 58–59.

Chevruta as Spiritual Practice

Beth Huppin

The Talmud reports that when Choni the Circle-Maker woke after seventy years of sleep, he discovered all his study partners were dead. Nobody recognized him or treated him with respect. God mercifully allowed him to die. The story ends with Rabba commenting that Choni's fate is the source of the "well known" saying: או חברותא או מיתותא ("Either *chevruta* [study partners] or death!") Without his study partners, he preferred death (*Taanit* 23a).

Though I never saw this "well known" saying anywhere else in Rabbinic literature, I deeply appreciate the sentiment and return regularly to study this story because it speaks directly to my experience with *chevruta*. A minimum of two or three times a week I study with dear friends. In most cases we live thousands of miles apart. Whether through various online platforms or in person, a central goal of our *chevruta* is to connect regularly on a level beyond updates about our jobs or family members. The texts we study together provide an occasion to open our hearts to the deepest parts of our inner lives so that when we conclude our studies, we will be more likely to bring our best selves into the world.

I learn about my own heart by noticing how I respond to a text. I learn about the heart of my friend by listening deeply to her response. No judgment. No fixing. No convincing. We don't decide matters of Jewish law. We examine matters of the heart. Our objective is not to cover material, but to uncover the ways in which we are connected and, in turn, how we can best connect to others in our daily lives.

Being human can be a lonely venture. No matter how many friends and family members we have, we rarely find opportunities to be vulnerable enough to share concealed parts of our fears, our

---

BETH HUPPIN is the director of Project Kavod, a Jewish education program of Jewish Family Service of Seattle. She is the recipient of a 2010 Covenant Award for Excellence in Jewish Education.

pain, and our joy. When we study together I feel my heart soften and calm. Our meaningful and substantive connection through *chevruta* study generally results in a sense of improved spiritual and emotional well-being as well as an easing of existential loneliness.

When studying in *chevruta* from a place of curiosity, our ancient texts provide a framework for openness. The text is a mirror, helping us see ourselves with greater clarity. We listen to the text and then to each other. Responding to the text, we wonder aloud, trying out words and phrases in an attempt to articulate ideas and feelings. We ask each other questions. Does this feel true for you? In what way? When? How might applying the truth of this teaching help us be more compassionate and open to others? Sometimes, especially when an idea feels true beyond words, we simply sit silently together in acknowledgment of that truth.

Chevruta is a place where vulnerability is safe. With mutual well-being as our goal, we strive to allow ourselves to explore hidden aspects of our inner lives, while also aware that whatever words we use will be insufficient. These discussions potentially expose places in our souls that are tender, sacred, and, until these conversations, unconsciously concealed. As our texts often teach, human language both conceals and reveals.

Our discussions are wide-ranging, always starting from the text, then reaching deep into our souls. We speak honestly, with certainty that what we discuss in *chevruta* stays in *chevruta*. Over the years, we develop a shared language based on the texts we've studied together. I discover language for aspects of my inner life I hadn't recognized or acknowledged before the study began. Culled from our ancient tradition, our shared new language is colored by our practice of study together.

I understand the many benefits of this type of *chevruta* though language from our Shabbat liturgy. During the Shabbat *Amidah* we ask God "to give us our portion of Your Torah" (ותן חלקנו בתורתך) and "to purify our hearts to serve You in Truth" (וטהר לבנו לעבדך באמת). *Chevruta* practice helps purify my heart so that I can offer my unique portion of Torah to the world. It helps clarify how I might more faithfully and usefully serve God and God's world, especially through enhanced and deeper service to others.

Each *chevruta* experience is unique, but there is a general flow. We begin with a quick check-in about the health and welfare of loved ones, followed by the Hebrew blessings for studying Torah. We then dive into our text. Since we don't want to waste time deciding what to study, an agreed-upon text forms the basis of our study. In most cases, we study a Hebrew text, often, but not always, with an English translation available. For me, there is power in tackling the text in the original Hebrew. Hebrew reaches a different corner of my brain, providing an opening to explore questions about the inner life through echoes from those who came before us. Those reverberations open my heart as well as my mind.

Depending on the text, I usually spend a short time preparing before our study. For a complicated text, preparation includes unlocking basic language issues. If a key word appears that I don't know, I look it up. I note the proof-texts embedded in the text, and those books are by my side for our shared study time. Our *chevruta* time is limited and precious. I prefer to discuss the issues raised by the text and my heart, not to work out technical Hebrew translation questions easily answered by a dictionary. The technical aspects are a means to a deeper end.

We always enter the text assuming it contains something to teach us. If the text is sexist or otherwise problematic, we try to redeem it with a modern interpretation. In some extremely troubling cases, we lovingly set aside the disturbing language and seek a deeper meaning in the overall message of the text.

Difficult texts don't frighten or anger us. We refuse to give them the power to cause us to reject the entire venture. On the contrary, we are secure enough in our love of the tradition and of each other that the experience of shared inquiry often elicits insights into our own truths in ways that would not be possible if we stayed with easier texts. Over months and years of study, we find that the sacred texts complement and comment on each other, sometimes solving earlier problems, as do the "texts" of our lived experiences.

This joint contending with difficult texts helps me when facing other challenging ideas or even challenging people. *Chevruta* study models seeing the possibility of revelation in difficult encounters outside of *chevruta* time. It works much the same way as any spiritual practice, training me to be curious, to listen, and not to take ideas and people at face value. There is context to a text, just as there is context to challenging ideas and people.

Chevruta study is a focused spiritual practice that grounds and nourishes me. In addition to the personal benefits, as a Jewish text teacher, the texts we study together often become the basis of classes I teach. The *chevruta* study keeps me fresh as a teacher, giving me confidence to teach texts that are difficult and challenging, and to treat students as group *chevruta* partners. My teaching improves as my *chevruta* study grows.

I've often thought of Choni the Circle-Maker trying to understand a world in which he outlived his *chevruta* partners, a world without anyone respecting him enough to study with him. I think of Rabba commenting on Choni's situation, understanding that without the possibility of study partners, death was his only option. Rabba expressed what those of us who experience the true beauty of this type of companionship know: our inner lives require this type of relationship. *Chevruta* is a rich spiritual practice from our tradition, providing a sacred and holy space for us not only to survive, but to flourish by growing our capacity to more fully serve both God and each other and to have a taste of experiencing the connection between them.

* * * * *

For more on this topic, see "Spiritual Friendship: 'Go Among People Who Are Awake and Where a Light Shines Brightly'" by Lawrence Fine in *Jewish Mysticism and the Spiritual Life: Classical Tests, Contemporary Reflections*, edited by Lawrence Fine, Eitan Fishbane, and Or N. Rose (Jewish Lights Publishing, 2011).

Slumbering at Sinai: Sleep as a Spiritual Practice

Jo Hirschmann

We learn in a midrash that the Israelites fell asleep on Erev Shavuot. To Moses' great dismay, they were still slumbering when it was time to receive the Torah.[1] To make amends for our ancestors' sleepiness, we stay up all night learning Torah on Erev Shavuot. The message of the midrash is clear: slumber equals missed opportunities, while wakefulness promises spiritual readiness and receptivity. This is not dissimilar to our contemporary approach to sleep. We live in a culture that sometimes valorizes sleep deprivation and regards sleep as an optional luxury. There are enormous demands on our time; we live in what Laura van Dernoot Lipsky calls "the age of overwhelm."[2] With so many people and things tugging at our time and attention, it is no wonder that, collectively, we are chronically sleep-deprived.

Arianna Huffington is, among other things, a prophet of sleep and her book, *The Sleep Revolution*, exhorts us to get more rest. Huffington reports that 40 percent of American adults are sleep deprived. She connects this to the increasing length of the workweek, reporting that, in the period 1990 to 2000, Americans added a full week of work to our year. Our collective sleeplessness is correlated with socioeconomic class, with poorer people getting less sleep than those with more economic resources. In Huffington's words, "sleep is not evenly—or fairly—distributed."[3]

Sleeplessness has serious health implications. According to Huffington, "the incidence of death from all causes goes up by 15 percent when we sleep five hours or less" each night, with lack of sleep connected to "an increased risk of heart attack, stroke,

---

RABBI JO HIRSCHMANN (NY09) is an ACPE Certified Educator who serves as the director of Spiritual Care and Education for Mount Sinai Downtown in New York City.

diabetes, and obesity." Sleep deprivation also negatively affects our mental health. It is associated with depression, anxiety, feelings of loneliness and helplessness, reduced cognitive performance, and compromised memory capacity.[4] Getting more sleep may improve our physical and mental health. It may also open doors to spiritual connectedness. This essay looks at several biblical and Rabbinic texts that suggest sleep might foster generativity and forge connections to holiness. We'll conclude by returning to the Shavuot midrash, to read it not as a rebuke of slumber but as a celebration of what sleep might usher into our lives.

Sleep Fosters Generativity

In the second creation story in Genesis, sleep is intimately connected with new life. Genesis 2:21–22 reads:

> And God caused a deep slumber to fall upon the human and he slept and God took one of his ribs and closed the flesh in place of it. And *Adonai Elohim* built the rib that he had taken from the human into a woman and [God] brought her to the human.[5]

While Adam slumbers, God is busy. In just two verses, God's actions are described with five different verbs: caused to fall (into a deep slumber), took, closed, built, and brought. The end product of God's labors is impressive: a new human, a companion for Adam. Through all of this, Adam has been so deeply asleep that the story requires two different words (*tardeimah* and *yi'shan*) to describe his sleepy state. Ostensibly, God is responsible for the creative process of fashioning Eve while Adam, in his deep slumber, contributes nothing but a rib to the process.

I like to think, however, that, rather than preventing activity, Adam's deep sleep might have facilitated it. Insights from the field of neuroscience teach us that, while we sleep, our neural connections are strengthened and reorganized, boosting memory, helping us to learn, and deepening our capacity for growth and change.[6] Perhaps God couldn't create a second human alone. Perhaps God needed Adam's sleepy state and the generativity sleep engenders. Perhaps God and Adam worked in partnership, one of them outwardly busy and active, the other inwardly making the invisible connections that drive transformation. In this way, the story of the creation of Eve becomes a metaphor for sleep-fueled creativity. It leaves us with this question: in addition to nurturing our neurons, what other kinds of growth might sleep facilitate?

Sleep Connects Us to God

If Genesis 2 invites us to soak up sleep's brain-strengthening functions, a unit of text from *B'reishit Rabbah* wonders about sleep's effects on the soul. *B'reishit Rabbah* 14:9 explores the nature of the soul and concludes by wondering about the changes our souls undergo when our bodies are asleep.

> Rabbi Bisni, Rabbi Aha, and Rabbi Yohanan said in the name of Rabbi Meir: Th[e] soul (*n'shamah*) fills the whole body and, when a person sleeps, it ascends and draws life to him from above. Rabbi Levi said in the name of Rabbi Hanina: Upon every breath and breath (*n'shimah ve'n'shimah*) that a person breathes, the person must praise the Creator. What is the reason? *Let every soul* (*n'shamah*) *praise God* (Ps. 150:6), [which means] let every breath (*n'shimah*) praise God.[7]

This aggadah imagines the soul leaving the body during sleep and rising up to be closer to God. From here, the soul draws life to its body *mi'la'malah* (from above, from the heavens, from God). The aggadah uses the verb *sho'a'val* (draws). This verb is often used to describe the act of drawing water, creating a powerful image of an inverted well from which the soul draws from the Source of Life buckets brimming with *chayim*.

Jewish meditation practices often play with the similar-sounding *n'shamah* (soul) and *n'shimah* (breath). Before God created Eve, God molded Adam from the earth and blew *nishmat chayim* into Adam's nostrils.[8] God's breath and our breath are one; our in-breaths are God's out-breaths, and vice versa. Similarly, this aggadah plays on *n'shama* and *n'shima*, implicitly wondering about whether the breath of wakefulness is different from the breath of slumber. The answer, it seems, is yes. In sleep, our breath-soul forms a different kind of connection with God, in which the soul leaves the body, ascends, and draws life directly from God. Speaking in the name of Rabbi Hanina, Rabbi Levi goes on to say that, when Psalm 150 exhorts every *soul* to praise God, this is the same as saying that every *breath* praises God. While we know that the soul-breath finds multiple ways to praise God when the body is awake, I read this aggadah to mean that sleep ushers in new kinds of praise-filled holy connections. I am left with this question: how might sleep connect us to God and deepen our praise of God?

Sleep as a Bridge between Life and Death

The notion of the soul's ascension during sleep evokes Jewish tradition's image of what happens after death as the soul ascends Heavenward. The Rabbis explore this connection between sleep and death in a teaching that lists things that are one-sixtieth of another thing.

> Five things are one-sixtieth of [something else] and these are them: fire, honey, Shabbat, sleep, and a dream. Fire is one-sixtieth of *Geihinom*; honey is one-sixtieth of manna; Shabbat is one-sixtieth of *olam haba*; sleep is one-sixtieth of death; and a dream is one-sixtieth of prophecy.[9]

The idea that sleep is one-sixtieth of death may echo Rabbinic notions about the soul's departure from the body during sleep. Alternatively, it may reflect premodern fears about the mystery of sleep and the ways—sometimes unsettling, sometimes reassuring—that death can look like sleep. I would like to suggest an additional reading: sleep may connect us to the world of the dead, offering a bridge between life and death.

In 2015, a hospice team from Buffalo, New York, published a study that describes their patients' end-of-life dreams and visions, a phenomenon that encompasses "visions occurring during a wakeful state or dreams occurring during sleep." In the words of this research team:

> People nearing the end of life often experience increasingly vivid and memorable dreams. This observation is consistent with the hypothesis that dreams and visions are intrinsic to the transition from life to death.

While some patients who participated in the study had dreams and visions that were distressing, most described them as a source of comfort. In some dreams and visions, patients reported that they were preparing to go somewhere. In other dreams, patients saw and interacted with deceased loved ones. Overall, these dreams and visions seemed to help patients accept their approaching deaths.[10]

If, as the Talmud proposes, sleep is one-sixtieth of death, perhaps it is a foretaste of the world beyond this one. According to the patients in the study, these dreams were gifts that eased their end-of-life paths. And perhaps these dreams hold a drop of prophecy —in the sense that they open a small and fleeting window into a usually-invisible world. For our purposes, we might ask: as we move through the cycle of our own lives, and as we support patients, congregants, and others who are approaching death, might we do more to embrace sleep and the dreams it can bring?

Returning to Sinai

This brings us back to our original midrash. While the *p'shat* reading teaches us that staying awake facilitates revelation, the texts explored in this article suggest a new reading in which sleep, in and of itself, may be a spiritual practice. There is no question that sleep is good for our physical and mental health; many of us can attest to the fact that we feel a lot better, and function more optimally, when we have had enough sleep. I invite us to consider also whether sleep increases our spiritual attunement, opens passageways to God, sparks creativity, connects us to our dead, and brings comfort as we face our own mortality. Far from meaning that we'll slumber through revelation, sleep may increase the likelihood that we'll find ourselves in the midst of epiphany, inspiration, and surprising new knowledge.

Notes

1. *Pirkei D'Rabbi Eliezer* 41.
2. Laura van Dernoot Lipsky, *The Age of Overwhelm: Strategies for the Long Haul* (Oakland, CA: Barrett-Koehler, 2018).
3. Arianna Huffington, *The Sleep Revolution* (New York: Harmony Books, 2016), 19–22.
4. Ibid., 26–28.
5. Author's translation.
6. Huffington, *Sleep Revolution*, 110–11.
7. *B'reishit Rabbah* 14:9. Author's translation.
8. Gen. 2:7.
9. BT *B'rachot* 57b. Author's translation.
10. Cheryl Nosek, Christopher Kerr, Julie Woodworth, et al., "End-of-Life Dreams and Visions: A Qualitative Perspective from Hospice Patients," *American Journal of Hospice and Palliative Medicine* 32, no. 3 (2014): 269–74.

Divorce: A Different Story

Lisa J. Grushcow

Introduction

There is no good text for this topic. At least, not one I've found. In my teaching, I often mention the fact that the Torah has more to say about the ritual of divorce than the ritual of marriage. Deuteronomy 24:1:

> When a man takes a wife and becomes her husband, it shall be, if she fails to please him, and he finds in her some shamefully exposed thing, and he writes her a document of divorce and puts it in her hand and sends her away from his house ...[1]

Rashi comments that in such a situation, it is a commandment for a man to divorce his wife (Rashi ad loc, citing BT *Gittin* 90a).[2]

Midrashically, the two most-cited texts seem to be the notion that when a man divorces his wife, even the altar sheds tears (BT *Gittin* 90b; *Sanhedrin* 22a); and the story of the woman who, when her husband reluctantly divorces her based on her infertility, gets him drunk and brings him back to her father's house as her most precious possession, and they live happily ever after (*Shir Hashirim Rabbah* 1:4).

What we see from Jewish tradition, inasmuch as it can be summarized, is that divorce is permitted and sometimes required—unlike Catholic doctrine, for example, in which there is a prohibition on divorce—but there is certainly no happily ever after for a story in which divorce is final.

As a pulpit rabbi six years after my own divorce, I'd like to write a different story: one that might be helpful to colleagues in similar

---

RABBI LISA J. GRUSHCOW, D. Phil. (NY03) is the senior rabbi of Temple Emanu-El-Beth Sholom, the Reform synagogue of Montreal. She also served as associate rabbi of Rodeph Sholom in New York City. She holds degrees from McGill and the University of Oxford, in addition to being a Rhodes Scholar, a Wexner Graduate Fellow, and a Hartman Senior Rabbinic Fellow.

circumstances; for all of us in our pastoral work with individuals and couples; and for each of us in our ever-evolving relationships with our rabbinates and with each other. There is so much I wish I had known, and though I am far from an expert, I would like to share what I have learned. I'll begin with the experience of divorce; go from there to life as a senior rabbi and solo parent; share some quasi-humorous reflections on dating and my own happy ending; and close with some theological and spiritual reflections. Dear reader, join me for the ride.

The Depths of Divorce

It is common knowledge that divorce is a loss: not only the loss of one's primary relationship, but the profound loss of an expectation of how one's life would unfold. For all the talk there is about divorce being undertaken lightly, I do not know a single person for whom the decision to end a marriage has been cavalier. That was certainly not the case for me.

Like many of us, I have often given sermons—especially on the High Holy Days—about all the unexpected changes that life throws at us. Loss of loved ones, yes, but also loss of health, loss of a job, and loss of a marriage. Clearly there are both similarities and differences on this list. But somehow I did not fully understand how different and how deep each of these losses can be. In the experience of divorce, I was not cavalier; I fear that in speaking about it as one more loss on a list of losses, perhaps unintentionally, I was. The experience of my own divorce taught me how important it is to care for people before, during, and after divorce. To reach out to them and ask if they want to talk. To realize how much divorce is an event that unfolds over time, and has its own stages of grief.

As rabbis, we have an extra layer to grapple with as we experience our own losses. Living through a divorce while leading a congregation, I had to figure out when and how and who I would tell. Would it be before the High Holy Days or after? (After; I didn't want the buzz to detract from the Days of Awe.) How would I ensure that my lay leadership heard directly from me, and most important, that my children (nine and three at the time) didn't hear it from anyone else? (I told my children first, then my executive director, president, and executive committee very soon after; I communicated to the congregation via newsletter later.) How could

I balance my desire for privacy with the recognition that people would talk and that it was better to tell the story than have it be told? (I still wish I had an answer on this one!).

On top of this, as much as I—again, like many of us—had taught that there should be no stigma around divorce, there is no question that stigma still exists. I was helped by the realization that many of my lay leaders were themselves divorced (and in happy second marriages, which was inspiring), as was my respected predecessor and rabbi emeritus. I feel especially fortunate that he, a trusted colleague, could help us through our *get*. But, I still felt like I had failed: first and foremost, in my marriage, but also as an exemplar for my congregation—plus the added layer of guilt that came with remembering how let down I had felt, as a young lesbian, when seeing same-sex relationships end.

Standing under the chuppah with couples, officiating weddings, I felt profoundly aware of the lack of a ring on my left hand. I had been married since before I was ordained, so this was an entirely new experience. I also found myself asking the same question that a couple would come to ask me in a premarital counseling session. It went like this: "Rabbi, with all due respect, we have to ask: We are each coming from divorced parents, and now, even our rabbi is divorced. How are we supposed to feel confident about our marriage?"

Fortunately, by the time they asked, I was a year post-divorce and had come up with this answer: "A marriage can end, but marriage is still worthwhile. With this, as with so much of life, we have no guarantees. The chuppah and *ketubah* are not impermeable defenses against divorce. But for me, if anything, the experience of divorce was tied to a realization of what marriage should and could be. Marriage is meant to be holy, a relationship unlike any other. The goal is not simply to be married, but to have a *good* marriage. Sometimes it takes a lot of work; sometimes, no matter how much work you put in, the marriage itself doesn't work. But I believe it is one of the most important and beautiful things we can try to do."

Two years later, when this couple was struggling in their marriage, they asked me to recommend a couples' therapist, and their relationship is now significantly stronger. I like to think that our conversation made them more open to asking for help.

As for me, the single best thing I did in the time leading up to the divorce was to reconnect with my therapist, to whom I had said a fond and confident goodbye when I left New York to take up a position in Montreal. A year after that goodbye, I called her as my marriage was starting to fall apart. She was, and continues to be, a vital support.[3]

Flying Solo

As rabbis, we often feel like we need to be two places at once. As a newly divorced rabbi, a year into a new position as senior rabbi of a large congregation with primary custody of two children, I felt pulled in multiple directions to the nth degree. There were practical challenges: I soon realized (with the help of advice from colleagues and friends) that I would do well to hire an au pair, given the unpredictability of my hours. This was a significant transition, and I was fortunate to be able to invest in hiring someone with part-time hours but full-time availability.[4] As much as I worked hard to continue my rabbinic responsibilities uninterrupted, I also sometimes erred on the side of being too available—in bed alone at night, I found myself answering e-mails at ridiculous hours. Work, in many ways, helped pull me out of my own sadness and give me a sense of competence and purpose.

At the same time, I discovered the need to reexamine my rabbinic boundaries. I had spent years preaching about the need to accept help, and how raising children takes a village—and yet I didn't want my congregation to feel like they needed to take care of me. I found a compromise in accepting help with my children, from unexpected quarters. Two women in their twenties, themselves raised by single mothers, stepped forward. One would pick one of my daughters up from school and take her to a Girl Guides program that she ran; another became an involved part of our household, and a big sister to my girls. I am grateful beyond words for these acts of kindness, at what was an exceptionally difficult time.

As someone for whom family and work had always been the two primary categories of life, I also found the need to reestablish old friendships and form new ones. I realized how much, during marriage, I had let my friendships slide, and I also realized, with great gratitude, that they could be rekindled. Reprioritizing friendships was a significant silver lining to the cloud of my divorce, and my life is so much richer now because of it.

Over these years, I benefited from resuming attendance at rabbinic gatherings, including the CCAR convention.[5] Reconnecting with colleagues, and learning from their experience, was very valuable. It did, however, lead to another realization: rabbis who are happily married tend to talk a lot about their spouses. This isn't a bad thing! But we might want to be more aware of how we speak about our relationships. Speaker after speaker, at the beginning or end of their remarks, would say: "I couldn't do this without my spouse." I am all in favor of recognizing goodness (*hakarat hatov*). But we might want to be more sensitive to the fact that not everyone has a spouse. As a student at HUC, I often felt it was easier to be gay and in a relationship, than it would have been to be straight and single. By all means, those who are so fortunate to be in healthy marriages should appreciate their partners, in public and in private. Just remember when you speak that there are those listening who are not so lucky, and who are putting one foot in front of the other, nonetheless.

There are other areas in which I have learned new sensitivity in language as well. A divorced congregant of mine mentioned this Facebook post from Jeff Brown, author of *Soulshaping and Grounded Spirituality*, and I think it's worth sharing:

> I grew up in a broken home. But not because my parents divorced. It was broken long before, when the love turned to hate. When they finally divorced, there was actually more room to breathe. All the energy that went into managing the breaks, could be channeled into healing. It's time we re-framed the shaming term, "broken home." It is riddled with assumption and judgment. And it neglects the fact that many single-parents held their families together beautifully. And that many seemingly intact families, are deeply broken. Because a home is not broken when parents separate or divorce. A home is broken when there is an absence of love. If there is love, nothing's broken.[6]

The author has had one experience; the person who shared it, another. I have had my own experience of divorce and raising children. My ex has her own story, and my children have theirs. I try to be careful not to project or impose my own experience on the people I meet, within the synagogue and my role as rabbi, and beyond. In this as in all things, the language we use matters; it shapes who speaks to us, about what subject, and with which fears and hopes.

Dating: A Tragicomedy with a Happy Ending

A friend of mine is a cantor at another congregation in Montreal. When he first started in his position, he was single, and on his first *hakafah* around the congregation, multiple people handed him slips of paper with phone numbers of eligible young women.

I would not want that experience. On the other hand, as a rabbinic gay divorcée, no one was coming to me with matches.

After a winter vacation in which I shared two weeks in a two-bedroom condo in Florida with my parents and children, I realized that I dearly loved my family and my work—and that maybe there could still be more to life. Clearly I could not count on being set up. Also, in a city in which I led the only Reform congregation (and one of two congregations that are fully LGBT-inclusive), anyone who might be a prospective match was also a prospective, or actual, congregant. Meeting up with someone in a coffee shop around the corner from my synagogue, the one time I tried it, led all too easily into a pastoral conversation, and definitely did not feel like a date. With significant prodding, I decided to venture online. Most couples I marry had met on dating sites; maybe, just maybe, it would work for me too.

In the words of a friend who is a divorced Anglican priest: "Online dating is a challenge. First, you have the people who aren't interested in you because you are clergy. Then, you have the people who *are* interested in you because you are clergy. Neither of these scenarios tend to work."

Nonetheless, I ventured onto JDate and match.com. I mention JDate because, when I entered my search parameters, I quickly got an alert in my inbox. "Good news! You have a 100% match." The bad news? They had matched me with myself. Apparently looking for a Jewish lesbian nonsmoker between the ages of thirty-five and forty-five in all of Quebec had turned up no one but me. Already out of my comfort zone, I had to expand my horizons. Gender and religion were nonnegotiable; smoking too (though I did spend much more time contemplating potential flexibility in these categories than I ever thought I would!). So I extended my geographical reach—and was lucky enough to find a beautiful, smart, and most of all, *kind* woman who speaks both Hebrew and Mandarin, a daughter of Israelis who was open to synagogue life and a move to Montreal. Reader, I married her. And with all due respect and affection for every couple at whose wedding I have been privileged to officiate, I have never been happier under the chuppah.

I thank God every day for my happily ever after. Having a second marriage has sensitized me to new realities, including the challenges faced by blended families, and the great courage of step-parents and rabbinic spouses. Hopefully this new chapter will help me become a better rabbi, a better parent, and a better wife.

Theological Reflections

For years, my core theological text was the exodus from Egypt. Having come out as a lesbian in my twenties, the exodus paradigm was the one that best described my experience of going from the narrow place (*mitzrayim*) of the closet, to the freedom of being true to myself. My God was *Ehyeh-Asher-Ehyeh*, the God of possibility and becoming. Not only did this approach resonate with me, I found it resonated with many others, gay and straight. Almost everyone could connect with the idea that we have times when we are not leading the life we are meant to lead, times at which we muster our courage to take a leap of faith into the wilderness, with dreams of the Promised Land.

One day, a few years after my divorce, I found myself having a theological conversation with a congregant, and I realized that this understanding no longer rang true for me. Much to my surprise, I turned to the Book of Psalms, and specifically, the translation by Pamela Greenberg.[7] In her introduction, she writes:

> The psalms are essentially about faith, but not as faith is often imagined. Many of us believe it to be an achieved state, a place on a spiritual map, a glow of unwavering belief in relation to God. But such a conception bears little resemblance to the real experience of religious life, which is always a vector, a way of directing and redirecting oneself toward God in various gradations of intensity and confidence.[8]

Now *this* resonated with me. My life had taken me to a place where I no longer saw a direct trajectory from narrowness to possibility, and slavery to freedom. Coming out of the closet, twenty years before, I had a clear sense of the closeness of God and the direction of my path. Twenty years later, in the wake of my divorce, I felt neither. I needed to be able to articulate my new experience: of a God who felt sometimes close and sometimes very far; of uncertainty about the purpose and direction of my life; of loneliness and exhaustion, combined with an emerging (albeit intermittent) sense of confidence and hope. Greenberg put this theological roller coaster into words, and helped me find a new theology in the psalms:

> Since all translation is part interpretation, bringing one's own ideas to the psalms is inevitable. The difficulty is that allegiance to preconceived ideas of piety has often resulted in a flattening of the richness and subtle poetry of the original. For readers of English, this has been a tragic loss. *It is precisely the psalms' refusal to engage in theological piety—their overflowing into wild jubilance or anger or deeply wrenching despair—that allows them to resonate as perennial expressions of the human desire to stand simply and unabashedly before God.*[9]

I felt that desire: "to stand simply and unabashedly before God." The most important part of the High Holy Day services, for me, became the moment of bowing down fully before the ark in the Great *Aleinu*, with a heart both breaking and full. To this day, I feel this new existential reality. We never know when the page will turn and we will find ourselves in a new chapter of our lives. We can only choose, moment by moment, how we will live our choices, and come to stand before God.

"Our prayer always begins exactly where we are," Greenberg writes.[10] This article comes from that place as well. I offer it with humility, hoping it is helpful to others.

Notes

1. This translation draws on JPS and Robert Alter. Alter points out that the "shamefully exposed thing" (*ervat davar*), is the same phrase used in Deut. 23:15, in a passage referring to the importance of proper disposal of excrement outside the camp. He notes that it is "specifically the term for prohibited sexual nakedness, which should never be exposed, and so carries a strong connotation of shame." Robert Alter, *The Hebrew Bible: A Translation with Commentary*, 993.
2. This is the origin of the title of Rabbi Perry Netter's book, *Divorce Is a Mitzvah*. The only other specifically Jewish book on divorce of which I am aware is Sanford Seltzer, *When There Is No Alternative*. There are many children's books on divorce, but here too I found few from a Jewish perspective. For young children, *A Tale of*

Two Seders by Mindy Avra Portnoy is excellent. In terms of general resources for parents experiencing divorce, I recommend *Helping Your Kids Cope with Divorce the Sandcastles Way*, by M. Gary Neuman and Patricia Romanowski, and *Why Did You Have to Get a Divorce? And When Can I Get a Hamster?* by Anthony E. Wolf. For those of us looking for a book featuring divorce in a family of Jewish, same-sex parents, I think it is yet to be written.

3. Two notes on the therapeutic relationship. One: My therapist shared with me the story of one of her colleagues, a couples and family therapist, who was divorced but wore a wedding ring for her clients' benefit. Acutely aware of my own bare finger while officiating weddings, I asked her what she thought of this strategy. It was tremendously helpful for me to hear her opinion that divorce can make one a better counselor and that there is no need to hide that aspect of oneself. Two: At some point in the process, I found that it took everything I had to wake up in the morning, be present for my kids, and be present for my congregation. At that time, my therapist helped me overcome my internalized sense of stigma and skepticism around medication. There is no doubt that this helped me be a better parent and rabbi. I share this in hope that it might help someone else with a similar struggle.

4. We ended up hiring two au pairs from Germany and one from Canada, with whom we have maintained a warm relationship, and to whom I will forever be grateful.

5. The best experience of professional and personal development came through the Hartman's Institute Rabbinic Leadership Institute, in which I was privileged to join the Class VI cohort. I could not have done this without the encouragement of Rabbi Lauren Berkun, Director of Rabbinic and Synagogue Programs, and the extraordinary friendship of Rabbi Michael Latz and his husband Michael Simon, who cared for my children like their own, enabling me to participate fully in the program as a single parent. My synagogue, Temple Emanu-El-Beth Sholom, and the Federation of the Jewish Community of Montreal, also enabled me to undertake this commitment. Their investment in my rabbinate continues to be a blessing.

6. Jeff Brown, Facebook posting, October 13, 2018, https://www.facebook.com/SOULSHAPING/posts/i-grew-up-in-a-broken-home-but-not-because-my-parents-divorced-it-was-brokenlon/10157218546105982/.

7. Pamela Greenberg, *The Complete Psalms* (New York: Bloomsury, 2010).

8. Ibid., xv–xvi.

9. Ibid., xvii (emphasis mine).

10. Ibid., xxiii.

Embracing Reality: Spiritual Preparation for Living with Dementia

Dayle A. Friedman

"If I get that way, just shoot me."

"I have taken care of both of my parents through Alzheimer's. I will *not* let my kids go through that."

These are just a couple of comments I have heard from people talking about the prospect of living with an illness that causes cognitive loss. Americans are terrified of getting Alzheimer's or other dementias. A 2017 study found that 38 percent of Americans are more afraid of dementia than any other illness.[1] We are scared, and we want to do anything to avoid this fate.

What causes our profound dread of dementia? Most of us have encountered some of the harsh realities of cognitive impairment. We have felt distress when a beloved no longer remembers who we are. We have seen agitation when a family member is disoriented. We have observed dear ones suffering indignities. We have run into inhumane care. Surely, there is much to worry about in contemplating dementia. More than all of this, though, we equate memory with personhood. We believe that without the capacity to remember, we cease to *be*. If we do not remember our friends, relatives, work, what we had to eat or where we went yesterday, who are we? *What* are we?

Our fears have been stoked by personal experience, and by a steady stream of film and media accounts of the tragedy of dementia. People with dementia are depicted as empty vessels, and their

---

RABBI DAYLE A. FRIEDMAN is a chaplain, spiritual director, and scholar of spirituality and later life. Her Philadelphia-based, national practice is Growing Older. Her most recent book is *Jewish Wisdom for Growing Older: Finding Your Grit and Grace Beyond Midlife* (Jewish Lights, 2015).

caregivers as suffering saints. We have a very limited picture of the experience of dementia, the "tragedy narrative."[2]

Dementia is far more complex than these simplistic images suggest. In my work as a pastoral caregiver for thousands of people with Alzheimer's and other dementias, and in my confrontations with dementia in my family, I have seen the sad and scary parts. I have also witnessed delight, growth, healing, and peace. In this essay, I invite us to face the intricate reality of dementia, and I challenge us to personally and spiritually prepare for it, so that we can live with ease and so that we can more compassionately accompany our congregants in this mysterious terrain. I am aware that such preparation is neither normative nor easy, and yet, I suggest that we may well reap unexpected blessings from it.

Costs of Fear

We are unlikely to successfully evade the experience of dementia, a complex of diseases, of which Alzheimer's is one type. Dementia currently affects about 5 million Americans; this number is expected to rise to 14 million by 2050. According to current estimates, about 10 percent of those over sixty-five and one-third of those over eighty-five live with dementia. One in three people over sixty-five die of dementia.[3] Dementia will touch us—if we live long enough, we will likely have it, and even if not, we will no doubt encounter it in our parents, partners, congregants, and friends—and the fear of it colors our perspective on our own aging.

This immense fear has a cost. In our trepidation of the prospect of dementia, we may do everything we can to avoid it. We don't admit that we could get dementia, so we don't plan for it. We don't talk about it with our families and friends. When dementia comes to us or our beloveds, we are drawn to denial. "She's just a little forgetful." "He is having a bad day." "I'm not so bad for my age." We may, despite our best intentions, gradually distance ourselves from dear ones or community members with dementia, thus increasing their isolation.

Avoiding reality can add to the suffering of the person with dementia and her family members. Because we have not explored, imagined, or planned for dementia, tough decisions become even more wrenching. A middle-of-the-night phone call suddenly prompts stressful choices regarding moves, medical treatment, or placement in a care setting, all without knowing what the individual might have wanted. How many families have struggled when an elder who, like my Dad, clearly was no longer capable but insisted on continuing to drive? How many people have insisted in staying in their long-time homes, even when they are not able to safely live alone? Denial and resistance can magnify our grief, confusion and agony.

Preparing for Dementia

How can we prepare for living with dementia? Alanna Shaikh, a courageous young woman whose father has early-onset Alzheimer's disease, recorded a TED Talk, "How I'm Preparing to Get Alzheimer's."[4] Shaikh is reaping guidance for herself from her Dad's journey. She wants to have enjoyable times when she gets Alzheimer's, so she is developing new, hands-on hobbies in which she could still engage if she were cognitively impaired. She is doing physical exercises to enhance her balance, so that she will reduce her risk of falling. And, most intriguingly, she is trying to be a better person. She says admiringly of her Dad, "When you take away everything he ever learned in this world, his naked heart still shines." She has work to do, she says, for "I need a heart so pure that if it's stripped bare by dementia, it will survive."

Jewish Spiritual Preparation:
The Wisdom of the Baal Shem Tov

Alanna Shaikh says that the process of approaching Alzheimer's head-on has brought her to "thinking more broadly about how to plan for a future that isn't the future you choose. How can you build a life that you're living right now that prepares you for both the best and worst possible future?" It seems to me that Shaikh's question is a spiritual one, and that we should be able to reach into our Jewish sources to find guidance in this task.

I wonder how we can prepare *spiritually* for the prospect of living with dementia. It occurs to me that we might find a framework from the Baal Shem Tov's three-fold approach to contending with unwelcome experiences. He taught:

> An individual should cultivate three ways of dealing with adversity: *Hachna'ah*/Yielding, *Havdalah*/Discernment, and *Hamtakah*/

Sweetening . . . If you are able to purify your thinking regarding what is good and pleasant about each of the occurrences that happen to you through Yielding, Discernment and Sweetening . . . you will then be able to hold your footing and you won't be toppled by the husks of evil. You will remain bound in oneness to the Blessed One.[5]

Hachnaah (Yielding)

Hachnaah, the first step in approaching unwelcome experiences, involves facing reality. The Gerer Rebbe teaches in *S'fat Emet* that even in moments of darkness we can connect to the vital divine power hidden within us by "submitting ourselves before truth" (1:246). We can resist the truth of our lives, or we can soften to it. This is not easy or even intuitive—we would certainly prefer to run away from darkness. Many of us are attached to the illusion of control, and we balk at the idea of submitting ourselves to anything.

This business of yielding to unwelcome reality is counterintuitive. It is natural, even reflexive, to deny, to stiffen. When you pull a muscle in your back, your body responds with alarm, attempting to protect the hurt, raw place by hardening around it. You want to make sure that nothing can get to that vulnerable place and injure it further. But a strange thing happens. Instead of feeling better, now you are not only sore but also stiff. You find you have trouble bending, turning, and eventually moving at all. You want to take to your bed; you pray that this will all just pass. Surprisingly, you should do anything *but* this. Stretch, move gently, your doctor tells you, and you will heal. This is yielding. The Baal Shem Tov teaches that *hachnaah* (surrendering to or allowing what is) brings redemption from imprisonment.

Yielding to dementia means including the possibility of having dementia in our pictures of our futures. I have been practicing saying, "When I get dementia . . ." as an invitation to my imagination. My guts rebel as I utter these words, but perhaps it is a tad easier for me than others, because I spent years hanging out in the land of dementia when I was a nursing home chaplain. I got to see people living with dementia as three-dimensional beings. I used to wonder which one I would be—the spirited woman who couldn't speak, but sang constantly; the agitated woman who asked every passerby, "what time is it?"; or the man who believed he worked there and constantly tried to help his fellow residents. Allowing for the prospect of dementia can empower us to discern our wishes, to make plans, and to collaborate with those who will be charged with our care.

Havdalah: Seeing Both Darkness and Light

If we yield to reality, we discover that what we are facing is not just darkness. The Baal Shem Tov calls us to discern the sparks that are encased in *k'lipot* (shards) as we face brokenness. I imagine this as a spiritual/emotional parallel to the phenomenon of our eyes adjusting to a darkened room; it turns out there is shadow, there are shades of darkness, and, if we try hard, we can make out tiny fragments of light.

Once we know the terrain of our sadness and we can let go of resisting it, we can begin to open ourselves to the totality of this complex experience. Another way of describing *havdalah* is bringing curiosity to the unwelcome reality. Having arrived in a place we hoped to avoid, we endeavor to take in and fully inhabit the landscape.

Jarem Sawatsky is a professor of peace and conflict studies who is living with, and reflecting on, Huntington's Disease. He watched his mother, uncle, and grandmother live and die with Huntington's, and he himself was diagnosed in his forties. In his moving memoir, *Dancing with Elephants,* Sawatsky writes, "Once you decide to embrace darkness, a different world comes into focus." He dedicates himself to living fully amid reduced capacities and with complete awareness that further decline awaits him. He insists that he is more than his disease. He works to befriend his forgetfulness and frequent falls, rather than to sink into constant anger. He aims "to be thrilled, grateful, wonder-filled and curious about life and living."[6]

Despite the losses and challenges of dementia, activist geriatrician Dr. Bill Thomas suggests that those of us who will live with dementia "have a choice. We can choose tragedy or we can choose joy."[7]

Hamtakah: Wresting Sweetness

When we have allowed ourselves to dwell in darkness and we have opened our eyes wide to sparks of light within it, the Baal Shem Tov teaches that we are ready to wrest some sweetness out of a bitter experience. It is interesting that the Baal Shem Tov changes his metaphor from darkness-light to bitterness-sweetness. Ultimately, he hints, what we can hope for is to harvest something of sweetness, something redemptive out of our most anguishing life experiences. Rabbi Burt Jacobson suggests that this sweetness can be seen as dispelling the darkness.

It is vital to note that the Baal Shem Tov is certainly not whitewashing the agony of suffering. He himself was orphaned as a young child, his first wife died, and he grew up in an atmosphere of deprivation and violence against Jews. This is not a Pollyannaish denial of suffering's sting. Rather the sage boldly reminds us that even the most wrenching agony may also contain goodness if we are able to be open to it.

Rabbi Burt Jacobson says that when we have done *Havdalah*, "The energy we have heretofore placed into identification with our adversity and with our suffering can now be released and transformed into joy. This sweetening may not always affect the physical conditions of adversity that impinge upon our lives. We may still find ourselves in a painful situation. But our act of *Havdalah* has brought about an inward change, and we are now able to cope with the external difficulties out of an inner sense of resolution, freedom, and joy."[8]

Perhaps *hamtakah* hints at the possibility that we can be transformed by our unwelcome experience, in this case, by living with dementia. When my late father entered a nursing home with dementia, I prayed that something would happen to his soul. I didn't exactly know what I meant. Dad had many accomplishments, but he was also a complicated person, with much pain in and around him. I could not have imagined what he would be like as a nursing home resident, but I would not have been surprised had he been demanding, impatient, and unhappy. Nothing could have been farther from the truth. Over the four years Dad spent in the nursing home, he was content, loving, and grateful. It was as if his personality burned away, and what was left was pure soul. Dad's sojourn with dementia afforded him a radically different way of being, and it gave me the opportunity to connect with him in a deep and healing way.

Not everyone who lives with dementia has such a profound or positive transformation, but I have witnessed many shifts in souls and relationships on the path. Nader Shabahangi, who works with people with dementia at AgeSong, a Zen-inspired eldercare organization, teaches about people with forgetfulness, "For those who can truly lay aside their aversion or discomfort and learn to accept what is, the gifts of the soul await; equanimity, intimacy with the dream-world and its magical ways, slowing down to the speed of soul essence."[9] My hope is that opening to dementia can defang our fears as we age, enable us to live more fully, and make us more compassionate and more resilient as we accompany family members, friends, and congregants on the journey of dementia.

Practice: Embracing Reality

The Baal Shem Tov's three-fold approach to unwelcome experience can be a guide for us in approaching the prospect of dementia. Although dementia might be far off, or perhaps not even part of our personal future, practicing embracing reality in the way the sage prescribed can help us to be present to all of what life brings us. We can gently invite ourselves to face that which we are avoiding, thus opening ourselves to choices and goodness, and putting down the burden of resistance and hardening ourselves. This practice of reflection can be a starting place.

I invite you to try this practice when you have at least twenty minutes. Sit comfortably. Breathe naturally and allow your body to relax as much as possible. Take some time to reflect on at least one of the following realms of your life:

- Intimate relationships: partner, parents, children, siblings
- Work
- Home
- Physical health
- Spiritual life

Ask yourself if there is something you are avoiding acknowledging or are resisting. If you become aware of something, notice the resistance. What does it feel like in your body? Is there an image or metaphor that describes it? Allow the resistance to "talk to you": What would be the worst thing that might happen if you faced the truth? What would be the best? Can you invite yourself to open a bit?

See if there is a hope that you have about this reality. If you wish, you can express that hope as a prayer, on the order of the following:

Makor HaChayim/Source of Life [or whatever name for the Divine suits you] who has sustained my ancestors and me, help me to face _____. Give me strength and courage; guide me on this path whose direction I cannot yet see. Open me to all that is before me; help me to be whole.

Notes

1. Alzheimer's Survey," Metlife Foundation, https://www.metlife.com/content/dam/microsites/about/corporate-profile/alzheimers-2011.pdf.
2. See Anne Basting's masterful work on developing deeper and more complex narratives of dementia, *Forget Memory: Creating Better Lives for People with Dementia*. (Baltimore: Johns Hopkins University Press, 2009).
3. Alzheimer's Association, "2019 Alzheimer's Disease Facts and Figures."
4. Alanna Shaikh, "How I'm Preparing to Get Alzheimer's," https://fellowsblog.ted.com/how-do-you-prepare-for-dementia-dc87f72be9ec.
5. Baal Shem Tov, as translated in Burt Jacobson, *This Precious Moment: The Wisdom of the Ba'al Shem Tov* (Piedmont, CA: Kehilla Community Synagogue, 2016), 52–53.
6. Jarem Sawatsky. *Dancing with Elephants: Mindfulness Training for Those Living with Dementia, Chronic Illness or an Aging Brain (How to Die Smiling Book 1)* (Red Canoe Press, 2017).
7. William Thomas, "A Hundred Miles in Their Shoes," https://www.edenalt.org/retrospective-bill-thomas-takes-tragedy-narrative/.
8. Jacobson, *This Precious Moment*, 56.
9. Nader Shabahangi. *Deeper into the Soul: Beyond Dementia and Alzheimer's Toward Forgetfulness Care* (San Francisco: Elder's Academy Press, 2008).

When the Rabbi Is Also the Caregiver

Eva Robbins

It is often easy to identify someone who is in pain, certainly when they are a congregant/patient in a hospital. The signs are all too visible. We feel compassion and concern for what they are going through, including the treatments and procedures that they must face. We are reminded of the importance of *bikur cholim* (visiting the sick), one of the things we should do in this world to which there is no measure (*Pei-ah* 1:1). In fact, the Sages teach that we remove one-sixtieth of illness when we tend to one who is sick.

But what about the caregiver? Often the caregiver is the silent patient in the background.

As a clergy person I have often found myself in the presence of those needing emotional and spiritual support. Being present for those I serve and for whom I care demands great empathy, as well as cultivating the ability to find enough distance not to be overwhelmed or emotionally drained by the pain of others. This is an ongoing challenge all clergy face. We use tools that help to keep our own emotional balance, including moments of intention or meditation before crossing the threshold of a hospital room, remembering we are just vessels for the Holy to flow through. Post visit we can perform a symbolic ritual or take a few moments before our next responsibility or before entering our own homes, using prayer or text or even the shower or bath, like a *mikveh*, to wash away the impact of caring for others on our mind, body or spirit.

RABBI CANTOR EVA ROBBINS was ordained as chazan in 2004 and rabbi in 2015 from the Academy of Jewish Religion, California, where she is on the faculty. She is co-founder and co-rabbi with Rabbi Stephen Robbins of N'vay Shalom and is a member of the Cantors Assembly, on the board of directors for the Sandra Caplan Community Bet Din, and a member of the Board of Rabbis of Southern California. Rabbi Eva is also a Reiki master and teacher of Jewish meditation. She is the author of *Spiritual Surgery: A Journey of Healing Mind, Body, and Spirit*, about the *Mishkan* as a vehicle for healing PTSD of the Israelites after leaving Egypt.

But how do we sustain our souls when it is our loved ones who are in need—a spouse, child, or parent—and we face the devastating reality of their critical and often unending chronic medical conditions? How do we answer that call for ongoing caregiving—perhaps while in the midst of serving others in our work, going to school, or raising a family?

In 2005 I faced such a reality. My husband of forty-six years and my work partner since 1993 faced a catastrophic illness that caused him extensive nerve damage and constant pain. Together, he as Rabbi and I as Cantor, had shared and thrived—and suddenly that partnership came to a shocking halt.

Steve had faced many other illnesses, most of which we both managed and in time watched pass. This time, however, the prognosis was not as positive. We were told that his shingles episode was one of a small percent in which the resulting post-herpetic neuralgia could last an unending number of years, demanding heavy-duty drugs, crawling into a cocoon, and drifting off to a life of pain, abandoned dreams, and isolation.

Stubborn, as we both are, we faced this new enemy in our lives without surrendering hope for the future. However, after various medications and treatments, along with inevitable aging, these past fourteen years have brought inordinate challenges along with other physical deterioration, creating enormous complexity and demands for both of us.

People with chronic pain and debilitating illness face not only physical challenges but professional and emotional losses as well. The inevitable changes tap into emotional and spiritual malaise, social isolation, and a devastating shift in what was once normal. Partners, parents, and children are impacted as well. Their reality as family members is often neglected and misunderstood.

The world I knew suddenly shattered, and I had to find a way to piece it back together by confronting not only the constant drain of physical caregiving but also the emotional and spiritual loss, grief, and changes I experienced on a daily basis. As a fellow caregiver shared with me recently, "It is so easy to lose your soul." Yes, living and caring for your loved one, 24/7, is a wholly (and holy) different challenge than visiting and supporting others in need. The thresholds blur while experiencing one deprivation after another. Healthy caregiving requires boundaries and an ability for the clergy person or chaplain to rest, recharge, refuel. Familial relationships are much more challenging and at times emotionally heartbreaking. Chronic illness has the capacity to stretch its hold over all those who live with it—the patient and the extended family. The work that Steve and I had shared needed to be redefined. I realized a few years in that I had to find a way to rediscover a sense of wholeness and hold on to my soul.

Claiming a new identity—caregiver—led me to research in order to get a better understanding of the demands of this role and my responses to them. I hadn't realized how many of us are out there. There are approximately 70 million people over 50 with at least one chronic health condition.[1] Of the approximately 325 million people in the United States, that is about one-fifth to one-quarter of the population; approximately 40 million to 50 million adults serve as unpaid caregivers.[2] Their work has an invaluable benefit and often saves unaffordable dollars for many families. With a growing "boomer" population, more and more people will face either their own debilitating illness or find themselves providing care for another.

Most disturbing is what the research shows caregivers confront: a myriad of issues crossing the total spectrum of their being: emotional, spiritual, mental, and physical. The role of caregiver demands acquiring knowledge of illnesses with their symptoms and prescriptive medications; finding and meeting a range of medical professionals, learning about procedures; amassing reams of forms and paperwork; dealing with insurance companies; organizing medical visits; facing the many strangers, often in the middle of the night, including paramedics and EMTs (emergency medical technicians); confronting devastating loss and grief; suffering from depression, guilt, and resentment; having feelings of helplessness and hopelessness, isolation, and loneliness; and often confronting their own health issues. The gravity of these challenges is reflected in a 63 percent higher mortality rate among caregivers.[3]

It's not a pretty picture. In fact, I discovered for couples faced with such a reality, where one person is chronically ill, the divorce rate is higher than the national average, reportedly as much as 75 percent.[4] The challenges of caregiving for a spouse demand incredible cooperation, listening, patience, and forgiveness. Communication, in its most honest and heartfelt way, is a critical pathway to shared understanding and problem solving. Sharing the vast array of feelings with each other makes it possible to better understand the often unspoken and nonverbal communication that is transmitted. The ability to listen and empathize with the other strengthens a couple's skills in navigating their new unchartered pathways in their marriage.

Steve and I often joke that he lives with pain, and I suffer. The distinction is an important one. One is physical, and the other is psychospiritual. As his life is consumed with pain, new medical conditions, and multiple forms of treatments and protocols, there are certainly emotional and spiritual challenges that he confronts; but his strength and spiritual toolbox help to combat their impact. I, however, generally pain-free, have confronted an ever-pervasive darkness and deep losses that continually challenge me.

As a child of Holocaust survivors, I am no stranger to darkness; and these past fourteen years have dragged me kicking into a cavernous pit, an image ingrained in me like that of the Joseph story. This trauma became part of my ever-evolving spiritual growth, reminding me that though my soul's survival often feels threatened, it would find a way to move forward and thrive. Like Joseph, I know God has brought me here. I also believed that the foundation of our friendship and consideration for each other would continue to help Steve and me face these new challenges.

During these past fourteen years I have discovered/developed unexpected skills, experiences, and emotions. None of us is trained or prepared for this role, but love, loyalty, and compassion help to both guide us to accept what we must confront. Self-care is the greatest gift we can give ourselves when the demands of caregiving envelop us like a dark cloud. Hillel's words ring so true, "If I am not for myself, who will be?" (*Pirkei Avot* 1:14). Judaism and its multiple pathways of spiritual practice have guided me on this journey.

My blessed tradition sustains me, lighting my path every step of the way. Becoming a bat mitzvah at fifty, I had always treasured the statement in Psalm 92, "The righteous shall flourish like a palm tree . . . they shall still bring forth fruit in old age."

As I was approaching my sixties when Steve faced his medical crisis, I held even more tightly to this wisdom. As a result of this radical shift in our lives, a voice whispered, I would face another crossroad. I had lost my work partner, whose words and teachings were extraordinary; and I couldn't imagine working with another rabbi as I continued to face our classes, and the expectations of congregants as well as the community members who we had served. They tended to see my role as limited, as only the cantor, a musical voice. I believed in order to continue my work I would have to hire a rabbi, or—perhaps even more audacious—become one. I chose the latter.

My suffering and grief found its way back into Torah and the depth of Jewish studies, expanding my skills and opportunities to serve in new ways. I decided to go back to school and was ordained in 2015 as rabbi, an enormous accomplishment under the circumstances and tremendous gift. Steve's enforced *tzimtzum*, contracting from the central role he played, pushed me forward in ways I could never have imagined. I found strength in leading and facilitating, channeling the compassion I discovered as a caregiver, towards those experiencing loss and grief, better able to walk them through the valley of the shadow of death. My empathy as a rabbi has grown exponentially because of this journey. Even as losses mounted, I found my "cup runneth over" in the work I could now do that nurtured my soul and gave it expanded meaning. Ezekiel's words gave me solace as I acquired a new heart and a new spirit: "I will remove the heart of stone from your flesh and give you a heart of flesh" (Ezek. 36:25). I was learning, over and over again, that even in the darkest of nights, in the most difficult of life's moments, light emerges as possibility breaks through.

I discovered the Aish Kodesh, the Piaszeczner Rebbe, Rabbi Kalonymus Kalman Shapira, who walked, taught, and held his people during the horrors of the *Shoah*. The Rabbi of the Warsaw Ghetto, his teachings not only reminded me that "the imminent presence of the Divine is in all reality," in pain as well as joy, but that even when one feels "crushed and trampled," they can find strength by taking baby steps to move forward. I could find strength to "pick myself up, dust myself off, and start all over again." The Piaszeczner remained silent for weeks at a time after suffering his own losses and tragedy. His example gave me permission to acknowledge my grief yet not let it overcome my life.

I delved deeper into my inner landscape, through meditation and yoga, as an entrance into moments of silence. Psalm 65:2 was a constant companion, reminding me that, *l'cha dumiyah t'hilah* ("To You silence is praise"). My moments of withdrawal and lack of words weren't just a reflection of my malaise but could be a gift to the Holy One and an entrance to the presence of the Divine. Alone in my garden, by my fountain, I sustained my meditation practice, hours of reading, and like Rebbe Nachman, touched the glory of creation. Sitting in the solace of quiet, reconnecting with the Divine, strengthened my resilience. Taking breaks from my husband's pain, both the sound and presence within the walls of our home, helped me to maintain some semblance of equanimity.

Jewish "triangular breathing," which my husband had taught years prior in our meditation classes, continued to sustain a deep well of gratitude and emotional presence for me. Using three Hebrew words, *ruach* (breath/wind), *nefesh* (physical life force), and *n'shamah* (the soul with the spark of the Divine), this focused breathing slowed me down and connected me with the Divine and my partnership in Creation. This triangular breath, *ruach*, breath in; *nefesh*, breath out; and *n'shamah*, pause, provided moments of spiritual healing and reinvigorated my spirit. Along with chanting Psalm 46:11, *harpu ud'u ki Anochi Elohim* ("refrain, stop, so that I can know God"), I had an opportunity to massage my inner being and tap into resilience once again. I was constantly replaying and reliving Genesis 2:7, the description of God forming the human and breathing life and soul into this being. Engaging spirituality brought me renewal.

Envisioning two of God's names are vehicles for me, like Ezekiel's vision of the chariot, both important for my survival. The first, the vertical *yod-hei-vav-hei* (*YHVH*) strengthens my inner structure, what I call the spiritual skeleton, as the letters look like the human body. The other name appears only once in Torah when Moshe hears the voice of the Divine coming from the Burning Bush. Moses wants to know what name to give the Israelites when he goes down to Egypt, and God replies, *Ehyeh-Asher-Ehyeh* ("I will be that which I will be"). This name, which is a verb, always inspires me with the hope of transformation and possibility.

Studying also reconnected me with mystic and kabbalistic language and images of prophetic visions and the *Eitz Chayim* (the Tree of Life). The human template with the *S'firot* guides new understandings of where in my body I might be blocked, needing attention. Navigating my own aging process and the various symptoms caregivers face, I must continue to be vigilant about my health and well-being, especially making sure I attend to my diet, exercise, and quality sleep, while also nurturing moments with friends and family, continuing to expand my mind and my spirit, and do the work that not only nurtures others but also enhances my sense of purpose and meaning in this world.

I choose to follow my soul's curiosity as well as support my partner in his new journey, which has brought its own surprises. At times it is like walking Rebbe Nachman's narrow bridge and remembering "not to be afraid." I can't say there aren't moments of fear and insecurity, but I work to intentionally hold on to courage and fortitude as much as possible. Other times I have a talk with God, sometimes questioning, sometimes complaining, sometimes expressing my anger. But most of time, like Hannah, I call out for help with Jeremiah's words flowing from my lips (shifting the pronoun), "Heal him, *Adonai*, and he will be healed; save him, and he will be saved; for You are my praise" (Jer. 17:14).

Through my own spiritual practice, risk-taking, and soul-expansion, I continue my Jewish journey, discovering new pathways to healing. I have also discovered a new voice, writing and sharing ways to support and inspire others who face their own challenges. I have become aware of and reconnected to the strength of my survivor parents, realizing it is a gift of inheritance on a cellular level. The darkness we often face is beyond comprehension, and yet the human spirit desires light and hope. My blessing has been that the darkness of fear and adversity continues to teach me not to let it defeat me. I am also blessed with the ongoing loving support of my partner, who in the midst of his own loss and pain encourages me to continue to grow.

We never know where our journeys will take us and how the darkness in our lives can surprisingly bring the light of surprise and newfound joy. "Those who sow in tears shall reap in joy" (Ps. 126:5). I encourage others to reach beyond the limits and boundaries they face, following in the footsteps of our early ancestors, known to us as *Ivri*, those who crossed borders and journeyed to an unknown land. Surrendering to the dark realties in our lives is no easy task—but there are rewards, mysterious and unknown, that await us.

I conclude with my Ten Commandments for Caregivers. Perhaps they can enlighten you, out there, alone, the silent patient and unsung hero, to support your journey of caregiving.

Ten Commandments for Caregivers

1. I surrender to now living a "new normal" that is anything but normal!
2. I must surrender to the unknown and the unpredictable and be in the "now."
3. I must relinquish all expectations, as nothing will ever be the same.
4. I must honor my new feelings: loss, sadness, fear, anger and guilt.
5. I must have compassion for the one I care for and their new road of difficulty, pain, trauma, dependency, and loss.
6. I must have compassion for myself as I navigate the new demands and responsibility I undertake.
7. I must recognize the impact this new role can have: exhaustion, stress, anxiety, PTSD, and grief.
8. I must take care of, not only my loved one, but also "myself" —physically, emotionally, and spiritually so I can sustain strength and resilience.
9. I must find appreciation and gratitude for moments of joy and pleasure, no matter how small.
10. I must discover my new bliss and create a life of meaning, productivity, and life-fulfilling activity.

Notes

1. AARP, https: assets:aarp.org/rgcenter/health/chronic condition.
2. Family Caregivers Alliance, www.caregiver.org/caregiver-statistics-demographics.
3. Populations at Risk, Family Caregiving Alliance, www.caregiver.org/caregiver-health.
4. Focus on Family, www.focusonfamily.com/marriage/facing-crisis/chronic illness.

The Professional Pursuit of Spiritual and Mental Health

Minding Our Behavioral Health for the Sake of Spiritual Fulfillment

Laura Stein

The first time I broached the subject with a colleague, I was suffocated by the stigma of it all. I was lamenting my experiences in the Jewish professional world, mindful not to sound histrionic, when I spoke the forbidden words—mental illness. "Yeah, but there's mental illness, and then there's *mental illness*," my rabbinical student friend responded. "And the difference?" I prodded. "Well, you know, there are those teachers who yell and throw things and we all kind of laugh, and then there are those people who talk to themselves on the bus and we all move away."

Sure. One is dysregulated behavior, and one is a sign of mental illness. But does the distinction matter? While it wasn't clear what to call it, what was clear was that we, as clergy, were struggling. As a cantorial student beginning additional professional training in mental health treatment, I started to take note of troubling behavior by Jewish leaders—behavior so disappointing I was beginning to lose faith in us as communal leaders and in our tradition's prescription for personal change and growth. I saw clergy texting each other while being led in prayer by colleagues, mentors showing a lack of empathy towards the suffering of people who were not powerfully situated or "important," and professors sacrificing

---

CANTOR LAURA STEIN, LMSW, was ordained from HUC-JIR's Debbie Friedman School of Sacred Music in 2018. She also holds a Master of Social Work from New York University. Currently, Laura works full-time as a social worker at Mount Sinai Hospital's Center for Transgender Medicine and Surgery and serves as cantor in various congregational, communal, and pastoral settings.

equitable education for ego. I watched a clergyperson spread gossip minutes before stepping onto the bimah to lead *Elohai N'tzor*.

I'm not naïve. What I saw was just people being people. *We are better than this.* I wanted to see Jews being Jews.

Newly oriented to behavioral health theory and evidence-based practice, I was learning to see people not in categories or camps, but as humans struggling with the human condition and with day-to-day ego functioning—the basic mechanism inside each of us that negotiates our impulses, regulates our emotions, engages us in problem solving, and allows us to stay grounded in what's true. As I immersed myself in my clinical training, I felt increasingly that we, as members of clergy, had lost sight of God's calls to treat each other with respect and compassion. Our human nature, gone unchecked, was getting the best of us.

What concerned me most was not that the disordered behavior was intrinsically damaging, but that it was creating barriers to true spiritual fulfillment—to bringing God's presence into our lives and into the world through acts of loving-kindness, compassion, and caregiving. I wondered: Are we living with integrity? More importantly, are we living Jewishly? Week after week we facilitate Torah study, worship, and holiday celebrations. We rededicate ourselves to the belief that the Jewish way is the best way. We strive to be fair and honest, inclusive and good, and, most of all, humble before God. And yet, we're human, which means we inevitably fall short.

How can we follow the behaviorally-focused commandments to treat others and ourselves with respect and kindness if we are constantly short-circuited by the human inclinations to compete, to win, to survive? These questions challenged me. I was desperate to address the seemingly unattainable behavioral directives posed by our tradition. *What is hateful to you do not do to another.*[1] The rest is commentary, right? Easy enough.

Not so easy. Being human is hard. Being a modern Jew is hard. Being a Jewish leader is hard. But when discussing what makes it challenging to live a meaningful Jewish life, we may hesitate to look inward and to evaluate the ways in which we distance ourselves from this ancient life-guide we so deeply treasure. We may hesitate to address how our behavior distances us from the commandments that God gifted us as tools for sacred living.

It's easy to take the moralistic approach—one that preaches perfection and lays blame on the inevitable shortcomings of ourselves and others. But this is not the point. If we are to continue to promote the Jewish way as one worth following, then we must address that which is spiritually corrosive. And we might start by looking at ourselves—by taking a moral inventory of our own relationships to Torah, to others, and to God; by assessing what really motivates us and, when necessary, recalibrating; and by addressing our personal behavioral health and incorporating behavioral health techniques into our spiritual and self-care practices. Only then will we bring our full selves to our Jewish journeys and show up authentically to our congregants as we guide them on theirs.

The Struggle Is Real

We see a staggering amount of mental illness and psychiatric diagnosis in the Jewish community. In fact, a study from the 1990s found that members of the Jewish community are 2.5 times more likely to develop a psychiatric disorder and 40 percent more likely to develop an affective or mood disorder than their non-Jewish counterparts.[2] While more recent statistics are not as readily available, another study posits that Ashkenazi heredity predisposes anxiety disorders.[3] In a population already at-risk for prejudiced mistreatment by society, and as leaders who carry the burden of protecting our institutions from external attack, this predisposition to anxiety can make it that much harder for us to practice and to serve.

But mental illness need not be a barrier to Jewish living. The Jewish community has proved adept at responding to crisis and helping those in critical need. From the Disabilities Inclusion Learning Center to Beit T'Shuvah's Addiction Treatment Congregation, we have developed resources to help those outside the camp find their way home. At our best, we bestow compassion on those with a diagnosis or seeking a diagnosis. We have overcome societal stigma and now serve as a model for and champion of inclusivity. So why do we as Jewish leaders struggle to address our own behavioral and mental health? Is it only ego, or do we feel personally ashamed? I know this struggle all too well, for it is a personal struggle at its core.

I grew up in a nurturing and progressive Jewish community in Scarsdale, New York. Jewish values were the bedrock of my family's culture, and I came to know the Jewish responsibility as one centered on the Golden Rule. Along with holidays and study, our observance manifested as we welcomed the stranger, cared for the environment, and sought a life of integrity and service. Familial, communal, and congregational messaging taught me that above all else, God wants us to treat each other with respect, kindness, and compassion. This became my personal mission and the foundation of my cantorial career. I was a young person with a dream.

I was also a young person who struggled. My early trauma was so severe that at age eight, I was diagnosed with panic disorder, a condition that was introduced into the Diagnostic and Statistical Manual of Mental Disorders[4] (DSM III) less than a decade before I was born. A disorder so little understood I often had to teach my parents and providers about the perils of living with panic. In the 1990s, I had multiple panic attacks a day, leading me to lock myself in bathrooms, run home from school in the middle of class, and threaten suicide. I was so scared of panicking that I would panic in anticipation, summoning the very panic attack I worked so hard to stave off. I was exhausted from simply trying to breathe. I remember talking to myself in the mirror of my bunk at sleepaway camp: *You are not going to die. You are not going to die.*

It felt hard to be good during this period of my life. (It's still hard now.) It was and is easy to let go, to act out, to isolate. But my "bad" behaviors—my ways of coping—did not seem to disqualify me from participation in Jewish life, so I participated. Judaism was a safe place and Jewish music my tonic. Even there, though, I was aware of my struggle. *I want to be a cantor. But a cantor wouldn't act this mean and angry. Come on, Stein. Try harder.*

I tried so very hard to be a kid others could be proud of —whom God could be proud of —and yet, I was struggling in ways beyond the reach of my Jewish teachings. The question wasn't whether to be a kind and holy person, but rather how to do so when my spirit was depleted of its childhood innocence and replaced with rage for all of the trauma I had endured.

Years later, the struggle returned. While in cantorial school, I found myself acting out again, reactive to the behavior around me and unable to disrupt my reaction. I tried my best. I prayed and sang, studied and taught, engaged in spiritual direction and psychotherapy. But I feared for my ability to sustain life in a clergy role when I felt so deeply damaged. I feared I couldn't access Judaism, couldn't even qualify for its foundational stepping-stones. *Be slow to anger like God.* How could I overcome a lifetime of anger towards a world that had forsaken me? *Do not remove yourself from the community*.⁵ How could I do that when the greater community didn't always make space for my special kind of experience? *Treat others the way you would want to be treated.* Why is this burden on me when I haven't received the same courtesy?

When I applied to New York University's Silver School of Social Work at the end of my second year of cantorial school, I hoped that the additional master's degree would provide some answers to my questions. People asked why I decided to switch my focus. But social work *became* and *is* my Judaism. I could not engage with our Jewish teachings without the support of the mental health community. Social work school was the most healing experience I've ever had, for it made Judaism make sense.

I feel blessed to stand here twenty years later as a person who not only overcame struggles but also harnessed her pain to begin a career devoted to healing others. As a cantor and a social worker, I straddle two philosophies, both of which have been incredibly helpful in my own healing journey: Judaism guides us with ritual, text, and prayer to live in the image of God while the mental health tradition teaches skills that build on our core beliefs to maximize our potential.

This approach has been especially effective in my work at Mount Sinai Hospital, where I currently work as a social worker in its Center for Transgender Medicine and Surgery (CTMS). The patient population at CTMS suffers from a great deal of trauma and often lacks the social resources many of us take for granted. The approach we use to support our patients is one I've come to appreciate, for it is nonjudgmental, holistic, and integrative. On a spiritual level, my patients are seeking inner peace and wholeness—to align their physical bodies with the gender identity they've always known themselves to be. This alignment depends not only on their psychological stability and capacity but also on their medical eligibility for surgery. Spiritual, physical, and psychological wholeness are interdependent; and behavioral decompensation can provide substantial barriers to surgery. We see these behaviors as adaptations in the service of survival—as compensating for lack of skill. We help our patients to mitigate these disturbances and reach their full potential by strengthening their mental health in order to achieve their spiritual goals.

I have a strong conviction for this dual approach. As a social worker, I believe that behavioral health strategies can help by bolstering our ability to connect to others and by teaching us to regulate our humanness so that we may embody the moral qualities of God and more closely adhere to God's commandments. The Jewish community would greatly benefit from integrating stigma-free psychosocial evaluation and behavioral health practices into our spiritual life,[6] starting with clergy leadership. As a clergyperson, my faith is renewed by what has been possible in my own personal growth and the growth of my patients. Let us apply this same process to all of our journeys, no matter the level of support we each may require.

Where Faith-Based Meets Evidence-Based

Real healing becomes possible when the pastoral meets the clinical, for this is where faith-based strategies intersect with evidence-based ones. We can marry our beloved textual and musical traditions, our prayer customs, and the rituals that calibrate us with the treasure trove of evidence-informed modalities that train people to live happier and healthier lives. In so doing, we can get closer to ourselves, to our tradition, and to God.

Dialectical Behavioral Therapy (DBT), developed by Dr. Marsha Linehan in the 1980s, is an approach that I have found to be particularly effective in healing from trauma and in reconciling the person I am with the person I want to be. Though Linehan's model was first designed to treat severely disordered populations, its science can be applied to all people.[7] DBT aims to reduce impulsive behaviors and regulate emotions, prioritizing the goal of succeeding in one's current environment. Considered ethical treatment because it is fair and nonjudgmental, DBT is a perfect complement for Jewish healing resources.

DBT teaches four core skills: interpersonal effectiveness, distress tolerance, emotion regulation, and mindfulness. All four of these skills can greatly improve our adherence to the commandments that relate to our treatment of each other. Specifically, we can teach interpersonal effectiveness to stay self-possessed while maintaining proper boundaries and meeting our own needs. Distress tolerance would be especially useful when facing the challenges surrounding the communal and collegial practice of Judaism. Emotional regulation refers to regulating one's reactions to be commensurate with the situation at hand. And mindfulness asks that the person stay present instead of becoming distracted by past events, which may become triggered by current circumstance.

I think of us clergy who engage in *l'shon hara*. If we possess the skills to tolerate our jealousy of a colleague's superior positioning, for example, we might not escalate so. If we can emotionally regulate, we might not speak aloud our disapprovals. Perhaps, then, my colleague's recitation of *Elohai N'tzor* could have retained its integrity, for the prayer to control one's slanderous speech would have been practiced in that very moment, with the help of a behavioral modification technique such as DBT.

Acceptance and Commitment Therapy (ACT), developed by Dr. Steven C. Hayes in the 1980s, is another modality that proves especially effective in human behavior change and could improve our relationships to each other and to our Jewish practice. ACT promotes psychological flexibility, the idea that we can modify our responses to be more adaptive to the present situation.[8] We engage in psychological flexibility by discovering the values that are important to us, taking action to pursue those things, accepting the difficulties in our situations, showing up as witnesses to our thoughts without becoming subordinate to them, and being present in the moment.

ACT can be especially effective for clergy when confronted with a congregant we find off-putting or whose needs feel overbearing. If we are able to orient ourselves towards the values of welcome and kindness we hold dear, and adapt them to the situation through psychological flexibility, we may find ourselves not only adhering more closely to Jewish values, but also enjoying our experience with a fellow Jew and human being. It's crucial to recognize the humanity in others in order to understand their motivations and to have compassion for their struggle. This approach can help.

Both DBT and ACT are evidence-based in that they are supported by research, strengthened by the wisdom of the practitioner, and reinforced by the client's personal experiences. Jewish living requires us to show up as vulnerable people who are both flawed and striving towards holiness. By practicing these strategies, we can model for our congregants the practice of growth.

The Role of Clergy Modeling and Its Inherent Limitations

As leaders in our communities, clergy play an essential role in modeling the integration of skills into Jewish practice. It is important, however, not to overvalue the use of self in such modeling. As ACT teaches, it is important to use self-as-context and not self-as-content.[9] Self-as-content would encourage a person to draw on personal experience as supporting evidence of the lesson they're teaching. Self-as-context, on the other hand, teaches that we are not the problematic behaviors we exhibit. *The person is not the problem. Let the problem be the problem.*[10] Clergy can model this idea by staying open to feedback and publicly acknowledging, through appropriate use of personal detail, our own efforts toward behavioral improvement. This distinction is important, for it asks us clergy to use ourselves, our stories, and our sense of professional calling not as the content for our sermons, music, or interactions, but rather as context to help us engage with and model practice of the tradition. We're all human and therefore, we all struggle. We can allow the context of that struggle to give us context for the struggles of those to whom we minister.

In addition to modeling the process of self-improvement, we can integrate a more clinical approach into our pastoral interactions. We clergy can commit to engagement, alignment, and attunement as a way to minimize the isolation of our constituents. Engagement refers to the communication between the clergyperson and congregants as a way to facilitate understanding. Alignment occurs when the congregant and clergyperson share goals for the conversation. Attunement means staying open to changes in the congregant's situation and letting the "client" remain the expert in their own experience. Borrowing from the therapeutic model, we can remember the wisdom of Jeff Levy, a clinical social worker who taught at University of Chicago's School of Social Service Administration: "It's not about you bringing your knowledge to them, it's about them bringing their lived experience to you."[11]

Unfortunately at this time, the opportunity for clergy clinical training is limited. Cantorial students at HUC-JIR, for example, are required to take only a single semester of Pastoral Care, and Clinical Pastoral Education is not required of cantorial nor rabbinical students. I hope that HUC-JIR, and all graduate-level institutions training Jewish clergy, will shore up their offerings in this area. In the meantime, while pastoral care can do more to incorporate clinical skills, it is not a substitute for expert clinical intervention administered by a licensed mental health professional.

Recognizing Our Common Humanity

It is crucial not to make false distinctions, as though we human beings are divided into broad categories. There's no such thing as mental illness and *mental illness*. There is no such thing as the anointed and the unwashed.[12]

Our society seems to believe that there are people who are unwashed—those who talk to themselves on the bus and we move away; and that there are people who are anointed—ordained with special protection and privilege, who are impervious to the normal slings and arrows of life—such as, perhaps, ourselves, the clergy. Even as a survivor of childhood trauma and lifelong panic disorder myself, I erroneously make such distinctions. But the lesson here is that one does not have to suffer from mental illness to mind his or her mental health. In fact, as clergy in pursuit of wellness and wholeness, it is our responsibility to mind our mental health. In order to truly live and serve with integrity, we must integrate the clinical into the pastoral.

I always return to the same question: does the labeling really matter? Who cares what the cause of someone's distress is? We owe it to ourselves to show up with compassion and a commitment to do better. The best path forward is to increase our competency in mental health assessment so that our individual and communal spiritual health may improve. We must find a way out to God. The only way out is in.

Notes

1. BT *Shabbat* 31a.
2. P. P. Yeung and S. Greenwald, "Jewish Americans and Mental Health: Results of the NIMH Epidemiologic Catchment Area Study," *Social Psychiatry and Psychiatric Epidemiology* 27, no. 6 (November 1992): 292–97.
3. E. Schnall et al., "Barriers to Mental Health Care: A 25-Year Follow-Up Study of the Orthodox Jewish Community," *Journal of Multicultural Counseling and Development* 42, no. 3 (2014): 161–73.
4. American Psychiatric Association, "Anxiety Disorders," in *Diagnostic and Statistical Manual of Mental Disorders*, 5th ed. (2013), https://doi.org/10.1176/appi.books.9780890425596.dsm05.
5. *Pirkei Avot* 2:4.
6. H. F. Unterrainer, A. J. Lewis, and A. Fink, "Religious/Spiritual Well-Being, Personality and Mental Health: A Review of Results

and Conceptual Issues," *Journal of Religion and Health* 53, no. 2 (2014): 382–92.
7. Behavioraltech.org.
8. S. C. Hayes, K. D. Strosahl, and K. G. Wilson, *Acceptance and Commitment Therapy: The Process and Practice of Mindful Change*, 2nd ed. (New York: Guilford Press, 2012).
9. Ibid.
10. Dr. Susan Bernstein, Director of Social Work Services at Mount Sinai Hospital.
11. Taught by a social work supervisor at the Educational Alliance's Project ORE.
12. Explained by Rabbi Kim S. Geringer, LCSW, in a private conversation.

Creating a Somatic Psychospiritual Practice

Karen Lee Erlichman

Wellness programs have been experiencing a renaissance in the last few decades. Complementary medicine has come into the Western mainstream; mindfulness practice has permeated workplace culture, psychotherapy, and health care settings, and yoga is enjoying enormous popularity. Even technology companies have developed tools to place wellness in our hands.

Wellness is typically understood as a continuum of physical, emotional, and psychosocial health supported by various beliefs, resources, practices, and remedies to optimize well-being. Jewish teachings and practices have explored wellness literally for thousands of years. Perhaps one of the most essential Jewish teachings promoting wellness and well-being is *b'tzelem Elohim*. Well-being is not merely for the sake of taking good care; it is a sacred obligation, protecting and tending to the divine nature of each one of us. This is the process of *sh'leimut* itself—practicing living fully *as tzelem Elohim*.

In *Sacred Therapy: Jewish Spiritual Teachings on Emotional Healing and Inner Wholeness*, psychotherapist and spiritual director Estelle Frankel offers a powerful kabbalistic framework for healing that integrates sacred text and stories with meditation and other psychospiritual practices. She writes of the mystical flow between brokenness and wholeness: "However broken and fragmented things may seem, all of life is in fact evolving toward a state of wholeness and . . . we humans have an active role and responsibility in furthering this evolutionary process."[1]

KAREN LEE ERLICHMAN, D. Min., L.C.S.W., provides psychotherapy, spiritual direction, supervision, and mentoring in San Francisco. She is a senior consultant for Ethics of Care and Resource Development with The Dinner Party and a faculty member in the Jewish Spirituality D. Min. program at the Graduate Theological Foundation. Karen's writing has been published in numerous journals, blogs, and anthologies, including *Presence: An International Journal of Spiritual Direction*, *Feminist Studies in Religion*, *Tikkun*, and in the interfaith anthology *Spiritual Guidance Across Religions*.

Embodied wholeness offers an explicitly psychospiritual framework for holding paradox between inner and outer, self and other, brokenness and wholeness, with a unique sustainable impact on social justice and *tikkun olam*.

My Personal Journey of Embodied Wholeness and Wellness

When my mother died a few years ago, I experienced the range and depth of emotions that one might expect after the death of a beloved parent. What I was not prepared for was my body's way of grieving. Grief moved deeply and emphatically into my body. One early morning I woke up and the room was spinning. There was a pressure in my left ear and my head and neck felt as if they were being squeezed. Nerve pain shot across my neck and head.

Over the next two months I saw numerous doctors, all of whom misdiagnosed me. Finally, I met a neurologist who began to crack the somatic mystery. He explained that the enormous psychosocial stress of my mother's illness and death had triggered a lasting neurological response.

I researched "grief in the body," and found very little useful information. Fortunately, I did find two articles that emphasized the importance of engaging the right brain in processing grief, using creative expression, ritual, and movement/somatic practices. I decided to add an embodied healing practice to my morning prayer and meditation, using the ancient practice of anointing. I created a spiritual guidebook to use daily during the seven weeks of counting the Omer between Passover and Shavuot and immersed myself in a nightly writing and meditation practice, using the scaffolding of the Omer to hold my grief.

Even as I engaged in all of these practices, the pain and pressure persisted. My body seemed to be wailing and crying out.

One night in early June, my wife and I went to a comedy show. During that ninety-minute show, I forgot about my grief and my physical pain. I experienced something I had not felt in months: I felt *joy*.

I woke up the next morning and something had profoundly changed. I scheduled an appointment with the neurologist immediately and told him the story of the comedy show. He did not seem surprised. In fact, he said, "Oh yes, we actually have data going back to the era of the Marx Brothers about how rigorous laughter resets the nervous system." Could laughter and joy actually have recalibrated my nervous system? Apparently they had.

Five Aspects of Embodied Wholeness

Rarely do people report being seen or cared for in their wholeness. White Western American culture and its major institutions tend to carve people into compartmentalized pieces, and the parts rarely communicate with one another. The following five aspects of psychospiritual and somatic experience are key dimensions towards wholeness and wellness. Each aspect includes some sample embodied wholeness practices for further exploration.

1. Embodied Knowing

Black lesbian feminist poet and activist Audre Lorde wrote about the power of women's eroticism as a source of embodied knowing and used the example of the common phrase "It feels right to me." This expression is akin to having "a gut feeling" about something, and Lorde urged women to harness the "strength of the erotic into a true knowledge, for what that means is the first and most powerful guiding light toward any understanding . . . The erotic is the nurturer or nursemaid of all our deepest knowledge."[2]

In the last few decades researchers like pioneering somatic practitioners Peter Levine, Pat Ogden, and others have recognized that approaches to healing trauma are incomplete without including somatic practices and embodied mindfulness tools. Some of these somatic approaches include meditation, mindfulness, generative somatics, various movement practices, and somatic psychotherapy modalities such as creating a somatic barometer, which begins with a mindful, embodied awareness of the very simple everyday decisions and choices one makes. Psychotherapist Eugene Gendlin developed Focusing, linking inner body sensations and somatic awareness with psycho-emotional intelligence and spiritual depth. These practices enable us to recognize our "gut feelings" and to trust and utilize them in our quest for understanding, knowledge, and wellness.

Practice Suggestions for Embodied Knowing

- Develop or deepen a mindful discernment practice for embodied knowing.

- Experiment with a movement, gesture, pose, or posture that engages your body.
- Draw a body map, ideally by laying on a piece of paper large enough for someone to trace your body. Identify where in your body you experience your somatic barometer, the locator of connection between the felt sense of the body and the internal decision-making process from within. Feel free to also paint and decorate the body map.

2. Identity/Felt Sense of Self

To experience wholeness is to include all parts of a person's identity: The question *Who am I?* is an ongoing process that continues across the life span. A body contains and metabolizes multiple coexisting identities; lived experiences are held as cellular memories of gender, culture, race, sexuality, disability, internalized oppression, and trauma. The journey toward wholeness is about fully embodying our unique manifestation of the Divine within. This includes shedding others' projections and expectations of who and what we should be and allowing the light of our wholeness to shine fully.

When we integrate the body and its erotic wisdom into our experience of self, we experience greater connection to wholeness. This is especially meaningful for people whose embodied selves are devalued, even demonized, by mainstream culture.

I like to think of the erotic self as inextricably connected to the soul. The daily liturgy affirms and blesses the soul we are given as pure. Two Hebrew words for "soul"— *ruach* and *nefesh*—also have an embodied aspect. *Ruach* can be translated as breath and wind, and *nefesh* is understood as the body and flesh of a living being, reflecting the essential interconnectedness of body and spirit. A felt sense of self and soul in the body is a process of *t'shuvah*, of returning to wholeness.

Practice Suggestions for Identity/Felt Sense of Self
- Keep a dream journal next to your bed and write or draw in it every morning upon waking for a month.
- Journal a conversation between your soul and your body.
- Experiment with walking or movement meditation in which you express gratitude for each part of your body. Start with your feet and end with the top of your head.

3. Relationship/Trustworthy Community

In *A Hidden Wholeness: The Journey Toward an Undivided Life*, Parker J. Palmer writes about the importance of "trustworthy relationships to sustain us."[3] Palmer calls these communities of support "Circles of Trust" and has crafted ethical guidelines, principles, and practices for these powerful relationships. Embodied wholeness has an opportunity to take root and thrive within such sacred circles.

Jewish practice includes many examples of and opportunities for creating and supporting "Circles of Trust." The minyan exemplifies the power and holiness of a group of trusted souls. *Chevruta*, at its best, is a relationship in which people are learning partners in mutual trust, seeing the other person in their divine wholeness and reflecting it back to them. Ideally, these "circles" will reflect Rabbi Shefa Gold's description of this type of sacred relationship as a "a mishkan, a dwelling place for God, by stepping back in awe of my beloved, and trusting the space between us as holy, by stepping forward in service, by taking responsibility for my own triggers."[4]

Longtime spiritual director, teacher, and psychotherapist Dr. Barbara Breitman has described the tender qualities of relationship that lend themselves beautifully to healing: "When people can be with one another, imbuing the time and space they share with presence, the possibility for holiness is manifest. Being with another creates the basic condition for healing or sacred encounter."[5]

Practice Suggestions for Relationship/Trustworthy Community

- Invite another person to be your *chevruta* or create an embodied wholeness *chavurah*.
- Identify a possible wholeness mentor, particularly someone who has a somatic or movement practice.
- Participate in an authentic movement or sacred dance group or workshop.

4. Practice: Ritual, Prayer, and Meditation

Creating a psychospiritual embodied wholeness practice includes contemplation and silence but is not limited to it. Contemplative practice is often described as gentle, spacious inner reflection, but can also take other forms of prayer and rituals that connect us directly to the Divine. New and innovative rituals enable those who may have felt excluded from the community to forge these sacred connections.

Jewish feminist and queer reclaiming of traditional practice have included such topics as *mikveh*; healing from illness, abuse, and loss; ceremonies and blessings for gender transition; and more.[6] For example, Rabbi Elliot Kukla has crafted several blessings for gender transition, Noach D'Zmura has written and taught about transgender *tahara*, and Rav Kohenet Taya Shere offers sessions and classes on Jewish ancestral healing, Embodied Presence, and Sex and the S'firot. Mayyim Hayyim and Immerse NYC have also breathed new life into the ancient traditional practice of *mikveh*. Finally, Kolot: Center for Jewish Women's and Gender Studies at the Reconstructionist Rabbinical College created an open source ritual database called Ritualwell in partnership with May'an Jewish Women's Project.

Ritual, prayer, and meditation facilitate the mutual flow between left brain and right brain, mind, body and spirit, and inner and outer experience. The embodied engagement with symbols, stories, elements, liturgy, movement, and *kavanot* enliven our senses, thoughts, emotions, and bodies, connecting us to sacred tradition and innovative creativity.

Practice suggestions for Ritual, Prayer, and Meditation

- Write your own liturgy/prayer/blessing for wholeness that includes a movement practice.
- Create a wholeness altar.
- Write a letter to God about your vision of wellness and wholeness. Read it out loud and notice your inner body sensations.

5. Connection to Sacred Dimensions of Time/Space

Historical persecution and multigenerational trauma impact present and future generations' health, behavior, emotions, and spiritual lives. A foreshortened or truncated future is a common experience of people who have experienced trauma. Yet Jewish tradition has always emphasized a capacity to vision a future—*l'dor v'dor*—accessing wisdom that exists in nonlinear time, in imagination and dreams, a seed of hopefulness and trust in the possibility of healing and wholeness in *olam haba* (the world-to-come).

In addition to cultivating a connection to past and future, present moment awareness practices and teachings ground us in the now. These include rhythm and regularity of daily prayer and liturgy, the cycle of Torah and our sacred holidays, dreams, Rosh Chodesh, and perhaps the essence of Jewish mindfulness: Shabbat. Engaging the body in these observances of time facilitate wellness transmuting over the life span.

Sh'leimut includes a multidimensional connection with self and other; inner and outer; past, present, and future; the individual and the community; the everyday and the Sacred.

Practice Suggestions for Connection to Sacred Dimensions of Time/Space

- Join a Rosh Chodesh group
- Write a poem a day or paint/draw forty-nine parts of the body during the forty-nine days of counting the Omer.
- Make a set of three visual timelines for your life: physical, emotional, and spiritual. Plot on each line the important moments, experiences, and relationships in each of the three dimensions. Notice the flow over time. Be sure to include important embodied experiences too. Observe the connections between and among each of the timelines.

Creating an Embodied Psychospiritual Wholeness Practice

Like daily prayers and blessings, creating a psychospiritual embodied practice connects us to the flow of life, to God, to others, and to Creation. I use the word "practice" knowingly because at its core, practice liberates us from expectations of perfectionism and emphasizes the organic, evolving quality of our intentions and actions.

Here is a set of simple steps to create your own practice:

1. Build Your Cornerstones

The first step in building your practice is to identify the ethical guidelines, intentions, and values and priorities that matter most to you. Be as specific as possible and remember these can be changed and modified later. These will serve as cornerstones for your practice.

Here are a few examples:

- Bring your whole self to the practice.
- Recognize the limits of your comfort zone and risk stretching a little bit.
- Be present with your delight *and* your discomfort.
- Find freedom in making mistakes.

2. Take Time for Reflection/Journaling

Consider:

- What does your body need right now?
- How does your body respond to the flow of Jewish and natural time and seasons?
- When have you felt the movement of divine flow in your body? How would you describe it?
- What would wellness and wholeness feel like from the inside out?

3. Create a Practice Compendium

Create a practice compendium, tool kit, or collection. This collection of practices is an ongoing archive of resources that you can expand, modify and develop over time.

Sacred Embodied Activism

Activism is an embodied wholeness practice in the service of the healing and repair of the world. Social justice work calls us to full awareness, reflection, and action—conscious engagement with ourselves, others, and the planet as *whole*, and taking action to realize that vision. Activism has the power to lifts us out of hopelessness and reminds us we are not alone in the struggle. We can bring a *kavanah* of holiness to our activism as well as the passion for social justice to our prayer.

Too often spirituality and social justice activism are viewed as disconnected from one another, despite the fact that our tradition teaches otherwise. Rabbi David Jaffe, a social worker, longtime spiritual seeker, and activist, has written a book called *Changing the World from the Inside Out: A Jewish Approach to Personal and Social Change*, blending Musar, Chasidic wisdom, and Jewish spiritual practices with social justice activism: "How do we walk a holy path that integrates deep spiritual awareness and righteous action in the world? . . . Just as an individual becomes holy by walking in the ways of God, so too does a society become holy by reflecting the ways of God in its social arrangements."[7]

More than simply religious people engaging in social justice activism, embodied wholeness offers an authentic integration of the two without compromising the integrity of either. This integration can also be seen in social justice initiatives within Jewish denominations and seminaries such as the Religious Action Center[8] and Reset 2019[9] and the work of multifaith organizations like the Auburn Seminary[10] in New York City, where as dean, Rabbi Justus Baird is at the forefront of multifaith movement, building programs at the nexus of spirituality and social justice.

In his article "Leaning Toward Justice," Rabbi David Stern wrote about the demands rabbis experience in communal leadership and names several embodied resources for sustenance and self-care in the spirit of moving toward wholeness: "What sustains us as rabbis for the challenges of this work? We have the blessing of the relationships that nourish and center us. We have loved ones beyond the work and allies in the work . . . we have the sacred grounding of our own spiritual practices, from prayer and chavruta study to meditation and yoga, from long walks to deep texts. It's hard to imagine doing this work without some kind of spiritual mooring beyond the work itself."[11]

While there have been numerous books,[12] articles,[13] workshops, and retreats[14] about wellness and self-care *for* activists, activism can also be a powerful action step in the service of healing and wholeness. Wholeness and well-being are not just about healing the individual or making one person whole, but about healing and unifying all of Creation. And when the world is being healed, it heals us in return.

Notes

1. Estelle Frankel, *Sacred Therapy: Jewish Spiritual Teachings on Emotional Healing and Inner Wholeness* (Boston: Shambhala Publications. 2004), 4.
2. Audre Lorde, "The Use of the Erotic: The Erotic as Power," in *Sister Outsider: Essays and Speeches* (Trumansburg, NY: Crossing Press, 1984), 56.

3. Parker J. Palmer, transcript from interview with Krista Tippett, https://onbeing.org/programs-the-soul-in-depression-mar2018/.
4. Shefa Gold, "*Shechinah and Mishkan*," http://www.rabbishefagold.com/shechinah-mishkan/.
5. Barbara Eve Breitman, "Foundations of Jewish Pastoral Care: Skills and Techniques," in *Jewish Pastoral Care: A Practical Handbook from Traditional and Contemporary Sources*, ed. Dayle Friedman (Woodstock, VT: Jewish Lights Publishing, 2001), 97.
6. These have included siddurim created by LGBTQ synagogues such as *Siddur Sha'ar Zahav* and groundbreaking texts such as *Twice Blessed: On Being Lesbian, Gay and Jewish Engendering Judaism, The Red Tent, Life Cycles Volumes 1 and 2, She Who Dwells Within, Balancing on the Mechitza: Transgender in Jewish Community*, and many more.
7. David Jaffe, *Changing the World From the Inside Out: A Jewish Approach to Personal and Social Change* (Boulder: Trumpeter Books, 2016), 10.
8. https://rac.org.
9. https://www.reconstructingjudaism.org/reset2019.
10. https://auburnseminary.org.
11. David Stern, "Leading Towards Justice," *CCAR Journal: The Reform Jewish Quarterly* (Summer 2019): 127.
12. Loretta Pyles, *Healing Justice: Holistic Self-Care for Change Makers* (New York Oxford University Press, 2018).
13. https://ejewishphilanthropy.com/fight-like-a-mensch-integrated-social-change/.
14. https://kripalu.org/presenters-programs/hanukkah-renewal-retreat-activists-and-organizers-tending-fire.

Watering the Earthly Garden with Sacred Flow: Tending to the Mental Health of Our Jewish Communities

Nancy E. Epstein and Elisa Goldberg

Introduction

As we consider the challenges of mental health in our Jewish communities and in the larger world, we are drawn to the story of Creation.

וְנָהָר֙ יֹצֵ֣א מֵעֵ֔דֶן לְהַשְׁק֖וֹת אֶת־הַגָּ֑ן וּמִשָּׁם֙ יִפָּרֵ֔ד וְהָיָ֖ה לְאַרְבָּעָ֥ה רָאשִֽׁים׃

"Now, a river goes out from Eden, to water the garden, and from there, it divides and becomes four stream-heads."[1]

Water is a powerful metaphor for God's presence throughout our tradition. In this verse, we imagine that God is the water that flows from Eden into the earthly world; it is the *nahar* that provides spiritual sustenance for us on our life journeys. The *nahar* is also a powerful Source from which we rabbis draw strength and insight as we provide care, spiritual support, education, and healing to our Jewish communities and to the people with whom we work.

RABBI NANCY E. EPSTEIN (RRC 06) is professor of Community Health and Prevention at the Dornsife School of Public Health at Drexel University. She is also a spiritual director at the Reconstructionist Rabbinical School, former vice-chair of the Faith and Spirituality Advisory Board at the Philadelphia Department of Behavioral Health and Intellectual disAbility Services, and a contributing author to the textbook *Why Religion and Spirituality Matter for Public Health*.

RABBI ELISA GOLDBERG (RRC 99) serves as spiritual leader of Temple Micah in Lawrenceville, New Jersey. She is also director of Rabbinic Career Development for the Reconstructionist Rabbinical Association, the Pastoral Care specialist at the Reconstructionist Rabbinical College, and author of *A Guide to Leading Spirituality Support Groups in Behavioral Health Care Settings*.

The *nahar* divides into four stream-heads that are emblematic of four roles that rabbis frequently play. These are:

- Pastoral Caregiver
- Community Educator
- Spiritual and Ritual Leader
- Advocate and Social Activist

In order to fulfill these four roles that predominantly require engaging actively with others, it is essential that we first attend to self-care. We draw on the waters of the *nahar* for our own spiritual vitality and, in turn, share that wellspring with others. Many articles in this special edition of the *CCAR Journal* explore ways to tap into the *nahar* to care for ourselves. We will explore how to draw the *nahar*'s sacred flow actively into our rabbinic lives to water the earthly gardens of self, family, community, and society with these heavenly waters.

Background on Mental Health

Our health is multifaceted. According to the World Health Organization (WHO), "Health is a state of complete physical, mental, and social well-being and not merely the absence of disease or infirmity."[2] This globally recognized definition emphasizes the importance of mental health and social well-being and ties closely to our Jewish concept of *shalom*—complete well-being.

The WHO goes on to define "mental health" as "a state of well-being in which every individual realizes his or her own potential, can cope with the normal stresses of life, can work productively and fruitfully, and is able to make a contribution to her or his community."[3] These definitions stand in stark contrast to the fact that depression is the leading cause of disability throughout the globe and the American Psychological Association's 2018 report "Stress in America" cited stress as "an impediment to the nation being healthy." It identified numerous connections between stress and a whole series of health symptoms.[4]

When we say the words "mental health," we often mean many different things across a continuum that ranges from the stresses of everyday living to serious mental illness. Mental health can mean chronic low-grade stress and anxiety or more extreme emotional stresses associated with acute pain, disability, and ongoing trauma or various labeled mental health challenges (e.g., depression) or a serious mental illness (e.g., schizophrenia). What we know is that in the United States, mental health challenges are prevalent. Recent data describes an American population in which:

- Over 44 million people (18 percent) have a mental health condition.[5]
- Nearly one in twenty-five adults in the United States (11.2 million) lives with a serious mental illness.[6]
- Nearly 60 percent of adults with a mental illness did not receive mental health services in the previous year.[7]
- One-half of all chronic mental illness begins by age fourteen; three-quarters by age twenty-four.[8]

Along with this descriptive population data, the American Psychological Association also stated in 2018 that a shortage exists in the mental health workforce.[9] With limited access to professional mental health treatment, the American Psychiatric Association also reported in 2018 that "people experiencing mental health concerns often turn first to a faith leader."[10]

In recent years, there has been growing recognition of the important roles that religion and spirituality play in promoting the health of individuals and communities. Research evidence from thousands of population-based studies supports positive associations between religion and spirituality with lower rates of depression, anxiety, suicide, dementia, and stress-related illnesses.[11]

Recognizing the importance of religion and spirituality in these larger communal contexts of health and mental health and acknowledging the vital roles that faith leaders can play on the frontlines of communities, rabbis are well situated to actively promote mental health and well-being in our congregations, universities, hospitals, long-term care facilities, and other types of community-based and advocacy organizations.

Four Rabbinic Roles That Flow from the *Nahar*

While being sure to first tend to our own mental health and well-being, rabbis can play critically important roles by drawing on the *nahar*'s sacred flow to help individuals and families experiencing mental health challenges. In addition to the indispensable rabbinic role of pastoral caregiver, we are community educators, spiritual and ritual leaders, and advocates and social activists dedicated to fostering communities that promote resilience and spiritual well-being, reduce stigma, and provide safe spaces for people to recover and flourish. We can provide a valuable service by making referrals that help people identify and access mental health services and supports. And, we are uniquely poised to advocate to improve public education about mental health, expand mental health funding, and assure full access to quality mental health care for all.

Just as we draw upon the *nahar* to nourish ourselves, rabbis can help others access these heavenly waters for their own sustenance. Like the four stream-heads that issue from the *nahar*, we see four roles for rabbis in addressing mental health in our communities: pastoral caregiver, community educator, spiritual and ritual leader, and advocate and social activist.

A Parable (*Mashal*)

Dr. Cohen[12] had been an active member of the Jewish community his whole life. He and his wife belonged to a suburban synagogue where he served as past president and was a regular attendee at Shabbat services. He and his wife sent their kids to Jewish day school and Jewish camps and watched with pride as they raised their own children with the same values. He traveled to Israel many times and generously supported Jewish causes.

At sixty-five, he had decided to retire from his successful dental practice and was looking forward to traveling and enjoying life abroad with his beloved wife of forty years. Unfortunately, only months after his retirement, his wife was diagnosed with cancer and died within a year.

Dr. Cohen was bereft. He had lost his love, his best friend, and he was angry. He had done everything right; he had been a mensch, a good father and husband, and a good Jew. He had dedicated his life to helping other people. He couldn't understand what he had done to deserve this. The question kept coming to him unbidden: "Why did God let this happen?"

Dr. Cohen became depressed. He stopped going to synagogue. The prayers that he once enjoyed felt empty, and he was terribly lonely without his wife. He shrugged off the rabbi's attempt to reach out and didn't answer calls from the synagogue president and the chair of the *chesed* committee. He felt that no one understood how he felt, and he did not believe he had anything to talk about with anyone. He grew isolated from the Jewish community that had once anchored him. The synagogue members and the rabbi eventually stopped calling. They labeled him "depressed" and then left him alone.

One Shabbat morning, he decided to go to synagogue to try and reconnect. It had been over a year since he was last there. He was stunned when only three people came over to say hello to him and ask how he was. Most glanced across the aisles, simply waved, and walked on. He was devastated.

Dr. Cohen had no language to express his grief and his anger. He had never developed spiritual tools or a spiritual vocabulary to draw on during dark times. Coupled with his profound disappointment in the synagogue community that had once been a center of his life, his depression worsened. One night, he had a few drinks, took a bottle of over-the-counter sleeping pills, and didn't wake up in the morning. His daughter found him unresponsive, called immediately for an ambulance, and Dr. Cohen was taken to a psychiatric hospital.

How can we rabbis best support someone like Dr. Cohen?

Rabbi as Pastoral Caregiver

For Dr. Cohen, Judaism was all about behaviors and belonging. He knew how to do "Jewish," and he valued being part of the Jewish community. For many years these Jewish paths nourished him. But, like many Jews, particularly those of his age group, he had never developed a spiritual life, a personal relationship with God or cultivated a sense of the sacred. Belief was not part of his vocabulary. For Dr. Cohen, personal God language felt foreign. If asked, he likely would have said either that he didn't really believe in God or that God was unfairly punishing him.

Research has demonstrated the important role religion and spirituality can play in the promotion of mental health.[13] The opposite is true as well. Spiritual or religious conflict can lead to mental health challenges. As Dr. Cohen began to feel less able to connect, was more alienated from his religious community, and bereft of spiritual language to make sense of his situation, his mental health worsened.

As rabbis, we are called to be empathic listeners and pastoral caregivers who help people develop a personal relationship with

God and draw the sacred into their lives. We liken this to watering the earthly garden with sacred flow.

Pain, loss, and suffering are inevitable life experiences. It is necessary that we provide opportunities for others to discover Jewish knowledge and tools that promote healing and meaning. Given the intense pressures on young people today, even more so it is imperative to start this at young ages so that people can cultivate spiritual resources throughout their lifetimes. As Rabbi Abraham Joshua Heschel taught, "the attainment of wisdom is the work of a lifetime."[14]

Best Practices and Tips for the Pastoral Caregiver

- *Engage in Continuing Pastoral Education*
  Pastoral counseling and caregiving are at the heart of most rabbinates and require ongoing education and training. Many rabbis frequently offer formal and informal supports, guidance, and pastoral counseling, particularly with regard to grief, loss, and mental health challenges. While many rabbis receive some level of pastoral training during seminary, it is vital to continuously develop these skills throughout one's rabbinate.

- *Participate in Ongoing Supervision*
  In almost every other professional counseling role, individual or peer supervision is required. Supervision offers necessary professional support to deal with difficult situations, explore issues of transference and countertransference, and learn to maintain appropriate boundaries, and supervision also provides a confidential setting to discuss situations that the rabbi cannot talk about elsewhere. Supervision can be individual or group, peer or professionally led, and made up of rabbis, other clergy, and mental health professionals. Ongoing supervision can alleviate burnout and isolation, prevent ethical violations, and support healthy boundary-setting.

- *Recognize and Honor the Limits of Our Rabbinic Role*
  It is important for rabbis to recognize the limits of the rabbinic role and know when to refer people with ongoing mental health challenges to mental health professionals. We should remember to stay in the lane of pastoral and spiritual care and make referrals appropriately. This doesn't mean that

we shouldn't support people with mental health challenges; rather the opposite. We should make sure they are getting professional mental health care while we continue to support them pastorally and spiritually.

- *Learn to Be Present to Existential Pain*
  One of the greatest challenges of providing pastoral care is learning to be present to the brokenness of the world. As we accompany people living with mental health challenges and mental illness, we open our hearts to their pain. One of the most important tools that we can develop as pastoral caregivers is remembering to turn to the sacred flow of the *nahar* to deal with our own existential pain and grief. Doing so prevents burnout and enables us to stay present to those whom we serve.
- *Make Referrals to Local Mental Health Professionals*
  In order to make appropriate referrals for professional mental health services, rabbis must spend time becoming familiar with local mental health professionals and resources and know how to help people access services and supports during times of stress, mental health challenge, or crisis.

Rabbi as Community Educator

Dr. Cohen is not alone in being a synagogue member dealing with mental health challenges. In conversations with many rabbis and mental health leaders, we learned that it is not uncommon for Jews to easily share physical health challenges in their congregational settings. But they tend to be more reluctant, even withholding, about sharing the mental health challenges that they or their family members face. One powerful reason for this is stigma. Just as Dr. Cohen sadly discovered, this reluctance, partnered with stigma, can lead to loneliness, isolation, and even thoughts of suicide.

This is true for people of all ages; both adults and youth are experiencing growing rates of mental health challenges. According to the American Psychological Association, Gen Z (young adults under age twenty-four) are experiencing stress at a greater intensity than any other age group and are less equipped to deal with it.[15]

Rabbinical school does not train rabbis to be mental health counselors or therapists. Nor does rabbinical school train us to recognize the signs and symptoms of mental illness. This lack of training can lead to missed opportunities to intervene and to offer support. It is incumbent on us, as rabbis in today's increasingly stressful society, to become mental health literate, understanding and effectively using mental health knowledge and information. Rabbis can be "first responders" when individuals and families experience a mental health challenge or crisis.

One way to become mental health literate is to take an eight-hour course on Mental Health First Aid (MHFA), which is offered across all fifty United States by many mental health agencies and community-based organizations. Just as CPR helps a person learn to assist someone who is having a heart attack, MHFA helps one learn to assist someone having a mental health or substance use challenge or crisis. Topics include how to recognize warning signs, symptoms, and risk factors associated with anxiety, depression and mood disorders, psychosis, trauma, and substance use, as well as learning how to listen effectively and make appropriate referrals to mental health and substance use services. MHFA is offered in several different modules: adults, adults who work with youth, veterans, those who work in public safety (e.g., police, fire, EMS), and those who work in higher education. MHFA is also offered in Spanish. A three-year national certificate as a Mental Health First Aider is offered to those who complete the training.

As we rabbis further our own knowledge about mental health, we gain self-knowledge that can help us as individuals, which in turn makes us better community educators. Understanding our own emotional landscapes and our family histories and drawing on the sacred flow from the *nahar* allows us to recognize our limitations and the possible topics with which we may need to seek support for our own *n'shamot*. It is important to remember that self-care is an important foundation for providing effective education to others in our communities.

Best Practices and Tips for the Community Educator

- *Take a Mental Health First Aid (MHFA) Course and Become Certified*
  A MHFA course will expand your knowledge of signs and symptoms of mental health challenges and mental illness and build your skill set of how to effectively respond and intervene. MHFA will build on and enhance any prior training you

have in pastoral care and chaplaincy. The training will also provide you with a list of local referrals for dealing with different types of mental health challenges and crises.

- *Bring MHFA to Your Congregation and to Other Settings*
Train your congregational community, your universities and Hillels, hospitals, long-term care facilities, and community-based and advocacy organizations in MHFA. Bring Adult MHFA, Youth MHFA, Higher Education MHFA, Elder MHFA and Veteran MHFA to appropriate audiences. Offer refresher courses or other kinds of opportunities for those who have taken MHFA to come together and share stories and continue to learn from and support one another.

- *Partner with Mental Health Professionals to Offer Programs to Deal with Stress*
Join with mental health professionals in your community to offer education programs on stress management and mindfulness training designed to build capacity, strengths, and prevent experiences of stress from becoming more critical.

- *Develop and Offer Peer Support Groups*
One of the most effective ways for providing mental health support is to offer peer support groups for those who are dealing with crisis, loss, pain, depression, or any kind of mental health challenge. Sharing one's story and being heard by caring and compassionate listeners who have experienced something similar can be very healing. Peer support groups can also help people become involved in their own self-care and be a source of hope and wellness to others. Rabbis can develop both mental health and spiritual peer groups for persons of all ages or for specific populations, such as youth and elders.

Rabbi as Spiritual and Ritual Leader

During Dr. Cohen's many years in synagogue life, mental health and mental illness were not discussed publicly. Perhaps he had heard whispers about another congregant who was "crazy" but otherwise nothing positive or informative about mental health was ever said. As he himself began to struggle, he found the synagogue community uninviting. He no longer enjoyed the big crowd, the lengthy sermons, the intellectual engagement. Nothing at the synagogue signaled that there might be a place for him to find support. After the shivah ended for his wife, members of the synagogue *chesed* committee called once or twice and then disappeared; no one reached out to him again. The rabbi called him and left him a message and then didn't call again when he wasn't immediately responsive.

As spiritual and ritual leaders, rabbis can provide leadership to create healthy community norms that include people experiencing mental health challenges and their families and create trauma-informed practices in communal spaces. We know from experience that the care, warmth, and acceptance of communities can provide a healing balm even when the painful realities and struggles of life cannot be changed. Inclusion is one of the most important qualities of a health community.

Creating awareness of the mental health challenges facing people in our communities is vital to both of our roles as community educators and as spiritual and ritual leaders. One important way to reduce stigma and create inclusive communities and welcoming environments is to speak positively from the pulpit about mental health and mental illness and incorporate the values of inclusiveness into our liturgy and text study. Through sermons, liturgy, and text study, rabbis can explore the experiences of people living with mental health challenges and teach about the role of spirituality in recovery. Some questions to ask yourself: When you say the *Mi Shebeirach* during services, do you include mental health? When you offer *divrei Torah*, do you educate your community about the loneliness, burdens, and challenges of stress, mental health conditions, and mental illness?

Rabbis are also beginning to explore how we can bring an awareness of trauma and its impact to our rabbinates.[16] As we begin to understand the far-reaching impacts of trauma and the way trauma manifests intergenerationally and collectively, we can actively draw upon trauma-informed perspectives to inform the culture, programs, and rituals of our Jewish communities. The success of being trauma-informed depends on incorporating the following principles into all facets of our organizations and religious communities:

- Safety
- Trustworthiness
- Transparency
- Peer support
- Collaboration

- Mutuality, empowerment, voice, and choice
- Awareness of the intersectionality of culture, history, gender, and race.[17]

As Jewish spiritual and ritual leaders, we can draw upon these principles in everything we do—from running staff meetings to leading services, offering religious school programs, supporting youth group meetings, and delivering High Holy Day sermons. We can infuse these activities with the sacred flow of heavenly waters that come from the *nahar*.

We have Jewish rituals that naturally align with trauma-informed practices. For example, sitting shivah is a trauma-informed practice that facilitates peer support and acknowledgment of loss. Chanting the *Mi Shebeirach* in community gives voice to difficult personal experiences and reinforces peer support. An awareness of trauma-informed approaches helps us strengthen the healing nature of our existing religious and spiritual rituals and creates new opportunities within our communities to address the suffering and pain that is so real and prevalent.

As we address trauma in our communities, we must recognize that our own personal and familial experiences of trauma may arise. Once again, we note that our ability as rabbis to provide meaningful care to others is dependent on creating space for self-care that draws from the sacred flow of the *nahar*. Self-knowledge about our own experiences of trauma, knowing our own limits, turning to others for support, and nurturing our connection to the sacred are essential foundations for ritual and spiritual leadership.

Best Practices and Tips for the Spiritual and Ritual Leader

- *Speak Publicly about Mental Health*
  Use sermons, *divrei Torah,* text study, newsletter articles, and other teaching moments to address issues of mental health, reduce stigma, and encourage health-seeking behaviors. Share stories of people living with mental health issues that exemplify the challenges and the supports.
- *Apply Trauma-Informed Practices*
  Integrate the tools of trauma-informed practice to the ritual, educational, programmatic, and administrative activities of your Jewish community. Invite experts in trauma-informed

practice to help you and your community assess, plan, and implement this most effectively.

- *Provide Healing Programs and Rituals*
  Over the last two decades, many different models have developed in the Jewish community to facilitate healing. These include healing circles, spiritual support groups, and group spiritual direction, as well as classes in spiritual autobiography and Musar. Engage community leaders to develop healing programs and rituals or expand those that already exist.
- *Encourage Sharing Stories*
  Encourage people, when they are ready, to speak about their mental health challenges. Sharing stories helps normalize the experience, provide social support, and reduce stigma. At the same time, it is important to note that we must maintain people's confidentiality when they share their experiences directly with us until the time when they are willing to be more public about their experiences.
- *Promote Preventive Spiritual Care and Self-Care*
  Speak publicly about your own spiritual journey and practices of self-care and encourage others to do so as well. Encourage God talk and the development of personal faith. Make referrals to spiritual directors or pastoral counselors and actively educate people about the existence of these modalities.
- *Cross-Pollinate Work Between Rabbis and Mental Health Professionals*
  Work collaboratively with mental health professionals to promote the integration of spirituality and mental health in your community. Invite mental health professionals into your Jewish communal space to offer services, perhaps using a parish-based health care model or fee-for-service. Offer support groups led together by rabbis and mental health professionals.

Rabbi as Advocate and Social Activist

One set of issues underlying Dr. Cohen's experience is insufficient funding for mental health programs along with limited mental health resources and a shortage of mental health professionals, all of which seriously impact the mental health system. When one adds the prominence of discrimination and social injustice, it quickly becomes clear that the rabbi's work is not finished by working to promote mental health within our Jewish communities. We must also dedicate ourselves as advocates and social activists who embody how to "welcome the stranger" and embrace the role of the prophet in bringing about justice and social change.

Religious communities have a long history of activism as a pivotal way to address social injustice and inequality issues and advocate for funding and community resources at the local, state, and national levels. In today's world, where the clamor for justice is strong and prevalent, rabbis are natural partners to join other clergy and health professionals to advocate for positive change. Rabbis are also well-positioned to promote faith-based community organizing that engages the members of our Jewish communities to advocate for comprehensive health care for all and better access to mental health care, treatment, and funding.

Engaging our Jewish communities in advocacy for mental health can have positive outcomes for all. According to the American Psychological Association (APA), current tensions from the political, social, and natural environments are having negative effects on people's stress levels. In the APA's 2018 national report, 69 percent were worried about the future of our country, which was up from the previous year. The APA found that the more engaged one is around the issues that one is stressed by, the more likely one can manage the stress.[18]

Sometimes, advocacy and social activism can lead to despair and burnout when we don't see the change for which we are working so diligently come to fruition. That is when we must tap into the sacred flow of the *nahar* for nourishment and spiritual sustenance for the long haul. Working with others in faith-based community organizing is not only effective for social justice and social change, but can also help the rabbi feel less alone and isolated. Partnering with other faith-leaders can provide important personal connections, as well as inspiration as we listen to others share what keeps them going. Addressing systemic issues requires a long-term vision and the ability to nourish the place of hope and spirit within us.

Best Practices and Tips for the Advocate and Social Activist

- *Join a Faith-Based Organizing Network*
  Faith-based networks, such as the PICO National Network, the Industrial Areas Foundation, and Gamaliel, that focus on

policy advocacy and funding for an array of health and social-justice oriented programs can transform our society starting with neighborhoods and cities and expanding to states and the nation. These nonpartisan faith-based organizing networks build coalitions that address the root causes of health problems and provide strong leadership and advocacy training for the grassroots. They utilize the dynamics of power and the importance of social media to advocate for a broad array of health-related issues, including mental health, physical health, jobs, and neighborhood safety. Power is in numbers! Look to join a local chapter and contact a lead organizer. Explore how the coalition's interests align with your community's concerns, particularly those related to mental health, social justice, and serving vulnerable populations.

- *Participate In (or Advocate to Create One If None Exists) a Faith-Based Advisory Group for Your Local Mental Health Agency*
  The power of faith-based collaboration and advocacy is exemplified by the Faith and Spiritual Affairs (FSA) Advisory Board of the Philadelphia Department of Behavioral Health and Intellectual disAbility Services (DBHIDS). The FSA builds ongoing partnerships with diverse religious leaders and faith communities across the city to promote behavioral health, reduce stigma, and provide a strengths-based recovery approach to substance use and addictions. DBHIDS works with religious leaders to develop collaborative training and offer mental health education programs, such as Mental Health First Aid, to faith communities throughout Philadelphia. They also plan an annual Faith and Spiritual Affairs conference that focuses on mental health and substance use education and promotes trauma-informed practices and capacity-building programs that strengthen, inspire, and mobilize an expanding network of religious leaders and faith communities.

- *Use Multiple Sources of Media to Convey Your Message*
  Remember that widespread and continual media coverage is important to educate the public, influence policymakers, and keep attention focused on vitally important mental health–related issues. Rabbis can use their social and political clout to advocate for mental health parity and to promote civil engagement of their communities.

Conclusion

וְנָהָר֙ יֹצֵ֣א מֵעֵ֔דֶן לְהַשְׁק֖וֹת אֶת־הַגָּ֑ן וּמִשָּׁם֙ יִפָּרֵ֔ד וְהָיָ֖ה לְאַרְבָּעָ֥ה רָאשִֽׁים׃

"Now, a river goes out from Eden, to water the garden, and from there, it divides and becomes four stream-heads."[19]

We are living in *galut* (the Diaspora), searching to find our way back to *Gan Eden* and an experience of *sh'leimut* (wholeness). As rabbis, we have the extraordinary privilege of helping others during their life journeys as pastoral caregivers, community educators, spiritual and ritual leaders, advocates, and social activists. Each of these roles is a stream-head of the *nahar* that flows from *Gan Eden*. Each role is different, yet all are related and unified at the river's Source.

Given the large number of people in the United States living with mental health conditions, it is incumbent on us rabbis to take up our multiple roles on the frontlines and develop the tools we need to foster supportive, healing communities. As we draw spiritual nourishment from the unceasing flow and life-supporting waters of the *nahar*, we strengthen our capacity to address mental health challenges in our communities and serve as effective guides and supports for others. None of the care we offer to others is possible without also cultivating our own abilities to stay connected to the sacred flow that sustains us.

As we encounter the mental health pain and struggles of those we serve, it is inevitable that we will also be reminded of our own pain. Tending to the mental health in our communities and encountering the brokenness of the world requires us to tend to our own emotional and spiritual landscapes. For rabbis, this tending necessitates watering our own spiritual thirst and feelings of drought and depletion by drinking from the sacred waters of the *nahar*, cultivating compassion for the loneliness of our rabbinic roles, and lifting up our personal and existential grief to share with our colleagues so that we don't carry this alone. As we deepen our spiritual reservoirs and fill them with the flowing sacred waters of the *nahar*, we gain insight and strength to stay the course on the frontlines of community by continuing to be present to others. In turn, as we accompany others, we become stronger guides and often find balm for our own pain.

As we deepen our relationship with the *nahar*, we strengthen our abilities to be present in our multiple rabbinic roles to tend the earthly gardens of our Jewish communities. And as the sacred flow of the *nahar* ripples through all of our encounters, we are given a taste of the beauty and wholeness of *Gan Eden*.

* * * * *

The authors would like to acknowledge the following authors from whose wisdom they drew for this article:

Dr. Melila Hellner-Eshed, *A River Flows from Eden: The Language of Mystical Experience in the Zohar* (Stanford, California: Stanford University Press, 2009)

Rabbi Toba Spitzer, "God and Metaphor," www.myjewishlearning. com/article/god-as-metaphor/

Notes

1. Everett Fox, "Genesis 2:10," in *The Five Books of Moses* (New York: Schocken Books, 1995), 19.
2. World Health Organization, "What is the WHO Definition of Health?" https://www.who.int/about/who-we-are/frequently-asked-questions.
3. World Health Organization, "Mental Health: Strengthening Our Communities—Key Facts," https://www.who.int/news-room/fact-sheets/detail/mental-health-strengthening-our-response.
4. American Psychological Association, "Stress in America—Generation Z" (October 2018), https://www.apa.org/news/press/releases/stress/2018/stress-gen-z.pdf.
5. Mental Health America, "The State of Mental Health in America" (2019), https://www.mentalhealthamerica.net/issues/state-mental-health-america.
6. National Alliance on Mental Illness, "Mental Health by the Numbers," https://www.nami.org/learn-more/mental-health-by-the-numbers.
7. Ibid.
8. Ibid.
9. American Psychological Association, "A Summary of Psychologist Work Force Projections" (July 2018), https://www.apa.org/workforce/publications/supply-demand/summary.pdf.
10. American Psychiatric Association, "Mental Health: A Guide for Faith Leaders," https://www.google.com/search?q=mental

11. +health+a+guide+for+faith+leaders&oq=mental+health+a+ guide+for+faith+leaders&aqs=chrome..69i57.5974j0j4&sourceid= chrome&ie=UTF-8.
11. Doug Oman, "Reviewing Religion/Spirituality Evidence from a Public Health Perspective: Introduction," in *Why Religion and Spirituality Matter for Public Health*, ed. Doug Oman (Springer Publishers, 2018), 25.
12. Dr. Cohen is a fictitious name whose story is drawn from a compilation of people with whom the authors have worked.
13. Doug Oman and David Lukoff, "Mental Health, Religion, and Spirituality," in *Why Religion and Spirituality Matter for Public Health*, ed. Doug Oman, 225–43.
14. Abraham Joshua Heschel, "To Grow in Wisdom," in *The Insecurity of Freedom* (Philadelphia: Jewish Publication Society, 1986), 84.
15. American Psychological Association, "Stress in America—Generation Z."
16. The Reconstructionist Rabbinical College is currently piloting a program, Trauma-Informed Rabbinic Training, directed by Rabbi Jessica Rosenberg.
17. U.S. Department of Health and Human Services, Substance Abuse and Mental Health Services Administration (SAMHSA), "SAMHSA's Concept of Trauma and Guidance for a Trauma-Informed Approach," https://store.samhsa.gov/product/SAMHSA-s-Concept-of-Trauma-and-Guidance-for-a-Trauma-Informed-Approach/SMA14-4884.html.
18. American Psychological Association, "Stress in America—Generation Z."
19. Fox, "Genesis 2:10."

Addiction and Recovery

Addiction Is a Spiritual Malady and Judaism Is a Spiritual Solution

Mark Borovitz

We are in the midst of what is being called an "Opioid Epidemic," and it is being spoken about as if it is a newer phenomenon. Yet, in 1971, Rabbi Abraham Joshua Heschel wrote: "We have a major curse in America today, the epidemic of drug addiction." He went on to say: "I interpret the young people's escape into drugs as coming from their driving desire to experience moments of exaltation."[1] These words, which were reprinted in the book *Moral Grandeur and Spiritual Audacity* edited by Dr. Susannah Heschel, give us a great insight into the cause and the "cure" for our current and ongoing crisis.

Be it drugs, alcohol, gambling, food, sex, work, etc., all addictions come from a deep place of psychic pain that the drugs, alcohol, etc., quiet for a moment, an hour, or a day. The underlying psychic pain is true for all people. Most people live with this pain in quiet suffering; I call it low-grade misery. One of the main characteristics of this suffering is the blame, shame, discontent, that people exhibit. The "If only I had ___, my life would be good" syndrome. The first alcoholic was Noah, of course. Yet the first example of psychic pain of loneliness, isolation, "not good enough" is Cain, and we know what he did with this pain: he killed his brother and walked around with a mark. We all still have this 'mark of Cain' within us.

RABBI MARK BOROVITZ is senior rabbi of Beit T'Shuvah, an alcoholic and criminal in Recovery, a father, grandfather, husband, uncle, and brother. Rabbi Mark has spoken all over the United States on this topic and others. He is the author of three books: *The Holy Thief*, *Finding Recovery and Yourself in Torah*, and *You Matter*.

Many of us have studied *Sanhedrin* 37a and quoted the verse: "Whoever destroys a single soul it is as if they destroy an entire world, and whoever saves a single soul it is as if they save an entire world." I learned from Rabbi Yitz Greenberg that this teaches us that every soul has infinite worth and dignity. The next verse: "So no one can say my father is better than yours" teaches us that we all have equal worth and dignity. The last verse: "Unlike humans when they mint coins from the same mold, every coin comes out the same, when God mints humans from the mold of Adam, no one resembles their fellow person. Therefore every single human is obliged to say: The world was created for my sake." Rabbi Greenberg taught us that this means each human has unique worth and dignity.

I have used this teaching to remind myself and the people that I spiritually counsel that there is no comparison or competition. There is only one you: who can you compete against and compare yourself to? Yet we do this all the time, again a remnant from Cain. In comparison and competition, we can only experience exaltation when we "win"; and there is always going to be someone better, faster, etc., than we are, so this experience lasts seconds, minutes at best. Drugs, alcohol, and other addictive substances and processes are the only way to prolong the exaltation for most people, so they eventually become addicted. It is important to know that what is the problem was originally a solution to the real problem—psychic pain—and we have to treat that underlying condition so people can live in recovery.

This is why I and we at Beit T'Shuvah treat addiction as a spiritual malady. Many people want to make it a brain disease and give pills—in fact this way of treating people is very financially lucrative—yet there is no pill that cure the psychic pain of competition, comparison, loneliness, isolation, "not good enough," shame, discontent, etc. This psychic pain has to be dealt with through our spirit and connection to God and another human being(s). I am sure of this for many reasons: my own story, my experience of thirty years in Jewish recovery, and on a bottle of whiskey/booze it says "distilled spirits"!

While the pharmaceutical and medical Industry are peddling pills and "brain disorder" as the cure and cause of this epidemic, we in the treatment field know that at its core, addiction is a spiritual malady and we have to heal the underlying causes of this disease. It is a dis-ease of mind, body, and spirit. The addict/alcoholic doesn't feel "at home" anywhere in their body, their thoughts, their emotions, and their spirit as well as in society. We feel different and believe that no one can understand us, sometimes not even another addict. We are dis-regulated in all areas of our life.

In the first chapter of Genesis, we are told that the earth was/is *tohu vavohu* (unformed and chaotic, in my understanding). We are still *tohu vavohu*! We are seeking exaltation, as Rabbi Heschel says, in all the wrong places, and Judaism has taken a back seat in our "war on drugs."

Johann Hari, in his book *Chasing the Scream*, says the opposite of addiction is connection. Judaism is all about connection, connection to God, connection to community, connection to self. Yet, we are not teaching this to our people in ways that they can hear. Yes, we are in the forefront of many of the social justice movements. Yes, we talk about *tikkun olam* in regard to caring for our planet. We are not, however, teaching our people how to deal with the eternal psychic pain all of us feel because we are disconnected from our source, God. We are not teaching people how to be immersed in our texts and see ourselves as if we were redeemed from slavery, we are standing at Sinai, we are filled with Holiness, etc.

So, what is the solution? It is simple: live our tradition in our daily lives. I am going to give some examples of spiritual values that I have found in our tradition that have helped people recover from their addictions, how their families have healed from the destructive effects of addiction and how we can all live them and teach them to our congregants as prevention from addiction and the low-grade misery of "quiet desperation."

In our tradition, *t'shuvah* is a foundational concept, according to some sages. Tractate *Yoma* is all about *t'shuvah*, Yom Kippur is all about *t'shuvah*, the month of Elul is all about *t'shuvah*, the Rambam wrote an entire book about *t'shuvah*, and Rabbi Yonah has his *Gates of Repentance*. Yet, other than speak about this on Rosh HaShanah and some people doing *kaparot*, little attention is paid to this important practice. Rabbi Abraham Joshua Heschel says: "The most unnoticed of all miracles is the miracle of *t'shuvah*. It is not the same as rebirth; it is transformation, creation."[2] He goes on to say that *t'shuvah* is done in remorse, responsibility and truth. *T'shuvah* is, according to Rambam, a *chesbon hanefesh* (an accounting of our soul). As any accountant will tell you, a true accounting lists liabilities and assets. This means we have to see what we have done well and where we have missed the mark. We, at Beit T'Shuvah have developed a sheet to do this work, which is included as an addendum to this article.

In Tractate *Shabbat*, we are taught by Rabbi Eliezer that we should do *t'shuvah* one day before we die and since no one knows the day of their death, we should do *t'shuvah* every day. Yet, how many of us do this? In *The Big Book* of Alcoholics Anonymous, there is a story by Dr. Paul where he states that he is sober one day at a time based on his spiritual condition. The program also says that doing a fourth step inventory and following it up with a daily tenth step is how we stay spiritually fit. Eighty-four years ago, Bill Wilson and Dr. Bob Smith followed the teachings of Rabbi Eliezer without even knowing it!

The challenge for us as Jews and as rabbis is to live this teaching ourselves, model it for our congregants, and teach our children the power of *t'shuvah*. Rabbi Heschel says that "the power of *t'shuvah* causes time to be created backward and allows re-creation of the past to take place. Through the forgiving hand of God, harm and blemish which we have committed against the world and ourselves will be extinguished, transformed into salvation."[3] These words written in 1936, reverberate within me and, I pray, within all of us. Recovery can only happen when we are in truth with ourselves and others. *T'shuvah* is one of the most powerful paths to truth. *T'shuvah* is translated as return, repentance, and response. It means, to me, repair, change, and hope. *T'shuvah* is one of the greatest spiritual path to wholeness and acceptance.

Doing *t'shuvah* gives me the courage to face myself and know I can change. It gives me the opportunity to meet my higher and lower self and find the way back as well as the way forward. In doing *t'shuvah* I give myself (and others) the gift of transparency and truth, hope and change, community and connection. I no longer have to hide from me and from you. I no longer need to believe that I am stuck and I can't get out of the mud. I no longer have to be lonely and isolated. What a relief!

Yet, we are not teaching this path, preaching this path, and living this path. Is it out of fear? Is it out of ignorance? Is it because we don't believe in the power of *t'shuvah*? Judah is the quintessential example of a complete *t'shuvah*. When he approaches Joseph in order to save Benjamin, he is doing the exact opposite of what he did with Joseph. How great an act was this? Well, we are called Jews and our tradition is called Judaism after this hero of *t'shuvah*. What is our reluctance to live *t'shuvah* in our daily life? I think it is a lack of belief in change and to be in recovery, we have to believe in change.

In my thirty-plus years of being in recovery, I have changed greatly. We believe, as my wife, Harriet Rossetto, founder of Beit T'Shuvah, often says: "The only constant is change." Without a belief in change, how can we live with ourselves? This is one of the major reasons that recovery is a spiritual solution for the spiritual malady of addiction. I continue to use the sheets that you can use at the end of this article each day. Each week at Beit T'Shuvah the residents and staff engage in a weekly *t'shuvah* group where we use the sheets and discuss where we missed the mark and where we hit the mark. Can you imagine doing this with your board, your staff, your congregation? It will allow each person to see the humanity of another person and, where there is competition and comparison there will be compassion and camaraderie. The change is miraculous.

Another spiritual solution to the spiritual malady of addiction is the Holiness Code. In our tradition, holiness is defined in Leviticus 19. To be holy, is an imperative. We become holy through our actions. This is known as *imitatio Dei* (imitating God). Just as God feeds us, so too do we have to feed the poor. Just as God honors us, so too do we have to honor our parents. Just as God observes the Sabbath, so too do we have to observe Shabbat. Just as God calls for us, so too do we have to call to and for God. Just as God does not favor rich or poor, so too do we have to show each person equal justice. Just as God rebukes us without hate, so too do we have to rebuke others without hate. Just as God loves us, so too do we have to love our fellow humans. This is a very hard beginning for most of us. We have regulated holiness to the purview of clergy and "saints." This thinking is clearly in violation of the words of God to us in Leviticus: "You shall be holy because I, the Lord am holy" (Lev. 19:2). We are called on to be a nation of priests, a holy nation. This teaches us that God doesn't expect perfection. God is holy and we **will be** holy. God is telling us that we are a work in progress. The Hebrew is in the imperfect tense—proving that God knows us as imperfect beings. The imperfect tense in biblical Hebrew denotes an action that is not yet completed. The use of the imperfect tense comes to tell us that God knows and loves us with our imperfections! How are we following God's teaching and being holy through being okay not being perfect? We read this *parashah* each year, yet do we realize that we are holy already and our actions bring us closer to God, to our authentic selves, and to each other?

Recognizing that we are holy and how we live our Holiness Code each and every day helps us to realize that we have intrinsic value and esteem. Since God is telling us that we are holy, like God is holy, low self-esteem is like spitting in God's eye. I know this because I did this for over twenty years. We are holy teachers and holy men and women. Acknowledging our own holiness allows us to take our proper places in the world and letting everyone know that we recognize and acknowledge their holiness and holy souls gives people a sense of well-being, hope, and joy.

Another spiritual value of our tradition is surrender. Surrender does not mean "giving up" or quitting. As a spiritual principle, I found the meaning of "surrender" to best be described by Rabbi Soloveitchik in his essay "The Lonely Man of Faith": "Redemption is achieved when humble man . . . lets himself be confronted and defeated by a Higher and Truer Being."[4] I say, surrender happens when humble humans allow themselves to be confronted and defeated by a higher truth. Surrender is a practice of being right-sized and not needing to always be right. It is a practice of opening myself up to higher truths that I can't get to on my own. I surrender each day to God to teach me how to be a better partner and fulfill the divine need God created me for. I surrender each day to other people who know more and/or are better equipped for a particular skill. This is such an important way of being in the world. It reminds me/us that we are **not** God! It is similar to the story of God holding the mountain over the heads of the Israelite people to coerce them to accept Torah.

True acceptance of Torah is our surrender to the truth that we all need help in managing our inclinations. We are told two stories of creation in Genesis: one is Adam who is able to subdue and use the environment and the other is Adam who is seeking connection. Neither of these two are bad, just as our two major inclinations are not bad. We need both parts of ourselves to live fully and completely in the world. An addict is unable to manage and integrate these parts: we swing wildly from one extreme to another. Recovery is integrating our inclinations and our two Adams so that we are able to move from binary thinking (i.e., either/or) into recovery/Jewish thinking (i.e., both/and). The realization that none of our traits are endowed with good or bad, rather their values are in the ways we use them, necessitates the need for a spiritual solution.

These are but a few of the reasons that addiction is a spiritual malady and Judaism is a spiritual solution. I welcome your comments and am available for consultations and speaking as well as assistance with any colleague or congregant that is in need of this spiritual solution. The *t'shuvah* sheets are on the following pages, please feel free to use them for yourself and your congregants.

Name: _____   Date: _____

Spiritual Counselor: _____

"The secret of spiritual living is in the sense for the ultimacy of each moment, for its sacred uniqueness, for its once-and-for-allness. It is this sense that enables us to put all our strength into sanctifying an instant by doing the holy."
—Rabbi Abraham Joshua Heschel

	How Did I Hit the Mark?	
T R U T H	What/How did I do well?	
	What made it right/okay? (Why was this important to do well?)	
E F F E C T	Who was impacted?	
	How were they impacted?	

RESPONSIBILITY	What was learned?	
	What's the plan? (for enhancing, sustaining, growing, etc.)	

"The most unnoticed of all miracles is the miracle of repentance. It is not the same as rebirth; it is transformation, creation. In the dimension of time there is no going back. But the power of repentance causes time to be created backward and allows re-creation of the past to take place. Through the forgiving hand of God, harm and blemish which we have committed against the world and against ourselves will be extinguished, transformed into salvation."
—Rabbi Abraham Joshua Heschel

	How Did I Miss the Mark?	
TRUTH	What/How did I miss the mark?	
	What made it right/okay? (What was your justification in the moment for this action?)	
REMORSE	Who was impacted?	
	How were they impacted?	

R E S P O N	What was learned?	
S I B I L I T Y	What's the plan? (for not repeating, changing growing, etc.)	

Notes

1. Abraham Joshua Heschel, "In Search of Exaltation," in *Moral Grandeur and Spiritual Audacity*, ed. Susannah Heschel (New York: Farrar, Straus and Giroux, 1996), 228.
2. Heschel, "The Meaning of Repentance," in ibid., 68.
3. Ibid., 69.
4. Joseph B. Soloveitchik, "The Lonely Man of Faith," *Tradition* 7, no. 2 (Summer 1965): 24.

Addiction and Recovery in the Minds of the Rabbis

Annie Belford

Addiction, in its many forms, is an increasingly common occurrence in our communities. While decades ago Jews were first beginning to meet with their rabbis about alcoholism, and those rabbis first began to speak about Jews who were addicts, today we would be hard-pressed to find any congregation, college campus, army base, or other setting where addiction in one form or another has not made itself known. Drugs, alcohol, and nicotine often get the most media attention, but today we know that people can become addicted to food, sex, pornography, shopping, gambling, and more. We think these behaviors, compulsions, and even consequences are new; reading our ancient foundational Rabbinic texts shows us they are not.

The Rabbis of the Talmud did not address addiction the way we do, because they do not share our language or understanding. One cannot search through midrash or responsa for the word "addiction," because there would be no results. However, this is not an indication that the Rabbis, or the Jews living at the time they wrote, had no experience of the behaviors and patterns that we would describe as addictive.

Today, we define addiction as compulsive, habitual behaviors that have a deleterious impact on a person's physical, emotional, and spiritual well-being, with far-reaching consequences and devastating results. In their day, our Sages recognized that people's lives could be consumed by compulsive, habitual behavior; they

---

RABBI ANNIE BELFORD (NY04), an El Paso, Texas, native, received a BA in Creative Writing from the American Jewish University (1998), an MA in Hebrew Letters from HUC-JIR/New York, and rabbinic ordination in 2004. Rabbi Annie has served Temple Sinai since July 2009 as the first full-time solo female rabbi in a Houston congregation. She is an avid reader, adores our national parks, and loves nothing more than spending time with her three amazing children.

also recognized that people were filled with natural urges that could, if they were not controlled, become extreme. Indeed, the way the Rabbis speak of *yetzer hara* (the will-to-evil) shows their understanding of the fine balance of our natural urges.

A well-known midrash from *B'reishit Rabbah* (9:7) lays the groundwork for the belief that all our natural urges can be used for our benefit, if they are kept in balance:

> Rabbi Nahum said in the name of Rabbi Samuel, "'Behold it was very good'—this speaks of *yetzer tov*. 'And behold, it was very good'—this speaks of *yetzer hara*." Can *yetzer hara* really be very good?! Yes, because were it not for *yetzer hara*, no one would build a house, or marry, or have children, or do business. This is what Solomon was referring to when he said, "I have noted that all labor and skillful enterprise come from men's envy of each other."

According to this dominant view, *yetzer hara* is not inherently bad. Because of a person's natural urge for sex, children are born; because of a person's feeling of envy, business is conducted and money made. These inclinations are labeled *yetzer hara*, but if they are held in check by the *yetzer hatov*, they can produce good things. Our urges, in and of themselves, are not bad and do not lead to compulsive, imbalanced behavior. So, too, "addiction taps into the most fundamental of human processes. Whether the need is to be high, to be sexual, to eat, or even to work, the addictive process can turn creative, life-giving energy into a destructive demoralizing compulsivity."[1] Hence, in both the Rabbinic and the modern view, the woman who has sex with her partner is acting from a natural, life-giving impulse; the man who cooks and enjoys a sumptuous meal is also acting from natural, life-giving energy. However, when the woman's sexual behaviors or the man's feasting change in intention or frequency, what our Sages called the *yetzer hara* can take hold and assert control. What we today call addiction can begin.

A balance between and *yetzer hatov* and *yetzer hara* was essential in the minds of the Rabbis because they recognized that either inclination could lead to compulsive behavior. For example, the *Y'rushalmi* (*Pei-ah* 3a) tells the story of a man who wanted to donate money to charity, something we can easily ascribe to the *yetzer hatov*. However, his *yetzer hara* did not keep his *yetzer hatov* in balance, and the need for financial security failed to moderate his desire to help others. As a result, he gave all his belongings away until he was himself destitute and in need of charity. With this example in mind, it seems as though the Rabbis saw "addiction" as a state when a person's natural inclinations, for either good or bad, were unbalanced. This led to far-reaching and devastating consequences as the person compulsively acted on his or her inclinations, until physical, emotional, and spiritual health were compromised. The result is that this imbalanced individual becomes an addict.

We see evidence of this imbalance and its consequence in Rabbinic responsa relating to who may serve as witnesses in a *beit din*. *Mishnah Sanhedrin* 3:3 declares, "These are the [categories of people] who are disqualified [from serving as witnesses]: those who play with dice [i.e., those who gamble], those who loan with interest, those who race pigeons. . . ." This text is not concerned with the internal experiences of the gambler or the progression of his or her behaviors; rather, it is concerned about the status this person holds in a legal system. The Rabbis believed that habitual gamblers could not serve as unbiased witnesses. Elsewhere (*Sanhedrin* 24b), the rabbis "denounce gambling as a way of life."[2] The problem of compulsive gambling seemed to plague Jewish communities throughout time, as we can see in Rashba's Responsa 1:180:

> Another question: A wise person, a teacher, who preached before the people, taught illogical lessons, and played with dice. He made an oath (*sh'vua*) that he would never gamble again, but he transgressed his oath. Then he said before the public that any oath that is sworn over a possession is not a valid oath. Because of this, many in the community have transgressed, and made their oaths with lies and falsehoods, and they are saying that every vow not made over a possession is not really a vow . . . Before this happened, everyone was very cautious lest they transgress their oaths . . . They were very strict about this matter before the law of this fellow came to them. What is the law? The answer: Every person who does this and teaches this way should be excommunicated. For this [so-called wise person] leads people to stray from a good path to a bad path, and he sins and causes others to sin . . . Heaven forfend! He is not a scholar or a teacher but an evil person and a dolt. Every person who listens to him and believes his word causes himself to slip.

This responsum should not be taken as advice on how to respond to an addict suffering from his or her addiction. Heaven forfend! Rather, this responsum is evidence of the consequences addictive behavior had for one individual and his community. This responsum shows a man who was a teacher, once well-regarded, who became consumed by gambling. He tried to stop by making an oath, which he then transgressed. In order to cover this transgression, he created an entire system of lies—that is, his ruling regarding oaths being sworn over possessions. This led to other people sinning and eventually to his own excommunication, perhaps the greatest punishment for a Jew in the thirteenth century. This man lost everything he had—his livelihood, his reputation, his community—because he could not stop gambling. Rashba never calls this man an addict, but we can certainly recognize the painful characteristics and terrible consequences of *addictive behavior* in this description.

The Rabbis describe other kinds of addiction as well. In describing compulsive eating, they teach in *Bavli P'sachim* 49a:

> Any Torah scholar who eats excessively in every place—in the end he will destroy his home, widow his wife, and orphan his young. His learning will be forgotten, and many arguments will come to him, and his words will not be accepted. He will desecrate the name of heaven and the name of his rabbi and the name of his father. He brings a bad name upon himself, his children, and his children's children until the end of time.

This brief description of the consequences of addiction on the addict and his family is intended as a moralistic teaching, preaching the necessities of living with moderation. Again, this text's harsh tone and punishing attitude is not the prescribed way one should treat addicts today; we know that moralizing and condemning only serve to deepen the shame with which most addicts are already deeply familiar, thereby perpetuating the cycle of addiction rather than interrupting it. Instead, this text shows the havoc addiction can wreak on one's work, family, reputation, and well-being. The Rabbis never use the word "addiction," but they clearly understand addictive behavior.

Rabbinic texts also point to what we might describe as workaholism. *Bavli K'tubot* 62b tells the story of Rav Rahumi, who spends every day studying in the *beit midrash*—even Shabbat, when most scholars would return home to be with their wives and engage in cohabitation. Rav Rahumi, however, only returned home for Yom Kippur, a day on which sexual relations are forbidden. One year on Yom Kippur, however, he was "drawn into his studies" and did not go home. His wife waited anxiously for his return, but as time passed, "her resolve weakened, and a tear fell from her eye." In a dramatic episode so poignant it could have been scripted for Hollywood, the roof of the *beit midrash* upon which Rav Rahumi stood completely collapsed at the exact moment that tear from Rav Rahumi's wife fell. The roof collapse resulted in his death.

A dominant reading of this text indicates that the Rabbis use this story to emphasize the importance of a scholar's maintaining a sexual relationship with their spouse. In her landmark book *A Bride for One Night: Talmud Tales*, Ruth Calderon hints at the addictive nature of Rav Rahumi's behaviors. She calls him "possessed" with his studies,[3] repeating his studies to himself "like a madman."[4] She observes that, perhaps, "Rav Rahumi's devotion to learning also serves as an escape from the dark depression within."[5] This catalogue of behaviors may allow us to see ourselves in this text. How many of us have interrupted our family vacations to assist congregants in times of need? How many of us spend longer hours in our *b'tei midrash*, synagogues, and houses of worship than in our own homes? Surely, like Rav Rahumi, our desire to serve our communities comes from our *yetzer hatov*, but we must strive to keep this life-giving energy in balance, lest we use our work as a tool for avoidance or numbing or to "escape from the dark depression within." Was Rav Rahumi a workaholic? The Rabbis of the Talmud do not use this word. However, they recognized the need for balancing the multiple needs and inclinations present in one's life; they also recognized the devastating consequences of imbalance, of what we might call addiction.

Perhaps the most dramatic Rabbinic stories describing addiction also contain an element of recovery. The first of these can be found in an amplification of *Bavli Avodah Zara* 17a:

> They said of Rabbi Eleazar ben Dordiya, that he did not let even one prostitute rest without coming to her. One time he heard that there was one prostitute in a city by the sea, and she required a purse of *dinar* to lie with her. Ben Dordiya took up a purse of *dinar* and set out. He crossed over seven rivers. At the time when they

ADDICTION AND RECOVERY IN THE MINDS OF THE RABBIS

began their sexual union, she blew out a breath and said, "Just as the breath can never return to its source, so too Eleazar ben Dordiya will never be received in repentance."

He went and sat between two hills and mountains, and said, "Hills and mountains, ask for mercy on my behalf!" They replied, "We cannot ask on your behalf, for we ask on behalf of ourselves," as it says, "for the mountains may move and the hills be shaken [but My loyalty shall never move from you, nor My covenant of friendship be shaken, said the Lord, who takes you back in love]" (Isa. 54:10).

He said, "Heaven and earth, ask for mercy on my behalf!" They replied, "We cannot ask on your behalf, for we ask on behalf of ourselves," as it says, "though the heavens should melt away like smoke, and the earth wear out like a garment [My victory will stand forever, My triumph will remain unbroken!]" (Isa. 51:6).

He said, "Sun and moon, ask for mercy on my behalf!" They replied, "We cannot ask on your behalf, for we ask on behalf of ourselves," as it says, "the moon will be ashamed, and the sun will be abashed [for the Lord of Hosts will reign . . . and the Presence will be revealed]" (Isa. 24:23).

He said, "Stars and constellations, ask for mercy on my behalf!" They replied, "We cannot ask on your behalf, for we ask on behalf of ourselves," as it says, "all the hosts of heaven shall wither" (Isa. 34:4).

Eleazar ben Dordiya said, "Then this matter depends only on me!" He rested his head between his knees and burst forth in tears until his soul departed. A *bat kol* (a heavenly voice), came out and proclaimed, "Rabbi Eleazar ben Dordiya is invited to life in the world-to-come!"

Here was a case of a sin [other than heresy] when the sinner died. In this case, too, because he was so deeply attached to pleasure, it is as if he had committed heresy. [When he heard this,] Rabbi cried and said, "One can achieve eternity after many years, and one can achieve eternity in just one hour." Rabbi also said, "It is the law that not only will one who repents be accepted, but also that we will call him Rabbi."

This is a painful story in many respects, in part because the "hero" of the aggadah dies. It can also be read as a painful illustration of a sex addict "hitting bottom." The fact that this text emphasizes that Rabbi Eleazar ben Dordiya has seen *every* prostitute constitutes enough evidence of an addiction. The text also shows that the addict is not really in control of his behavior: others feel that his actions are not normal, as evidenced by the need to cross seven rivers—indicating a long, expensive, and arduous journey; the cost of the prostitute is extreme, an entire bag of gold coins; and finally, the consequences of his actions are deeply destructive in that they risk his eternal life. It seems from the text that Rabbi Eleazar ben Dordiya takes very little physical or emotional pleasure from his compulsive behavior, yet he still cannot desist. However, this text does offer some glimmer of hope in that it also shows a kind of recovery from addiction.

One of the most common paths to recovery from addiction is through a twelve-step program, the first step of which states, "We admitted we were powerless over [the substance of choice, be it alcohol, sex, narcotics, food, etc.]—that our lives had become unmanageable"[6] Rabbi Eleazar ben Dordiya certainly seems to make this step when he realizes how out of control his pursuit of prostitutes had become and how much it had cost him. He then appeals to all manner of intercessors—the earth, sky, stars, suns, hills, and so on—to seek mercy for his actions and attempt to ensure his place in the world-to-come. Each of these attempts at intercession fails, and each is accompanied by a prophetic quote by way of explanation, the majority of which speak of the limitations of earthly matter. The hills, mountains, sky, earth, sun, and moon will all eventually "be shaken," "melt away," "wear out," and "be ashamed." These things, and by extension all things found on earth, are not lasting and cannot bring mercy to human beings. The second part of each of these verses reveal that human beings can find lasting support and mercy through God, and that God will take us back in love. These verses offer a powerful message to the recovering addict, who is depending on a Higher Power to help him or her maintain sobriety.

Most recovering addicts understand, however, that recovery does not happen in a vacuum; the community of support offered by twelve-step groups, the relationship between sponsor and sponsee, and the outpatient or inpatient recovery settings all prove vital in the process of recovery. One of the greatest tragedies of addiction is its isolation; the addict becomes separated from all that they love and know in their pursuit of their addiction. They no longer are a part of community. This is something Rabbi Eleazar ben Dordiya experiences, painfully, as well. However, he too finds community, though at first it seems he finds it only posthumously. Rabbi

Eleazar ben Dordiya's moment of repentance at the end of the aggadah, when he realizes that his path to return "depends only on [him]," can be likened to the moment a modern addict begins the first step and starts the process of recovery. At this point, he also reenters his community, and after hearing his story, Rabbi—the recognized Rabbinic authority of his time—declared that Eleazar ben Dordiya and any other person who truly repents is "accepted" into the community with respect. In Eleazar ben Dordiya's case, he should be given the title of "Rabbi." This indicates that a return to, participation in, and commitment to the larger community is part of recovery from what we call addiction both in ancient times and in modern days. For Rabbi Eleazar ben Dordiya, his recovery is not just a return to a community of people, but also a return to God.

Sadly, our text ends with Eleazar ben Dordiya's death, which leaves a less than promising message for those seeking recovery from addiction. However, it is possible to understand his death figuratively. Many addicts record an experience of an "ego death,"[7] which is simultaneously the ending of one life and the beginning of a new life. Everything that a person was—"all relationships and reference points, all rationalizations and protections"[8]—disappear, and the addict is left with nothing but surrender into the core of their being. "There is nowhere to go but up,"[9] and so the addict starts to rebuild a new life, without the addiction. When we view Rabbi Eleazar ben Dordiya's death as an ego death, we recognize that the only thing that has departed was his addiction. He is born into a new life, which the text calls "life in the world-to-come." This follows the pattern of many addicts who, for example, celebrate not their birthdays but their "sober birthday." This reading of the text certainly echoes that experience and provides more hope for recovering addicts.

Another familiar and powerful text that illustrates both the power of addiction and the promise of recovery can be found in *Bavli M'nachot* 44a:

> There is a story of a man who was strictly observant in the laws of *tzitzit*. He heard that there was a prostitute in a city by the sea who demanded four hundred gold coins as payment for lying with her. He sent her four hundred gold coins and set a time to be with her. When his time came, he went and sat by the entrance. Her maid entered and said to her, "The same man who sent you

four hundred gold coins has come and is sitting by the entrance." She said, "Please, come in. Seven beds spread out before him, six [filled] with silver and one with gold, and between each one was a ladder of silver, and the highest [of the ladders] was of gold. The prostitute ascended and sat on top of the highest ladder, naked. When he [began to] ascend to sit naked next to her, his four *tzitzit* slapped him on his face. He was startled and he sat down on the floor. She was also startled and sat on the floor.

She said, "By the Capital of Rome! I will not let you rest until you tell me what blemish you saw in me."

He said to her, "By God, I have never seen a woman as beautiful as you. But the Lord our God commanded one commandment, and that is the commandment of *tzitzit*. For it is written 'I am the Lord your God,' [Num. 15:41] two times. [The meaning of the repetition of 'I am the Lord your God is] 'I am the One who, in the future, will demand payment; and I am the One who, in the future, will give rewards.' Now, the [four *tzitzit*] appear to me as four witnesses [to my actions, which will be judged by God in the future]."

She said, "I will not let you rest until you tell me your name, the name of your city, the name of your teacher, and the name of the school where you learn Torah." He wrote all this information down and gave it to her. She stood and divided all her belongings. [She gave] a third to the government, a third to the poor, and she kept a third to herself, including those same beds.

She then went to the academy of Rabbi Hiya. She said to him, "Rabbi, teach me and make me a convert." He said to her, "My daughter, has one of my students caught your eye?" She took out the note and gave it to him. He said to her, "Go and take ownership of what you've purchased! The same beds that you once offered him illicitly, now offer him licitly. This is the reward in this world, and as for the reward in the world-to-come, I cannot say how much it will be [i.e., it will be immeasurable]!"

The similarities between the setting of this story and the previous story are immediately obvious. In both stories, there is a prostitute who lives "in a city by the sea,"[10] and in both stories men spend a great deal of money and time to pursue the respective prostitutes. The unnamed man in this story, whom we will call Ploni Tzitzit, is not described as having a history of seeking after prostitutes, unlike Rabbi Eleazar ben Dordiya, and it may be a stretch to call him a sex addict. In the context of Tractate *M'nachot*, this text is used to illustrate the rewards of following the Torah commandments, which are often commanded with little guarantee of a visible reward in this world, but with "immeasurable" reward in the world to come. However, for our purposes, this single incident in Ploni Tzitzit's life may suggest addiction. He is not in control of his behaviors, and his actions are extreme.

Ploni Tzitzit's actions also exhibit the typical addictive cycle. First, he hears about the prostitute and becomes *preoccupied*. Then, through the brief description of Ploni's preparations and the prostitute's arrangement of her chambers, the *ritualization* begins. The next step in the cycle is the *compulsive behavior*,[11] but at this moment Ploni's *tzitzit* slap him in the face and he has a moment of clarity. Ploni Tzitzit realizes he is not in control, and that he is powerless over his addiction. He does not complete the addiction cycle and engage in the compulsive behavior, or feel the *despair* of the fourth and final step. Instead, he stops the addictive behavior, and his recovery begins.

By recognizing he is powerless, he accepts the first step of the twelve-step program. Next, through the ritual meaning behind the *tzitzit*, he is reminded of a power greater than himself. By reciting the commandment associated with *tzitzit*, Ploni says, "I am the Lord your God," and thereby, as the second step counsels, comes to believe in a Power greater than himself. He also exhibits four spiritual traits that are central in the spiritual recovery from addiction. First, he acts with humility: when he is in the midst of the addiction cycle, he ascends to the highest bed, but when he accepts powerlessness, he sits on the floor. Second, he is honest: he truthfully answers the prostitute's questions, even when those answers could lead to his downfall. Third, he maintains his connection to community, returning to his *beit midrash* and his teacher. Fourth, he maintains his integrity and has stopped the duality that living with addiction requires. He does not keep the world of his addiction separate from the world of his learning; instead, he recognizes that his recovery demands integrity and acts accordingly. This Talmudic story is a powerful illustration of addiction and spiritual recovery and offers important guidance for contemporary addicts. Additionally, it has a "happy ending," which is testimony to the power of hope in the work of addiction and recovery.

Of course, there is no "ending" when working with addiction and recovery. Any addict will attest that recovery is a lifelong endeavor, with endless lessons and challenges. Just as our people have wrestled with Torah and its meanings for thousands of years, so to have we wrestled with addiction for thousands of years: this is evidenced in the texts above and the many more that could not fit in the scope of this article.

The attempt to live with integrity and moderation is also not new. The Rabbis sought to balance the *yetzer hara* with the *yetzer hatov*, believing a middle path would stave off extreme behavior. They used the tools they had, such as warnings, oaths, castigation, and excommunication; they also found none of these was effective. They did seem to find that faith, community, honesty, and integrity can be effective in challenging addictive behaviors, to some degree—a path that twelve-step groups rely upon to this day.

There is no one "right path" for every addict. Addiction is a brain disease, an emotional disease, and a spiritual disease. As rabbis, perhaps these texts can be our teachers as we become better informed in our efforts to help heal one of the greatest spiritual ailments of our time.

Notes

1. Patrick Carnes, *Out of the Shadows: Understanding Sexual Addiction* (Center City, NM: Hazeldon Press, 2001), 8.
2. Eliezer Diamond, "Wheel of Fortune: A Rabbinic Perspective on Gambling," *JTS Magazine* 7, no. 2 (Winter 1998): 10.
3. Ruth Calderon, *A Bride for One Night: Talmud Tales*, trans. Ilana Kurshan (Philadelphia: Jewish Publication Society, 2014), 35.
4. Ibid., 36.
5. Ibid., 38.
6. *Twelve Steps and Twelve Traditions* (New York: Alcoholics Anonymous World Services, Inc., 2002), 5.
7. Christina Grof and Stanislav Grof, *The Stormy Search for the Self: A Guide to Personal Growth through Transformational Crisis* (New York: G.P. Putnam's Sons, 1990), 106.
8. Ibid.
9. Ibid.
10. In both this aggadah and in the previous Talmudic aggadah, we find two Jewish men whose spiritual *t'shuvah* depends on the awareness of the non-Jewish prostitute. While this article's purview cannot encompass this element, it does bear mentioning that in both these stories it is a wise non-Jewish woman who seems to better understand the consequences of behavior and usher a new path for the supposedly more learned Jewish man.
11. Carnes, *Out of the Shadows*, 20.

Married to a Sex Addict

Anonymous

In the early years of our marriage, when I was in rabbinical school, I knew something was wrong when I got a busy signal on the phone. I would call home from a pay phone—this was in the days before cell phones—and the phone would be busy. For an hour, two hours, five hours, I would try to reach my husband for a banal or urgent matter, but the phone line would be busy. For some people, this would simply mean that he was making other phone calls or that the phone had fallen off the hook. In our marriage, though, it meant he had dialed onto the Internet and was perusing the web for pornography. My husband is a sex addict, and porn is his drug.

As the years progressed, the danger evolved into smart phones. We tried all sorts of adaptations and programs to make his phone "safe" and still allow him the flexibility and ease of this wonder of modern life. They worked as well as locking the computer modem in a box had worked in the early years of our marriage; he just found a way to break the lock, break the box, bypass the program, sneak through the safety features. He is smart, you see, and I think that smart addicts are the most difficult to treat.

He's also incredibly kind, and if you met him you would never know that he struggles with this addiction every day. He laughs easily and can discuss just about any topic at length, and he loves his children deeply and well. He just learned early in his emotional development that looking at porn obsessively was an easier way of dealing with his feelings than actually dealing with any of his feelings, and so that is what he has continued to do to this day.

He tried to become sober. He had worked twelve-step programs for sex addicts, of which there are many: SLAA, SLA, SRA, SA, SAA . . . he did them all. For periods of time he would refrain from pornography, but he was still never quite "with" us. He was emotionally detached, distracted, and volatile. He was passive-aggressive with me, and our fights—when they occurred—would be epic and leave me in tears. I carried almost the entire emotional, physical, financial, and organizational burdens of the family, so as not to add any stress to his life and thereby increase the likelihood of a relapse. For years he told me he was sober; for all those years he was lying.

I confronted him one night before heading to a work meeting, and he confessed that he had not been sober for the last ten years. You know the saying "it felt like the rug had been pulled out from under me"? That is exactly how it felt. My world spun off its axis. I felt the foundation of our life—which I thought was so stable—crack into thousands of pieces. I looked back on the years when our children were born, when we'd started new jobs and created a home together and realized that every single thing we'd created together had been a lie.

Despite this world-shaking realization, I took a deep breath and went to work. I had a bar mitzvah student to teach, a board meeting to attend. I hyper-compartmentalized that night, and even though I know I was not fully present with my student or my board, I also marvel that I was able to get through the next few hours. Actually, I marvel I was able to get through the next few years.

It took me a few years to get strong enough to say, "I want a divorce." I had bent my schedule, my life, my entire spirit so completely around him that I was the very definition of codependent. I couldn't articulate my own needs or wants if I tried. But I knew I needed to learn, so I went to intensive therapy and my own twelve-step group. (Did you know there's a twelve-step group for codependents? I didn't but I sure do now!) I read voraciously. My friends were supportive every step of the way. So was my family. I got stronger and stronger, and after years of my own growth I finally acknowledged how terrible our marriage really was. I admitted—not for the first time, but for the last time—how angry and tired I was. I asked for a divorce, and papers were served during the *Aseret Y'mei T'shuvah*. I moved into my own house shortly before the secular new year. What a year that was of growth and change; what a year of new beginnings.

As a congregational rabbi, very few people knew what was going on in our marriage. When news of our divorce spread, most people were shocked because we always presented ourselves and our family as a happy couple. I was exceptionally lucky, however, to find myself in a community that was curious but polite, supportive, and open-hearted. As my ex-husband and I continued to share space together peacefully, people remarked not on our divorce but on the model of peaceful coexistence we presented. I was and remain proud of that model we show. I also, I believe, have become a better rabbi. My boundaries have become stronger, and I am no longer willing to adopt other people's problems and make them my own. I am clear about what is important for our community and what is not, just as I am clear about what is important for me and what is not, and this clarity helps in my leadership and guidance. I was a codependent wife and I was a codependent rabbi, and doing both was deeply unhealthy physically, emotionally, and spiritually. Now that I am a recovering codependent and do not depend on other people's approval for my sense of self, I am stronger and centered. How could this not make me a better rabbi?

Now some time has passed, and I continue to grow. I continue to work on my own issues, of which there are many. My ex-husband and I co-parent very well, and the kids, as they say, are doing alright. When I moved out, I felt a freedom I have never experienced. I lost a dependent that day, and I have not looked back. I worry about his impact on our children but trust my example will have an impact as well. I know that I have never felt more joyous than I do now.

What I have learned about addictions is that they can take any form and create a path of destruction that is deep and wide. Addiction harms not just the addict but his or her family and friends. My husband's addiction destroyed our marriage and nearly killed my soul, and I am so grateful I was strong enough to leave. Many couples are not so lucky, and their marriages are festering in cesspools of shame, sorrow, and brokenness.

I have also learned that while our society is growing increasingly comfortable talking about alcoholism, opioid addiction, food addiction, and other addictions, our society's puritanical views on sex keeps sex addiction deep in the shadows of shame. This is a problem for us as clergy, because sex addiction in all its forms—obsessive pornography, compulsive one-night stands, "massage parlor" visits, and so on—is becoming a hallmark of our time. Sex addiction counseling is the fastest growing type of treatment in addiction therapy, but it is one about which we in the Jewish community know very little and hear about even less. How can we break this cone of silence and shame and allow our congregants and each other to feel safe sharing, addressing, and healing from this difficult addiction?

My story of being married to a sex addict is a defining story in my life, yet only a handful of people know the details, and I share this story here anonymously. Let my brokenness and healing be a light for all of us to open ourselves to the very real pain that is present in all of our communities, in Hillels and congregations and chaplaincies and every area we serve as rabbis. Sex addiction is real, dangerous, and disastrous. And with help, it can get better.

For more information on sex addiction and co-addiction, visit or read:

>   www.saa-recovery.org (Sex-Addicts Anonymous)
>   www.coda.org (Codependents Anonymous)
>   *Out of the Shadows* by Patrick Carnes
>   *In the Shadows of the Net* by Patrick Carnes
>   *Facing Codependency* by Pia Melody
>   *Intimacy Anorexia: Healing the Hidden Addiction in Your Marriage* by Douglas Weiss

A Daily Reprieve: Addiction, Recovery, and Finding God

Michael Richker

Each time I tell my story it is a little bit different.

I grew up in Houston, Texas, to Jewish immigrants. Both had escaped Nazi Germany. My parents were twice-a-year Jews. I attended Sunday school, became bar mitzvah (my largest gift was a $25 bond), and was confirmed. We observed the holidays, usually at my grandmother's house.

There was no love shown, no affection in my house. I cannot remember my parents ever holding hands or kissing. My father was verbally and occasionally physically abusive. He used to say, "Just do your best." I did, but it was never good enough. When he told me to do something and I questioned him, he hit me. I quickly learned that what I thought was worthless.

I remember my father often saying, "All I want you to be is a mensch." What ten-year-old knows what a mensch is?

Addiction is a disease that is often passed on genetically. I got mine from my mother, who took diet pills. When she stopped taking pills, she started drinking.

My first recollection of drinking was at Passover. I thought the four cups was a contest and tried to outdrink my cousins. I was also a good little boy and helped my parents clean up when they had a party: that allowed me to finish drinks on the way to the kitchen.

MICHAEL RICHKER is the past two-term president of Temple Emanu-El in Sarasota, Florida. Under his leadership, Temple Emanu-El overcame a crippling deficit, increased membership by 25 percent, and completed a successful capital campaign. He also oversaw a philanthropic initiative that raises hundreds of thousands of dollars annually and developed a *b'rit avodah* to enhance the sacred nature of serving on the Temple Emanu-El board of directors. He is a trustee of Jewish Family and Children's Service of the Suncoast and a counselor at Resurrection House.

I believe the feeling of abandonment played a great part in my turning to alcohol and drugs. When I was sixteen, my father died. I hated him for leaving me. At the end of my freshman year of college, I came home to find out my mother was getting remarried, selling the house and the family business, and moving to Chicago. I decided to shut down and never let anyone hurt me again.

When I was in college, we guys went out for a pitcher of beer. When it was done, I was the only one who wanted more. I always wanted more. I spent the next four years drinking every weekend, ending up with my head in the toilet, saying, "Dear God, if I live though this I will never drink again." I always drank again.

When I graduated and got married, I drank and actually tried to trade my wife for a woman down the hall. My wife left me—for good reason. I had no business being married. After my wife left, I started drinking heavily. Whiskey, every day, by myself, plus whatever I drank outside the house.

I moved to Chicago to work for my stepfather. But I took the long way via California, where my childhood best friend introduced me to marijuana. I loved it. I found my apartment in Chicago by smelling marijuana wafting under a door on the way to look at the apartment. I told the realtor, "I'll take it." She said, "Don't you want to see it?" I said no. I had found my source.

I like to say I only smoked marijuana once—from July 1969 to February 1981. I smoked every day, and even grew the stuff.

By 1975, I was married again and had two kids. I was a traveling salesman who drove with his knees while rolling a joint. In 1981 I was at a convention in Atlantic City and was introduced to cocaine. I came back to Chicago and called everyone I knew, asking them if they used cocaine. Finally, one guy said he did; and I said, "Next time you buy, buy the same amount for me." I started using occasionally, which led to daily. By 1989, I was drinking and snorting cocaine every day. Cocaine had such control over me that at the end I cared about nothing other than cocaine. Not my family or my business—nothing but making sure I had my cocaine.

When my children reached the age of kindergarten, I joined a temple, enrolled them in religious school, and became a twice-a-year Jew. I really had no regard for religion. I remember snorting cocaine in the men's bathroom during High Holy Day services.

The last day I used, my fourteen-year-old daughter came home from Sunday school. I was supposed to go out to lunch with her, but I heard her and her mother talking about me. I chased my daughter around the house, she locked her bedroom door, and I kicked it in. The police were called, and I was confronted about my use. My family asked me to leave and to get help.

I went to detox and slept for three days. They sent me to a treatment center. I relapsed in treatment because I was not there for myself; I was there for my family. My counselor said, "You have two choices. You can go home and the next hit may kill you, or you can go to a long-term treatment center for professionals." That was the day my recovery started.

My first encounter with God took place on November 26, 1989. I was forty-four years old, in detox for the second time in three weeks, and prayed to a God I did not believe in: "Take this from me. I cannot do this anymore." About the same time I was introduced to the twelve-step program. The program relies on the addict/alcoholic to believe in a power greater than themselves and turn their lives over to that God.

The first step is to surrender, admit defeat. The second step introduces the idea that we need to believe in a power greater than ourselves. The third step encourages us to turn our will and lives over to this power. When I was in that first treatment center, I asked my rabbi to come and talk to me. He suggested I raise my hand toward God and ask God to help me. So at first, my higher power was a hand. But over a period of time I came to believe in a power greater than myself, and today I call that Power, God.

The twelve-step program is one of spirituality, not religion. As I learned in recovery, there is a great deal of difference between religion and spirituality. In the rooms of recovery, we say: "Religion is for those people afraid of going to hell. Spirituality is for those of us who have been there."

My real connection with Judaism came when my sponsor—who is Jewish—gave me the daily read *Living Each Day* by Rabbi Abraham Twerski. *Living Each Day* has taught me more about Judaism than anything else. And the eighth and ninth steps in the recovery program are the same as we observe during Yom Kippur. Those sins committed against God must be forgiven by God. For those sins committed against another person, the recovering person must ask that person for forgiveness.

As I reconnected with my Judaism, I found new meaning in the stories and holidays. I identified with Jacob, as I had been just like him. I wanted what I wanted and would go to any length to get it, not caring what harm I did along the way. I saw Rosh HaShanah as the opportunity to begin anew and start a new year. I also viewed Passover in a new light: As the Jews were freed from slavery, I was freed from ADDICTION. Even my prayers reflected my recovery: The love of my life, Joyce, whom I married after I became sober and who passed away several years ago, used to ask me if I was praying to the God of Abraham, Isaac, and Jacob. My answer was no: I am praying to my higher power.

It is hard for an addict/alcoholic to get sober. All my life I thought the world owed me something and that I was entitled to do anything I wanted. It was only through recovery that I learned I had to live life on life's terms, not mine. It was very important for me to throw myself into the program of recovery, to surround myself with only recovering people. By going to meetings, working the steps, and surrounding myself with only sober people, I had the foundation to stay sober.

When I first got sober, I was ashamed of my past. I mostly kept my recovery a secret. But the longer I stayed sober, the more readily I was able to tell new acquaintances that I was in recovery. When a new rabbi joined my congregation, I told him immediately so that he knew and that I was available if anyone came to him needing help with addiction. Since then, he has asked me to talk to congregants about their own or a child's problem with addiction. Also, we changed what was in the Kiddush cup from wine to grape juice and have grape juice available at all of our Kiddushes and Onegs.

I think that rabbis and the organized Jewish community can do more to understand and welcome people in recovery. Please understand it is a disease and the person CANNOT JUST STOP. Please make sure that grape juice is available at all temple and community functions. And if asked, "Can the temple or community organization house a recovery meeting?" please be supportive in making that decision.

Early recovery was difficult. The disease kept telling me it was okay to use, to take, to drink, to use a drug. I am sober over twenty-nine years, and the disease still talks to me. My disease still tells me it is okay to do the wrong thing. I have only a daily reprieve, and this reprieve depends on my spirituality.

Lost in TV Land

Monique Mayer

I'd never thought of myself as being an addict. I've never taken drugs or smoked a joint. I steer clear of gambling and have seen how it almost destroyed the life of one of my congregants.

My life is pretty good. I have a loving partner; a warm, bright home; a few pets for comic relief and cuddles; and I like being the rabbi in my community. That said, when my rabbinic work begins to set me on edge, when I am overwhelmed by the problems that people share with me layered over my own, or when I am drowning in paperwork and e-mails and my to-do list, I become an addict.

My addiction is television. I go to our lounge, flop down on the sofa, and flip on the TV, scrolling through the innumerable options to binge-watch whatever series matches my mood. Subscription or catch-up services are dangerous because as soon as I finish one series, I'm on the hunt for another one. There are so many choices that—if left to my own devices—I could watch TV for the rest of my life.

The television keeps my brain from settling on my problems. It gives the illusion of relaxation. And it is an illusion. Jerry Mander, in his *Four Arguments for the Elimination of Television* (1978) writes that "television is not relaxing" and that "drugs provide escape while passing for experience and relaxation. Television does as well." Viewing actually does the opposite of what we think it does. It "inhibits your ability to think . . . and leads to a more exhausted mind."[1] Television pours images into our heads, taking up space and repressing other thought processes. So whatever reprieve from my problems I may have while viewing, they lurch back into my consciousness as soon as the television is turned off. And then

---

RABBI MONIQUE MAYER (Leo Baeck College 2009) is the spiritual leader of Bristol and West Progressive Jewish Congregation in the UK and author of the Liberal Movement's Ba'alei Tefillah program. She serves as a facilitator for the Season of Mussar course from The Mussar Institute.

I'm so wound up I can't go to sleep, lying there with my eyes fluttering between open and closed, debating whether to get up and watch something else.

Television has always been in the background for me since I was a child. I was a shy kid, and asthma and other childhood illnesses isolated me. I consumed hours of Saturday morning cartoons, afternoon horror movies, and Saturday night sitcoms. As a teenager, I used to do my homework in front of the television. It was my way of drowning out destructive thoughts or worries about my parents (who eventually divorced). Down through the years, television has continued to be my "drug of choice," as a way to self-medicate.

What appears to trigger my addiction is low self-esteem and isolation. I've battled with low self-esteem most of my life. Add to that the fact that I'm an American living in the UK now for over fifteen years away from family, who are in California. My rabbinate is in a small congregation away from major cities where there is a high concentration of Jewish people, culture, food, etc. Most of my dearest friends are in the United States; those in this country are at least two hours away because I met them either in rabbinical school in London or around London.

So instead of initiating contact with potential friends or reaching out to strengthen relationships I already have, I find myself getting caught up in the television show *Bones* and the fictional relationships between the characters. I feel like I know them as friends, and it gives me a warm fuzzy feeling akin to what I get when I spend a few hours with a friend over a cuppa or a nice meal. But the feeling I get from watching the television is only temporary, and my "relationships" with the characters are not real. And then my viewing becomes a vicious cycle because, when I binge watch, I might sit in front of the television until 1 or 2 in the morning. And then the guilt sets in; guilt about how I wasted my time, disappointed others by avoiding responsibilities, ignored friends or congregants, and—honestly—didn't even have the benefit of experiencing joy in the process.

Having a television addiction, like any addiction, means stopping is difficult. As I continue to binge, I become more exhausted, which challenges my ability to manage my responsibilities as a congregational rabbi. I end up skipping parts or all of my morning self-care regimen, I skip meals, I become more irritable and impatient with people who need me to show them patience and compassion . . . congregants, friends, my partner. Moreover, my ability to self-censor diminishes, and I am susceptible to expressing things to people I would never say when I am at full strength and taking proper care of myself.

As this behavior continues, I become more anxious, suffer panic-attacks, and start to doubt my abilities and my role as a spiritual leader. Up until I wrote this article, almost no one knew this about me and—to be honest—my partner doesn't even know the whole of it. I've mentioned my panic attacks, but don't want to burden him with the full story.

So, you may ask, what's the solution? How do you get out of the cycle of binge/exhaustion/ineffectiveness/self-sabotage?

There is no simple answer to those questions, but I can only respond by sharing what I've tried. No one technique works in isolation, but implementing all of them helps me to shift from binge/numb mode to more positive coping strategies.

Keeping a Daily Routine

The most important thing I can do is look after myself. Because self-care is one of the first things to go when my addiction kicks in, I need to discipline myself to change my habits and lifestyle. Sometimes it's as simple as following a checklist. I generally keep it in my head, but often I'm more successful when it's visual and in a prominent place. This means getting up at a reasonable hour, having a decent breakfast, meditating, showering, and going out for fresh air. My television addiction encourages general inactivity and poor diet. So ensuring that I eat three proper meals is essential.

And, of course, getting enough quality sleep is key. To do that I set a limit on watching and aim to go to bed by a certain time. I check my watch and say out loud, "Okay, two episodes and then the TV goes off" (somehow saying it aloud makes it more of a commitment). When I feel myself being seduced to watch more, I ask myself, "What time is it and what do I need to be doing right now?" Generally the answer at that point is "go to bed."

Getting Fresh Air/Exercise

When I get sucked into the television, I forget about the fact that there's a real world outside that I actually enjoy. The number of sunny days I've spent inside is embarrassing. If I make sure to take a walk first thing in the morning, I can clear my head and move my body (my dog is grateful, too). Then I am more able to sit down at my desk having enjoyed nature and fresh air. The other thing that pulls me out of a TV binge funk is to go dancing. I've never been a sports-oriented person, but I love to dance. Dancing is one of the closest things to prayer for me because I become completely at one with the movement and the music, and it is pure joy.

Keeping an Uncluttered Workspace

I collect papers. They seem to multiply overnight, threatening to take over both of my offices, synagogue and home. As things pile up on my desks, my immediate response is to close the door and walk away, and—of course—turn on the tube. In the meantime, I spend more and more time looking for things I can't find. If my workspace is clear and organized, I'm less likely to want to numb out. I'm a visual person, so items I need to access regularly I post on an oversized bulletin board directly in front of me at my desk. Every so often I clear it to keep it organized as well. And I intersperse pictures that lift my heart and a helpful phrase as one reminder of my spiritual practice. My current phrase is "Nurture my heart to speak my truth."

Maintaining a Daily Spiritual Practice

I mentioned under "Keeping a Daily Routine" that I meditate in the morning. I've practiced meditation since I was a teenager. And although the type of meditation has changed, the effect remains constant: I'm calmer, more focused, and less ruffled by challenges during the day. Most mornings I sit for a thirty-minute guided meditation known as a "body scan," in which I focus on body sensations in a planned progression. When I first sit down, my heart is racing and my mind is swirling around all the "better things" I could be doing with the half hour. But, truly, the only thing I need to be doing is meditating. Focusing on body sensations grounds me. Lately I've added some Hebrew chanting. It feels good to express myself in a Jewish way, and I find that music really does soothe my heart and my soul. The other aspect of my spiritual practice is Musar (Jewish ethics). The helpful phrase I post on my bulletin board is often tied to this practice, and I find that the Musar emphasis on improving the world around me also moves me from passivity to active participation.

Remembering You Are Not Alone

The last thing I do is get support. I've been working with the same life/professional coach for about a year and a half. She has helped me to look at my behaviors and how I can generate energy for change and have more success on a day-to-day basis. This is not about high-profile success; it's about the small, incremental steps that help me move from self-sabotage and doubt to a place of strength and empowerment. Additionally, I am in a rabbinic support group that has met quarterly for six or seven years now. I also have two really close friends with whom I can share these challenges. I don't feel embarrassed or inadequate with them; I share my feelings and my difficulties and then we talk about how I can move in a more positive direction.

Final Thoughts

Overcoming television addiction is an ongoing struggle. On my days of overwhelm, it would be much easier to give in and numb out. Yet I also don't want to spend my life being the person I turn into when I succumb to the pull of the screen: passive, anxious, overwhelmed, depressed. I would rather live life to its fullest and enjoy both the busy and quiet moments in ways that are life-affirming. Keeping a daily routine, getting fresh air and exercising, keeping an uncluttered workspace, maintaining a daily spiritual practice, and drawing on others for support enable me to develop, reinforce, and integrate the best parts of myself. They enable me to ignore and abandon the lure of television and be the best person, partner, friend, and rabbi I know I can and want to be.

Note

1. Jerry Mander, *Four Arguments for the Elimination of Television* (New York: William Morrow, 1978), 211, 213.

With the Blink of an Eye, I Finally Saw the Light

Edwin Goldberg

> *"Illness is the night side of life, a more onerous citizenship. Everyone who is born holds dual citizenship, in the kingdom of the well and in the kingdom of the sick. Although we all prefer to use the good passport, sooner or later each of us is obliged, at least for a spell, to identify ourselves as citizens of that other place."*
>
> — Susan Sontag, *Illness as Metaphor*

So, I was going to begin this essay in a "safe" way, recounting the probably apocryphal story of when the great professor of Jewish mysticism, Gershom Scholem, pulled out a ham sandwich during a class at Hebrew University. When a student inquired why a teacher of Judaism would break kashrut, he supposedly responded, "If I were teaching geometry would I have to be a triangle?" In other words, does a person who writes about emotional distress and addiction have to suffer as well from such maladies?

But anyone reading this essay deserves a more honest answer. At the risk of sounding like a dilettante in matters of personal suffering and addiction, I will share my truth. I am an addict. The worst kind, perhaps. Undiagnosed and relatively bereft of support. That is not to say I have not spent much of my inner life and a fair amount of my actual earthly activities involved in dealing with my addiction. But I don't want to make light of those with far more serious maladies and consequences of their conditions. So please know what I will share is not in any way meant to compare myself to others. And if there is still a whiff of such comparison then I hope you understand my intent is merely to explain myself.

RABBI EDWIN GOLDBERG, D.H.L., served as the coordinating editor of *Mishkan HaNefesh,* the new Reform High Holy Day prayer book. He served as the senior rabbi of Temple Sholom of Chicago from 2013 to 2019 and now serves as rabbi of Congregation Beth Shalom of The Woodlands, near Houston, Texas.

How am I an addict? I believe I am addicted to avoiding pain. This is probably common as addictions go. I suppose my greatest pain I face is neurotic guilt. This guilt is produced by two unrelated historical facts: (1) My mother should have died at Auschwitz. She was saved from this fate and I have always felt the need to do something with my life to reflect the miracle of her surviving. (2) My parents lost their first child to cancer when he was seven. Had he not died I never would have been born. I feel a lot of guilt for this fact even though of course I had nothing to do with his demise.

That is why I consider this suffering neurotic. However, I suppose every human being was created as a miracle and there is some existential core to my suffering. Nevertheless, I think I am outside the range of normal neurosis.

I have dealt with my fear of pain by trying to numb myself. My agent of choice has been neither drugs nor alcohol, although I enjoy the effects of liquor in moderation. I have confronted, or rather not confronted, my fear by the legal but ultimately unfulfilling practice of buying things. Not in order to go in debt but to occupy my mind with something other than reality. For many years I bought wristwatches. And then I would give them away. I kicked that habit and started buying briefcases. I would also give them away. Goodwill really loves me. At this point I own two watches and one briefcase, so I feel pretty "sober."

What changed? My exposure to the Institute for Jewish Spirituality slowly enabled me to appreciate the gift that pain can bring if we address it and stop numbing ourselves from it. Mindful meditation is very important to me. As is a practice of what I will call "the essence of strategy is denial." Saying no to things creates a space to say yes to what matters most. But every day is a struggle. And I literally live next door to a luggage store!!! (My back door also opens onto the part of the street with at least fifteen watch stores. God enjoys toying with me!)

When I was a rabbi in Los Angeles in the 1990s, I would teach at L'Chaim, a Jewish twelve-step support group, but I always felt I was an impostor. I got more out of the discussion after the text I shared than I did as a teacher. I had no way to express why at the time this was so but now I do.

I could say more about my inner struggles, but I fear one may think that perhaps my condition is too slight to consider. I admit I have suffered little from the outside besides my poor wife's confusion about why I need such things. And why they disappear. I am not the first annoying spouse with a collection addiction. Nevertheless, I do feel that sacred vulnerability that comes from knowing that whatever I do will never be enough. And it eats at me.

I used to think of myself as an owner of one passport, to paraphrase Susan Sontag, that of the emotionally strong and perpetually mentally fit. I had yet to suffer my only one bout of depression, again never diagnosed, when after my father died, I tried to act tough. Six months later the depression set in. I now take anti-anxiety meds, albeit a low dose, and really am not bothered by ups or downs. Nevertheless, I have learned a lot in these last few years about the second passport we all carry. And this land of suffering, brokenness, and vulnerability, of truth, is a very important place.

I have also often escaped into other people's writings to avoid direct confrontation with the pain, although sometimes what I read is very helpful. The late M. Scott Peck—a mentor of mine, albeit only through reading him—wrote that mental health is a dedication to reality at all costs. I often paraphrase him and say that spirituality is a dedication to reality at all costs. Increasingly I am enamored of reality. Which means I find its opposite—what Hamlet calls "seeming"—to be increasingly intolerable.

I am grateful that worship practices and sacred texts in Judaism (although not all of them) are so powerful in this regard. As the great and late Rabbi Alan Lew put it, "This is real, and you are completely unprepared." He was speaking in the context of the Days of Awe except of course he really meant every moment.

Another great teacher for me in my enlightenment has been the Baal Shem Tov. Born in the backwaters of the Carpathian Mountains, in what in the eighteenth century was part of Poland and is now in Ukraine, his teachings are an invitation inward, a map that allows us access to premodern and even prehistoric modes of religiosity, and to the transforming secrets of the Jewish esoteric tradition. The Besht believed that we find God in the ongoing story of one's own life, and he believed in the value of each individual life—a recipe for an engaged mystic, one who is of the world rather than withdrawn from it. Following his lead, even our struggles are to be seen in the context of the godly. Difficulties do not come from God, but God is part of our struggles with them.

The Baal Shem Tov did not leave behind many teachings but there are numerous stories told about him. Here is one: After he had been teaching for quite some years, his followers asked him, "Rebbe, what is different since you have come and shared your wisdom with us?" And he replied, "Before I came, when a thief tried to enter the house they would shout and scream and try and scare the thief away. Now that I have come"—the Baal Shem Tov went on to say—"when a thief tries to enter the house, they lie in wait. They trap the thief and they hand the thief over to the proper authorities." So that's the change: Shouting and trying to scare the thief away or letting the thief in before turning the thief over to the proper authorities. Of course, this is not an argument about literal thieves and literal houses. Rather it is a question about the nature of the human soul. What is going on in this parable of the Baal Shem Tov? Well the house is the body: me or you. And the thief? In Jungian terms the thief is our shadow: our messy stuff—our failures, our shortcomings, our embarrassments. It is the stuff we keep hidden from our conscious minds. It's not just the things we have done, but also the things we are drawn to do; the thief is the temptation to do unhealthy acts, our lusts and our temptations to hurt ourselves and others.

The ancient Rabbis saw the thief as the *yetzer hara* (the evil inclination). In Yiddish we might call it the schmutz. So in essence the Baal Shem Tov is saying this: Before I came, when people felt the evil inclination coming upon them, they would try and scare the evil inclination away. Now that I have come, he says, we let the schmutz in, we acknowledge that it can't be scared away, and we hand it over to the authorities. We work it over, and we own our schmutz. This is the great contribution of the Baal Shem Tov: helping us to "own our schmutz." Shouting and screaming and trying to scare the thief away is an immature attitude, and it won't work; the thief will duck around the corner and plot another heist. We are instead asked to admit that there is something to learn from letting the thief in. You see, there is always something to learn from our evil inclinations, from all of our actions, even the failures. Of course mindfulness is more than paying attention to the world. It is specifically about how we work so hard to avoid our inner truths, our schmutz, and how we might learn to confront our schmutz instead.

I have tried mindfulness meditation throughout the years. The basic discipline in this meditation is to concentrate on your breath and let your subconscious come to the fore. I always found it hard to do because it's hard to let go of one's conscious ego. Finally, last year I found myself more successful at the practice, but I was in for a nasty surprise. My meditation did not make me feel relaxed or good. Indeed, it seemed to be bothering me. I felt worse, not better, after meditation. Then I read Jeff Roth's book on Judaism and meditation and his words helped me. He observed that mindfulness meditation often is unpleasant precisely when it works. For him, the practice is like revealing all the garbage under the kitchen sink. It stinks. But here's the thing: when you see the garbage and you deal with it, you take it out of the house and you dispose of it. And that's a good thing. After all, it's better when it smells outside the house than inside the house!

My struggle with confronting reality will never end. Alas the burden of addiction. But I also take comfort in the teaching of another Chasidic work, the *Tanya* of Rabbi Shneur Zalman of Liadi. In chapter 26 he writes:

> As you arouse your heart by facing your shadow you may find yourself engulfed in a deep and troubling sadness. If so, do not be alarmed. Such sadness arises from and operates within the shadow of self, yet it draws energy from your innate yet hidden desire for God and godliness and thus kindles your passion for self-transformation. To work with sadness, say to yourself: "I feel utterly removed from God, yet within me is the light of God desiring only to return to God . . . Therefore I will cry out to God and God will end the exile of my two related selves. Shalom will come."

God. A Higher Power. However we situate ourselves in a world with great deception and lies, our heritage beckons us to see the light of truth and live for the first time in authentic wholeness and hope. We can say goodbye to the avoidance and addictions and hello to a more honest journey. It is sacred and scary but as real as it gets. As Rabbi Norman Hirsh has written, "We don't like leaving, but God loves becoming."[1]

Note

1. *Mishkan T'filah*, 231.

MAAYANOT (PRIMARY SOURCES)

T'filah Zakah: A Yom Kippur Eve Self-Evaluation from Head to Toe
Translation, Texts, and Commentary for Study and Meditation

Audrey R. Korotkin

Introduction

On the eve of Yom Kippur, as twilight approaches, Jews throughout the world gather in congregations large and small to prepare their bodies and souls for a twenty-four-hour period of fasting, praying, and reflection on their words and deeds, in accordance with the Rabbinic directive, "You shall afflict your souls."[1] The liturgical rubric most often associated with this time is *Kol Nidrei*, the hauntingly sung plea to God asking for divine forgiveness should we, despite our best efforts, find ourselves unable to fulfill our promises of elevated thoughts and behavior.

Yet we may overlook a prayer to God that immediately precedes *Kol Nidrei* (and follows the donning of the tallit) in traditional *machzorim*—and, for the first time in a *machzor* representing North American Reform Judaism, the CCAR's *Mishkan HaNefesh*—that encourages us to think deeply about how we have used every part of our body, for good or bad, before we embark on such an audacious request of God.

T'filah Zakah takes us on an intensely personal journal through our own bodies, inside and out, top to bottom. It is both a plea and a confession that forces us to consider and acknowledge how we have used each limb and each organ in service to God—or not.

RABBI DR. AUDREY R. KOROTKIN is the spiritual leader of Temple Beth Israel, Altoona, Pennsylvania, and earned both her *s'michah* (1999) and Ph.D. (2018) at HUC-JIR, Cincinnati. She is a longtime member of the CCAR Responsa Committee and a member of the board of the Solomon B. Freehof Institute for Progressive Halakhah. She writes frequently about Jewish ritual and legal issues for ReformJudaism.org.

Composed by Abraham ben Yechiel Danzig (Lithuanian rabbi, 1747–1820), *T'filah Zakah* appears in his widely influential *Chayei Adam*, a halachic guidebook that updates the material of two and a half centuries earlier in the *Shulchan Aruch*'s *Orach Chayim*. This treatise, designed to be accessible to lay people as well as to rabbis, deals with the laws of daily conduct, as well as prayers for Shabbat and holy days. Rabbi Abraham emphasizes the ethical imperatives of the mitzvot as well as their practical details.

The full version of Danzig's petitionary prayer was widely adopted in High Holy Day prayer books and appears in traditional contemporary *machzorim* such as that published by ArtScroll.[2] The published version of the CCAR's *Mishkan HaNefesh* includes an English-language adaptation written by the editors entitled "Prayer for Purity and Worthiness" preceding *Kol Nidrei*.[3] But early on in the editorial process, the core editorial team envisioned a fuller Hebrew-English version culled directly from Danzig's original text. As the leader of the team of talented rabbinic scholars providing the "below the line" commentary for the *machzor*, I took on the task of an extensive annotation of such a presentation of *T'filah Zakah*. I offer it now, along with my own translation, based on the Hebrew text as it was given to us in 2011 and with the permission of the CCAR, as a private meditation as well as a study text for individuals and groups alike. All commentary and translations are mine except where noted; all *Tanach* translations are from the New Jewish Publication Society edition. The footnotes to the text itself draw attention to allusions to traditional sources, while the annotations that follow provide a richer insight into particular elements of Danzig's prayer.

Such a detailed evaluation of ourselves at this already emotion-drenched moment in our liturgical observance can leave us feeling exposed and vulnerable. Will God hear my plea? Will God answer with a "yes" and the divine embrace we seek?

As Dudley Weinberg wrote, "We want to deserve what is given to us undeserved, what is conferred by God on faith, so to speak, through His grace. We may never succeed perfectly in this endeavor, but we desperately desire to succeed. If it were not so, no man would ever feel guilty about anything."[4]

Thus, the power of *T'filah Zakah* is in its deeply personal tone—its "I" language, which switches to "we" language only at the end as a segue into *Kol Nidrei*, which immediately follows. The worshiper acknowledges to God in clear, simple terms: I have misused the gifts

You have bestowed upon me and have shamed Your great name. But know, God, that I acted out of weakness, not out of rebellion, and I need Your strength now to guide me onto a better path.

If each of us takes these words truly to heart, we need not worry that our request of *Kol Nidrei*, asking God to annul our unkept promises, will be considered frivolous or dishonest by the Holy One of Blessing, Compassion and Forgiveness.

For those who wear the tallit:

בָּרוּךְ אַתָּה יְיָ אֱלֹהֵֽינוּ מֶֽלֶךְ הָעוֹלָם אֲשֶׁר קִדְּשָֽׁנוּ בְּמִצְוֹתָיו, וְצִוָּֽנוּ לְהִתְעַטֵּף בַּצִּיצִת.

Praised are You, *Adonai* our God, Sovereign of the Universe, who has brought us to a consciousness of holiness through Your mitzvot, as you command us to envelop ourselves in the embrace of these fringed garments.

T'filah Zakah

רִבּוֹן כָּל הָעוֹלָמִים, וְאַתָּה בָּרֵאתָ אֶת הָאָדָם לְהֵטִיב לוֹ בְּאַחֲרִיתוֹ; וּבָרֵאתָ לוֹ שְׁנֵי יְצָרִים, יֵֽצֶר טוֹב וְיֵֽצֶר הָרָע, כְּדֵי שֶׁתִּהְיֶה הַבְּחִירָה בְּיָדוֹ לִבְחוֹר בְּטוֹב אוֹ בְרָע, וּכְדֵי לָֽתֶת לוֹ שָׂכָר טוֹב עַל טוֹב בְּחִירָתוֹ. כִּי כֵן גְּזֵרָה חָכְמָתֶֽךָ, כְּמוֹ שֶׁכָּתוּב: רְאֵה נָתַֽתִּי לְפָנֶֽיךָ הַיּוֹם אֶת הַחַיִּים וְאֶת הַטּוֹב וְאֶת הַמָּֽוֶת וְאֶת הָרָע, וּבָחַרְתָּ בַּחַיִּים. וְעַתָּה אֱלֹהַי, לֹא שָׁמַֽעְתִּי לְקוֹלֶֽךָ, וְהָלַֽכְתִּי בַּעֲצַת הַיֵּֽצֶר הָרָע וּבְדַרְכֵי לִבִּי, וּמָאַֽסְתִּי בְטוֹב וּבָחַֽרְתִּי בְרָע.

Sovereign of all the worlds, You have created each of us so that we[5] may be rewarded when our lives have come to an end.[6] You have implanted within us two inclinations—the inclination to good and the inclination to evil—so that the choice would be in our hands whether we turn to goodness or wickedness, and so that we would be rewarded with goodness when we choose well. For this is the wisdom of your decree, as Scripture teaches us: *See, I have laid out before you today both life and good, and death and evil, that you choose life.*[7] But in this moment, my God, I must confess that I have not heeded your call; I have followed the counsel of the wicked inclination and the paths of my own desires, rejecting good and choosing evil.

בָּרֵֽאתָ בִּי מֽוֹחַ וְלֵב וּבָהֶם חוּשׁ הַמַּחֲשָׁבָה, לַחֲשׁוֹב מַחֲשָׁבוֹת טוֹבוֹת וְהִרְהוּרִים טוֹבִים, וְלֵב לְהָבִין דִּבְרֵי קָדְשֶֽׁךָ, וּלְהִתְפַּלֵּל וּלְבָרֵךְ כָּל

הַבְּרָכוֹת בְּמַחֲשָׁבָה טְהוֹרָה. וַאֲנִי טִמֵּאתִי אוֹתָם בְּהִרְהוּרִים רָעִים וּמַחֲשָׁבוֹת זָרוֹת.

You have gifted me with a mind and a heart with which to form ideas, so that I might formulate good thoughts and kind intentions; a heart with which to understand Your holy words so that I might recite my prayers and blessings with purity of purpose.[8] And yet I have defiled them with evil intentions and ignorant thoughts.

בָּרָאתָ בִּי עֵינַיִם, וּבָהֶם חוּשׁ הָרְאוּת, לִרְאוֹת בָּהֶם מַה שֶּׁכָּתוּב בַּתּוֹרָה, וּלְקַדֵּשׁ אוֹתָם בִּרְאִיַּת כָּל דָּבָר שֶׁבִּקְדֻשָּׁה. וְהִזְהַרְתָּ בְּתוֹרָתֶךָ: וְלֹא תָתוּרוּ אַחֲרֵי לְבַבְכֶם וְאַחֲרֵי עֵינֵיכֶם.

You have gifted me with eyes, and with them the sense of sight, so that I might see through them what is written in Your Torah, imbuing them with sanctity as they look upon every holy word. As you cautioned in Your Torah: *So that you do not follow your heart and eyes.*[9]

בָּרָאתָ בִּי אָזְנַיִם, לִשְׁמֹעַ דִּבְרֵי קְדֻשָּׁה, וְדִבְרֵי תוֹרָה. אוֹי לִי, כִּי טִמֵּאתִי אוֹתָן בִּשְׁמֹעַ דִּבְרֵי נְבָלָה, וְלָשׁוֹן הָרַע, וְכָל דְּבָרִים אֲסוּרִים. אוֹי לָאָזְנַיִם שֶׁכָּךְ שׁוֹמְעוֹת.

You have gifted me with ears with which to hear words of holiness and words of Torah. Woe is me, for I have defiled them by listening to obscenities and evil language and all sorts of forbidden talk. Woe to the ears that hear such things!

בָּרָאתָ בִּי פֶּה וְלָשׁוֹן וְשִׁנַּיִם וְחֵיךְ וְגָרוֹן, וְנָתַתָּ בָּהֶם כֹּחַ לְדַבֵּר בָּהֶם חֲמִשָּׁה מוֹצָאוֹת הָאוֹתִיּוֹת הַקְּדוֹשִׁים שֶׁל א"ב, אֲשֶׁר בָּהֶן בָּרָאתָ שָׁמַיִם וָאָרֶץ וּמְלוֹאָהּ, וּבָהֶם אֲרַגְתָּ תּוֹרָתְךָ הַקְּדוֹשָׁה. וּבְכֹחַ הַדִּבּוּר, הִבְדַּלְתָּ אֶת הָאָדָם מִן הַבְּהֵמָה, וַאֲפִלּוּ כַּבְּהֵמָה לֹא הָיִיתִי, כִּי טִמֵּאתִי פִּי בְּדִבְרֵי נְבָלָה, בְּלָשׁוֹן הָרַע, בִּשְׁקָרִים, לֵיצָנוּת, רְכִילוּת, מַחֲלֹקֶת, מַלְבִּין פְּנֵי חֲבֵרוֹ, מְקַלֵּל אֶת חֲבֵרוֹ, מִתְכַּבֵּד בִּקְלוֹן חֲבֵרוֹ.

You have gifted me with a mouth and tongue and teeth and palate and throat, enabling them to articulate the five different utterances of the holy letters[10] of the *alef-bet*, through which you created heaven and earth in all their fullness, and with which You assembled Your holy Torah. Through the power of speech, You differentiated human from beast—and yet I am not even a beast, for I have defiled my mouth with obscenities and with evil language; with lies, mockery, and gossip; sowing discord, shaming others, cursing others, and glorifying myself at the expense of others.

בָּרָאתָ בִּי יָדַיִם וְחוּשׁ הַמִּשּׁוּשׁ לַעֲסוֹק בָּהֶם בְּמִצְוֹת, וַאֲנִי טִמֵּאתִי אוֹתָם בְּמִשְׁמוּשִׁין שֶׁל אִסּוּר, וּלְהַכּוֹת בְּאֶגְרוֹף רֶשַׁע, וּלְהָרִים יָד לְהַכּוֹת.

You have gifted me with hands and the sense of touch, that I might engage in the performance of mitzvot. And yet I have defiled them through forbidden contact, striking with a vicious fist[11] and raising a hand to cause harm.

בָּרָאתָ בִּי רַגְלַיִם לַהֲלוֹךְ לְכָל דְּבַר מִצְוָה, וַאֲנִי טִמֵּאתִי אוֹתָן, בְּרַגְלַיִם מְמַהֲרוֹת לָרוּץ לָרָעָה.

You have gifted me with legs with which to walk the path of mitzvah. And yet I have defiled them, turning them into legs that hasten to cause trouble.

מִשַּׁשְׁתִּי אֶת כָּל אֵבָרַי וּמְצָאתִי אוֹתָם בַּעֲלֵי מוּמִין, מִכַּף רַגְלִי וְעַד רֹאשִׁי, אֵין בִּי מְתֹם.

I have examined every one of my limbs and have found them to be defective; from the sole of my foot up to my head, there is nothing sound within me.[12]

וְלִהְיוֹת שֶׁיָּדַעְתִּי, שֶׁכִּמְעַט אֵין צַדִּיק בָּאָרֶץ אֲשֶׁר לֹא יֶחֱטָא בֵּין אָדָם לַחֲבֵרוֹ, בְּמָמוֹן אוֹ בְגוּף, בְּמַעֲשֶׂה אוֹ בְדִבּוּר פֶּה, וְעַל זֶה דָוֶה לִבִּי בְּקִרְבִּי, כִּי עַל חֵטְא שֶׁבֵּין אָדָם לַחֲבֵרוֹ אֵין יוֹם הַכִּפּוּרִים מְכַפֵּר עַד שֶׁיְּרַצֶּה אֶת חֲבֵרוֹ. וְעַל זֶה נִשְׁבָּר לִבִּי בְּקִרְבִּי וְרָחֲפוּ עַצְמוֹתַי, כִּי אֲפִלּוּ אֵין יוֹם הַמִּיתָה מְכַפֵּר. וְלָכֵן אֲנִי מַפִּיל תְּחִנָּתִי לְפָנֶיךָ, שֶׁתִּתְרַחֵם עָלַי, וְתִתְּנֵנִי לְחֵן וּלְחֶסֶד וּלְרַחֲמִים בְּעֵינֶיךָ, וּבְעֵינֵי כָּל בְּנֵי אָדָם. וְהִנְנִי מוֹחֵל בִּמְחִילָה גְמוּרָה, לְכָל מִי שֶׁחָטָא נֶגְדִּי, בֵּין בְּגוּפוֹ וּבֵין בְּמָמוֹנוֹ, אוֹ שֶׁדִּבֶּר עָלַי לָשׁוֹן הָרָע, וַאֲפִלּוּ הוֹצָאַת שֵׁם רָע. וּכְשֵׁם שֶׁאֲנִי מוֹחֵל לְכָל אָדָם, כֵּן תִּתֵּן אֶת חִנִּי בְּעֵינֵי כָּל אָדָם שֶׁיִּמְחֲלוּ לִי בִּמְחִילָה גְמוּרָה.

Yes, I do know that there is hardly a totally righteous person on earth who never commits a sin between a person and his neighbor, whether monetarily or physically, by deed or by word. Regardless of this, my heart aches so within me, because for a sin committed against one's neighbor, Yom Kippur does not atone until one makes peace with one's neighbor.[13] Because this is so, my heart is broken within me and bones shudder, for even the day of death does not atone. Therefore do I fall in supplication before You. Have mercy upon me! Help me to find favor and kindness and compassion in Your eyes and in the eyes of every single person. I, in turn, extend complete forgiveness to anyone who has sinned against me, whether physically or monetarily, or who has gossiped against me or slandered me. And just as I forgive them all, so may You grant me favor in all of their eyes, so that every one of them may grant me complete forgiveness.

וּלְפִי שֶׁכָּל זֶה גָּלוּי וְיָדוּעַ לְפָנֶיךָ, כִּי אָדָם אֵין צַדִּיק בָּאָרֶץ, אֲשֶׁר יַעֲשֶׂה טּוֹב, וְלֹא יֶחֱטָא, לָכֵן, בְּרַחֲמֶיךָ הָרַבִּים, נָתַתָּ לָנוּ יוֹם אֶחָד בַּשָּׁנָה, יוֹם אַדִּיר וְקָדוֹשׁ, יוֹם הַכִּפּוּרִים הַזֶּה, הַבָּא עָלֵינוּ לְטוֹבָה, לָשׁוּב לְפָנֶיךָ, וּלְכַפֵּר אֶת כָּל עֲוֹנוֹתֵינוּ, לְטַהֵר אֶתְכֶם, מִכֹּל חַטֹּאתֵיכֶם לִפְנֵי יְיָ תִּטְהָרוּ.

Because this is all revealed and known before You—that there is no one on earth who is fully righteous, who does only good and does not sin[14]—therefore, in Your great compassion, You have given us one day out of the year, one holy and glorious day, this Day of Atonement. May it shower us with goodness, so that we may return to You in atonement, cleansed from all our sins: *You shall be clean before the Lord*.[15]

בָּאנוּ לְפָנֶיךָ בְּלֵב נִשְׁבָּר וְנִדְכֶּה, כַּעֲנִיִּים וְדַלִּים וְרָשִׁים, לְבַקֵּשׁ מִמְּךָ מְחִילָה וּסְלִיחָה וְכַפָּרָה עַל כָּל מַה שֶּׁחָטָאנוּ וְעָוִינוּ וּפָשַׁעְנוּ לְפָנֶיךָ.

We come before you with a heart utterly shattered,[16] as wretches, lowly and destitute, asking Your pardon and forgiveness, and atonement for every way in which we have sinned, transgressed, and rebelled before You.

וִיהִי רָצוֹן מִלְּפָנֶיךָ, אֵל מֶלֶךְ יוֹשֵׁב עַל כִּסֵּא רַחֲמִים, הָרוֹצֶה בִּתְשׁוּבַת רְשָׁעִים, שֶׁתִּתֵּן בְּלִבֵּנוּ וּבְלֵב כָּל עַמְּךָ בֵּית יִשְׂרָאֵל, אַהֲבָתְךָ וְיִרְאָתְךָ, לְיִרְאָה אוֹתְךָ כָּל הַיָּמִים. וּבְתוֹכָם, תְּרַחֵם עַל פּוֹשְׁעֵי עַמְּךָ בֵּית יִשְׂרָאֵל. וְתִתֵּן בְּלִבָּם פַּחַד הֲדַר גְּאוֹנֶךָ, וְהַכְנַע לִבָּם הָאֶבֶן, וְיָשׁוּבוּ לְפָנֶיךָ בְּלֵב שָׁלֵם, כְּמוֹ שֶׁהִבְטַחְתָּ עַל יְדֵי נְבִיאֶיךָ, לְבַל יִדַּח מִמֶּנּוּ נִדָּח.

Now, may it be Your will, God Most High, who sits on the throne of mercy and who desires the repentance of the wicked, that you implant within our heart and the hearts of all your children

T'FILAH ZAKAH

Israel love and awe of You that we may revere You all of our days. Be present in their midst,[17] and show compassion concerning the sins of your people the House of Israel. Place within their hearts reverence for Your great glory. Subdue their hearts of stone, so that they may return to You wholeheartedly as you assured us through Your prophet: *That no one may be kept banished.*[18]

וְטַהֵר רַעְיוֹנֵינוּ וּמַחְשְׁבוֹתֵינוּ, כְּדֵי שֶׁנִּהְיֶה אֲנַחְנוּ דְּבוּקִים בְּךָ תָּמִיד.

Purify our thoughts and desires so that we may cleave to you always.

* * * * *

For those who wear the tallit:

Bless the Lord, O my soul; O Lord, My God, you are very great. You are clothed in glory and majesty; wrapped in a robe of light. You spread the heavens like a tent cloth. (Ps. 104:1–2)

Erev Yom Kippur is the only evening service for which the worshiper is invited to don the tallit; the mitzvah otherwise requires daylight in which to see its fringes. Tonight, we see the fringes through the shining light of God's presence: It beckons us to turn in repentance and be embraced by God's love, like the beacon of a lighthouse guiding sailors through thick fog and hidden obstacles to the safety of harbor.

T'filah Zakah: Commentary

להטיב לו באחריתו   **"You created man to reward him when his life is ended."**

Understanding Rabbi Abraham's desire to imbue Jewish practice with a deep sense of moral integrity, perhaps we could understand this phrase as: "You created man that, when his life is over, he be remembered for goodness." This is, after all, the divine goal of the words that follow: for each of us to use our genetically encoded moral compass to choose a life dedicated to goodness.

כדי שתהיה הבחירה בידו   **"In order that the choice is in his hands."**

The choice, as well as the power, is always in our hands, but the task is not always easy: "Rabbi Levi bar Chama said in the name of Rabbi Shimon ben Lakish: A man should always stir up his impulse to good against the impulse to evil. For as it is written, *So tremble, and sin no more* (Ps. 4:5)" (BT *B'rachot* 5a). Other translations use the word "rage" rather than "tremble," and this may better fit the Rabbis' teaching.

שכר טוב על טוב בחירתו "That he be well-rewarded for his good choice."

Our good reward comes in the act of living righteously with others:

> *Two are better than one, in that they have greater benefit ("sachar tov") from their earnings. For should they fall, one can raise the other; but woe betide him who is alone and falls with no companion to raise him!* (Eccles. 4:9–10).

ראה . . . בחיים (Deut. 30:15–16) *"See, I have laid out before you . . ."*

God has made the path of righteous living accessible to all who make the choice to follow it, as Torah teaches in the preceding verses (Deut. 30:11–14): *Surely, this Instruction which I enjoin upon you this day is not too baffling for you, nor is it beyond reach. It is not in the heavens, that you should say, "Who among us can go up to the heavens and get it for us and impart it to us, that we may observe it?" Neither is it beyond the sea, that you should say, "Who among us can cross to the other side of the sea and get it for us and impart it to us, that we may observe it?" No, the thing is very close to you, in your mouth and in your heart, to observe it.*

Reform Judaism offers this as the scriptural reading for Yom Kippur morning as a parallel text to Leviticus 19, the Holiness Code, on Yom Kippur afternoon. The first is a call to believe that a life of goodness is possible; the second describes how to infuse the ethical tenets of Torah into everyday living.

ובדרכי לבי "And the paths of my desires"

"Give your mind to me, my son; Let your eyes watch my ways (Prov. 23:26). Why did the Holy One of Blessing ask of Israel that their heart and their eyes be directed to God? Because transgression is dependent on them. This is why Scripture teaches *that you do not follow your heart and eyes* (Num. 15:39): The eye and the heart are the two agents of sin" (*B'midbar Rabbah* 10:2).

מחשבות זרות "foreign thoughts."

Are we Jews to be punished for "lusting in our hearts"? Is ours not a faith of deed over creed? Yet the word *zarah*, meaning alien, foreign, or other, is used to describe both what we think and feel (as here) and what we do with those thoughts and feelings (as with Aaron's son's offering *eish zarah* [alien fire] or the worship of idols as *avodah zarah*). Corruption of the heart and mind may well lead us to destructive behavior—and it certainly distracts us from hearing God's call.

Yet this concept of the "other" need not be wanton. When we risk becoming absorbed in our own selfish wishes, tuning out both others and the call of the Divine, Proverbs (27:2) comes to teach us: *Let the mouth of another (zar) praise you, not yours; the lips of a stranger, not your own.*

אזנים לשמוע דברי קדשה "ears with which to hear holy words"

Moses summoned all of Israel and said to them: You have seen all that the Lord did before your very eyes in the land of Egypt, to Pharaoh and to all his courtiers and to his whole country: the wondrous feats that you saw with your own eyes, those prodigious signs and marvels. Yet to this day the Lord has not given you a mind to understand or eyes to see or ears to hear (Deut. 29:1–3).

How is it possible that, in forty years, the Israelites did not fully comprehend the miraculous magnificence of what they experienced in their journey to freedom? Perhaps, in the fullness of a lifetime, they simply overlooked or neglected what had become commonplace.

In our own lives, we may witness God's wonders and gifts all around us but do not take the time to appreciate their holy nature and their intrinsic worth. They may be in the people we meet, the food we enjoy, a poem we read, or the vibrant colors of nature—yet we take them for granted or soon forget about them. These, too, are personal failings that we acknowledge tonight.

דברי נבלה "obscene words"

The Torah uses the word *n'valah* to describe abominations to God, from mere folly to true wickedness and obscenity. It is related to the word *n'veilah*, the unclean animal carcass forbidden to Jews, reflecting the divine directive not only to refrain from engaging in such behavior but to stay far away from it.

חמשה מוצאות האותיות הקדושים של א"ב "Five different utterances of the holy letters of the *alef-bet*."

The Jewish kabbalistic tradition ascribes mystical power to the letters of the Hebrew alphabet; here, the "mouth," "tongue," "teeth," "palate," and "throat" signify not only the five basic sounds made by the *alef-bet* but the power of the words so spoken. Along with the wicked or frivolous acts for which we must atone tonight are the hurtful or base words we have used in attacking others, whether thoughtlessly or intentionally.

* * * * *

The midrashic tradition expounds upon this five-fold utterance in various ways. Here are two examples taken from the English edition of *Sefer Ha-Aggadah: The Book of Legends*:[19]

> The Gemara interprets the five-time use of the phrase *Bless, O my soul*, used in Psalm 103:1, 2, 22 and 104:1, 35:

> "With regard to whom did David say five times, 'Bless the Lord, O my soul'? He said these words with regard to the Holy One and with regard to the soul. As the Holy One fills the entire world, so the soul fills the entire body. As the Holy One sees but is not seen, so the soul sees but is not seen. As the Holy One sustains the entire world, all of it, so the soul sustains the entire body. As the Holy One is pure, so the soul is pure. As the Holy One dwells in chambers that are innermost, so the soul dwells in chambers that are innermost. Therefore let him [i.e., man] who has these five characteristics come and praise Him who has these five characteristics." (BT *B'rachot* 10a)

> The breath of life is called by five names: life, spirit, soul, the solitary, the one that lives on. "Life" refers to the blood, as is said, "For the blood is the life" (Deut. 12:23). "Spirit" refers to its capacity to go up and down, as is said, "Who knoweth the spirit of man whether it goeth upward" (Eccles. 3:21). "Soul" refers to man's distinctive character. "The solitary": while all other parts of the body are pairs, this one is solitary in the body. "The one that lives on": while all other parts die, it lives on in the body.

> The soul fills the entire body, and when a man is asleep, it goes up and draws new life for him from above. (*B'reishit Rabbah* 14:9)

* * * * *

הבדלת את האדם מן הבהמה "You distinguish human from beast"

God's utterances were mighty enough to create the universe and everything in it, including humanity, showing us just what power the simplest words contain. We, unique among the animals in that we were created in the divine image, are commanded to speak as God speaks, as well as to act as God acts: with thoughtfulness and with compassion.

"... **shaming others, cursing others, and glorifying myself at the expense of others.**" מלבין פני חברו, מקלל את חברו, מתכבד בקלון חברו

This concept of the power of trivial, evil, or malicious speech to spread harm is so crucial to our self-evaluation on Yom Kippur that the text here is extensive, as is the volume of Rabbinic literature on which it is based:

> "Rabbi Eliezer said: Let the honor of your fellow be as dear to you as your own." (*Pirkei Avot* 2:10)

* * * * *

From Sefer Ha-Aggadah (English CD):

> "Thou shalt love thy neighbor as thyself" (Lev. 19:18). Rabbi Akiva said: This is a great principle of the Torah. Ben Azzai said: The verse "This is the book of the descendants of Adam . . . him whom God made in His likeness" (Gen. 5:1) utters a principle even greater: You must not say, "Since I have been humiliated, let my fellow man also be humiliated; since I have been cursed, let my neighbor also be cursed." For, as Rabbi Tanhuma pointed out, if you act thus, realize who it is that you are willing to have humiliated—"him whom God made in His likeness."
> (JT *N'darim* 9:4, 41c; *B'reishit Rabbah* 24:7)

* * * * *

באגרף רשע "with a wicked fist"

Because you fast in strife and contention, and you strike with a wicked fist! (Isa. 58:4). For this reason, declares the prophet in Yom Kippur's Haftarah selection, *Your fasting today is not such as to make your voice heard on high* (Isa. 58:4b). Doing without food on this day means nothing to God if it is not accompanied by a parallel abstention from our daily doses of rancor and ill will.

Further, we must present ourselves to God the same on the inside as on the outside. For as our tradition teaches: "Rava said:

Any scholar whose inside is not like his outside is no scholar" (BT *Yoma* 72b).

ברדלים ממהרות לרוץ לרעה "legs that run swiftly to do evil."

Six things the Lord hates; seven are an abomination to Him: a haughty bearing, a lying tongue, hands that shed innocent blood, a mind that hatches evil plots, feet quick to run to evil, a false witness testifying lies, and one who incites brothers to quarrel (Prov. 6:16–19).

In *Pirkei Avot* 4:2, Ben Azzai teaches that one mitzvah leads to another and one transgression leads to another. That is, when you put yourself on one path or another, that road you've chosen becomes more comfortable to travel. With repetition, it becomes easier, even second-nature, to act according to God's will and as God's partner on earth; but also with repetition, it is all too easy to fall into a life of easy lies, arrogance, cheating, and even violence. Emotional, verbal, and physical abuse can become a regular part of everyday behavior—even, or especially, against those with whom you are closest. Recognition, acknowledgment, and ongoing resistance to *aveirah* is imperative, not only to protect ourselves but also others.

שנהיה אנחנו דבוקים בך תמיד "That we may cleave to You always"

The concept of *d'veikut* (attachment) is the ultimate attainment of the true penitent. It is, in the more mystical sense described by Adin Steinsaltz, "a state of mind in which all of one's powers of thought and feeling are exclusively directed to and attached to God," to the point where someone can lose awareness of being separate from God.[20]

The verb is *l'dabek*, to cleave or cling or hold fast, but the conjugation here, *d'vukim*, is better translated as "that we may *be held fast*," suggesting that it is God's powers of mercy, compassion and forgiveness—rather more than our behavior—that will make this happen. To be sure, that's not to obviate the need for our own behavior to change; we are reunited with God when both sides move closer to one another. Yet, as Dudley Weinberg noted (see above in the introduction), we often seek forgiveness before we have earned it.

Yom Kippur is, then, the starting point for being held fast to God. Although our prayer book may say at *N'ilah* that the gates are slowly closing, in fact we can understand that our prayers, attentiveness, and willingness to expose ourselves and our flaws to God in the presence of our congregation constitute the arduous and necessary work that opens the gates a crack, to let us glimpse what is possible if we continue on that path. On Yom Kippur, we take that first step. But God takes a major leap—from the throne of judgment to the throne of mercy—allowing us to "be held fast" while we pursue this life of mitzvah.

* * * * *

Here is a final meditation:

> When the rabbis departed from the academy of Ammi (though some say it was the academy of Rabbi Chanina), they would say to him: May you live to see your world fulfilled; may your latter days be for the life of the world-to-come and your hope for future generations. May your heart act with understanding, your mouth speak wisdom, and your tongue whisper songs. May your eyelids look straight before you, your eyes shine with the light of Torah, and your face glow like the splendor of the heavens. May your lips utter knowledge, your organs rejoice in uprightness, and your steps run to hear the words of the Ancient of Days. (BT *B'rachot* 17a)

Notes

1. BT *Yoma* 74b, from Lev. 16:31.
2. *The Complete ArtScroll Machzor Yom Kippur—Nusach Ashkenaz* (Brooklyn: Mesorah Publications, Ltd., 1986), 38–49.
3. *Mishkan HaNefesh Machzor for the Days of Awe* (New York: CCAR, 2015), vol. 2, 12–13.
4. Dudley Weinberg, "Meaning and Directions," *Understanding Jewish Prayer*, ed. Jakob J. Petuchowski (New York: Ktav Publishing House, Inc., 1972), 130.
5. Danzig's first paragraph initially uses the masculine third person, "to reward him when his life has ended." I have changed the English to make it both more inclusive and more personal.
6. See, for example, *Pirkei Avot* 4:1:

    בֶּן זוֹמָא אוֹמֵר...אֵיזֶהוּ עָשִׁיר הַשָּׂמֵחַ בְּחֶלְקוֹ, שֶׁנֶּאֱמַר (תהלים קכח), יְגִיעַ כַּפֶּיךָ כִּי תֹאכֵל אַשְׁרֶיךָ וְטוֹב לָךְ. אַשְׁרֶיךָ, בָּעוֹלָם הַזֶּה. וְטוֹב לָךְ, לָעוֹלָם הַבָּא.

    Ben Zoma says . . . who is the one who is rich? The one who rejoices in his portion, as it is written: *When you eat of the fruit of your labors, happy shall you be and well will it go with you*

(Ps. 128:2). [That is,] happy shall you be in this world, and well may it go with you in the world-to-come.

7. Deut. 30:19.
8. Prov. 19:21: *Many designs are in a man's mind, but it is the Lord's plan that is accomplished.*

רַבּוֹת מַחֲשָׁבוֹת בְּלֶב־אִישׁ וַעֲצַת יְהֹוָה הִיא תָקוּם

9. The full text of Numbers 15:39 is more specific in its warning, with a focus on lust and sexuality:

וְלֹא תָתוּרוּ אַחֲרֵי לְבַבְכֶם וְאַחֲרֵי עֵינֵיכֶם אֲשֶׁר־אַתֶּם זֹנִים אַחֲרֵיהֶם׃

The NJPS translates this: *So that you do not follow your heart and eyes in your lustful urge.* The context is that the Israelites should wear fringes on their garments and gaze upon them in order to remember and follow God's mitzvot. That is, one's eyes should be focused on God's presence in our lives so that we prioritize what God wants and not what we, more basely, might want to have. Danzig's original text, edited out here by the CCAR editorial team, continues: "Woe is me, for in following after my eyes I have contaminated them by looking upon women and everything impure"—a clear reference to the sexual context of the Numbers citation.

10. See the midrashic explanations below.
11. This the language of Isaiah 58:4, from the Haftarah portion read on Yom Kippur:

    Because you fast in strife and contention, and you strike with a wicked fist! Your fasting today is not such as to make your voice heard on high.

12. Isa. 1:6: *From head to foot, no spot is sound.*
13. BT *Yoma* 85b.
14. Eccles. 7:20.
15. Lev. 16:30. The text now turns from "I" to "we" as we pray together and for one another.
16. Ps. 51:19. NJPS translates this as *[You will not despise] a contrite and crushed heart.*
17. The word בְּתוֹכָם, "among them," is not grammatically necessary here. So I translate this as an allusion to its use in Exodus 25:8: וְעָשׂוּ לִי מִקְדָּשׁ וְשָׁכַנְתִּי בְּתוֹכָם, *Make for me a sanctuary that I may dwell among them,* signifying God's presence in the congregation, drawing near to each of us on the eve of Yom Kippur.
18. II Sam. 14:14.
19. *Sefer HaAggadah: The Book of Legends* © Copyright English Translation © 1992 by Schocken Books, Inc.; CD-ROM Version © 1995-2003 Davka Corporation.
20. Adin Steinsaltz, *Understanding the Tanya: Volume Three* (San Francisco: Jossey-Bass, 2007), 298.

Book Reviews

And God Created Recovery: Jewish Wisdom to Help You Break Free from Your Addiction, Heal Your Wounds, and Unleash Your Inner Freedom
by Rabbi Ilan Glazer
(St. Petersburg, FL: Maddix Publishing, 2019), 229 pp.

This book is unique. There are a number of excellent Jewish recovery books available. I have read many, and I recommend most.[1] *And God Created Recovery* teaches most of what we need to know to help our Jewish community address the tragic, growing, and often-ignored disease of addiction. Every Jewish professional should read this book, and keep it on hand.

Rabbi Glazer makes three primary arguments. First, the Jewish community largely continues to associate addiction with secrecy and shame. Jews are often ignorant about addiction/recovery, and few Jewish professionals are well equipped to support addicts or their loved ones. As a result, we as a community frequently isolate, stigmatize, and fail the large number of addicts among our people. Second, Judaism is entirely compatible with the twelve-step program of recovery, and Jewish wisdom is a valuable source that can support recovery. Finally, Rabbi Glazer advocates for an organized, public, accessible network of and for Jews in recovery, and he takes practical steps to launch it.

Rabbi Glazer has brought these different aspects together, along with a powerful, personal narrative. Previous authors have fought against the ignorance and fear that cause so many Jews to misjudge addicts, though as Rabbi Glazer demonstrates by citing research, negative stereotypes like "a *shikr* is a goy" (meaning that Jews aren't alcoholics) are still widespread among American Jews. Many rabbis have convincingly argued the second point, though sadly many Jews still believe that twelve-step programs are Christian or incompatible with Jewish observance. However, to my knowledge, nobody has initiated a worldwide Jewish recovery community of the sort Rabbi Glazer has recently launched.[2]

Rabbi Glazer's Our Jewish Recovery Network—now on Facebook —is unique. Though JACS,[3] Beit T'Shuvah,[4] and other organizations are well-known and do incredible work, they are largely tied to particular funders or geographic areas, leaving New York City and Los Angeles well-resourced and many Jewish communities underserved. Chabad has launched successful online connections and advocacy for Jews in recovery, along with other Orthodox institutions, but sadly, none of the liberal movements has yet done so. In the twenty-first century, with social media at our fingertips, and so many people getting their information primarily from the Internet, it is time for liberal Judaism to break the silence and save Jewish lives, in person and especially online.

And God Created Recovery is well-organized and divided into three main sections. Part 1, entitled "How Did We Get Here?" begins by citing statistics and scholarly research to provide a comprehensive and digestible overview of the reality of Jews and addiction. It then concludes with Rabbi Glazer's compelling narrative of his own addiction and journey of recovery—reason enough to read this book. His courage to share his personal story of recovery from multiple addictions is an inspiration to me, and I believe it will provide hope to many Jews who read this book.

Part 2 analyzes the twelve steps from a Jewish point of view. Rabbi Glazer brings the wisdom of our sacred texts to bear on one of the most significant books of the twentieth century, *Alcoholics Anonymous*. The texts he has collected here make it almost effortless to compile a text study, lesson plan, or sermon on this subject.

In Part 3, entitled "Additional Wisdom to Support Your Journey," Glazer presents Jewish principles and practices that are not always discussed as tools for recovery. These subjects include joy, surrender, Shabbat, and what Rabbi Abraham Joshua Heschel calls "radical amazement."

And God Created Recovery stands out from other books in the field for two reasons. First, while all recovery books written by rabbis focus on what rabbis are good at—teaching Torah—Rabbi Glazer also cites academic research on addiction in the Jewish community.[5]

Perhaps most importantly, Rabbi Glazer addresses a variety of addictive substances and compulsive behaviors, especially ones rarely discussed. While earlier contributions to the field have addressed compulsive overeating, compulsive gambling, and codependency, this book includes material on compulsions as varied and taboo as skin picking, pornography, and sex addiction. This honesty and realism is long overdue.

Nonetheless, no book is perfect. Part 3 is worthwhile, but quite disappointing relative to Parts 1 and 2. The section's title, "Additional Wisdom to Support Your Journey," is neither catchy nor inspiring. It is nonetheless accurate. Perhaps too accurate, as the word "additional" is sadly warranted. It does seem to be a collection of assorted add-ons.

Part 3 was occasionally repetitive. For example, Rabbi Glazer gives his website address three times in four pages (pp. 153–56). It is also filled with what felt like commercial plugs for what twelve-step fellowships refer to as "outside help." While most addicts (and lots of human beings who aren't addicts) benefit greatly from "outside help," one grows bored with the endless quotes from every podcaster or seminar leader Rabbi Glazer has found valuable. It's probably true that "learners are earners," and "the book you don't read won't help," but these pithy sayings do not, in my view, contribute to the book's holy purpose. The wisdom of Torah and the wisdom of Rabbi Glazer's own experience provides enough learning and inspiration.

And God Created Recovery is an inspiring resource all rabbis should have on hand to distribute to congregants struggling with addiction. It should be displayed prominently on the bookshelf, right next to *Alcoholics Anonymous*, to advertise that we are knowledgeable of addiction and welcoming to addicts and their families.

Notes

1. Rabbis Kerry Olitzky, Rami Shapiro, Paul Steinberg, Shais Taub, and Abraham Twerski have written extensively on these subjects. I particularly recommend Abraham Twerski, *Addictive Thinking: Understanding Self-Deception*, 2nd ed. (Center City, MN: Hazelden Publishing, 1997); Shais Taub, *God of Our Understanding: Jewish Spirituality and Recovery from Addiction* (Jersey City, NJ: KTAV, 2011); Rami Shapiro, *Recovery—The Sacred Art: The Twelve Steps as Spiritual Practice* (Woodstock, VT: Skylight Paths Publishing, 2009); and Paul Steinberg, *Recovery, the 12 Steps and Jewish Spirituality: Reclaiming Hope, Courage and Wholeness* (Woodstock, VT: Jewish Lights Publishing, 2014).
2. www.facebook.com/groups/ourjewishrecovery.

3. Jewish Alcoholics, Chemically dependent persons, and Significant others (JACS); jewishboard.org/listing/jewish-alcoholics-chemically-dependent-persons-and-significant-others-jacs/.
4. Rabbi Mark Borovitz is the Founding Rabbi of Beit T'shuvah, beittshuvah.org. See Rabbi Borovitz's piece in this issue, "Addiction Is a Spiritual Malady and Judaism Is a Spiritual Solution."
5. Example: Melanie Baruch, Abraham Benarroch, and Gary E. Rockman, "Alcohol and Substance Use in the Jewish Community: A Pilot Study," *Journal of Addiction* (June 16, 2015), https://www.ncbi.nlm.nih.gov/pmc/articles/PMC4487707/.

RABBI LAURIE E. GREEN (NY07) is the spiritual leader and education director at Kehila Chadasha in Montgomery County, Maryland. She served as an inspiration for the Addiction and Recovery section in this issue of the *Journal*, and frequently trains her colleagues on topics ranging from addiction/recovery and trauma, to feminist midrash and the needs of the transgender Jewish community. Rabbi Green is blessed to be an educator, activist, *ima*, organizer, counselor, spiritual guide, and aspiring yogi.

Recovery, the 12 Steps and Jewish Spirituality: Reclaiming Hope, Courage and Wholeness
by Paul Steinberg
(Woodstock, VT: Jewish Lights Publishing, 2014), 176 pp.

My first exposure to the masterful writing of Rabbi Paul Steinberg was his award-winning three-volume series, *Celebrating the Jewish Year*. Here I found the breadth of his Jewish wisdom and his belief in the spiritual possibilities of Jewish living. I have returned to this series numerous times.

I return even more frequently to *Recovery, the 12 Steps and Jewish Spirituality*.

In this important and personal endeavor, Rabbi Steinberg examines a difficult subject. The pages are full of helpful understandings of the twelve steps and recovery, considered through the lens of Jewish tradition. As well, the book carries a striking narrative: the author's own recovery from the depths of the disease of alcoholism. Sharing his own journey into and out of suffering, the author invites the reader to join him on a journey of Jewish spirituality.

The book is easy to navigate. From the opening Foreword and Preface by Rabbi Abraham Twerski and Harriet Rossetto, the reader is assured they are engaged with a work of substance. Throughout the book, the author honestly and courageously approaches the complex challenges of addiction and alcoholism with a grounded approach rooted in Jewish thought and text. Rabbi Steinberg allows himself to be exposed and raw in the public square, writing at times from his rabbinic voice and at times as a person in recovery. Writing out of both his professional and personal experience, his voice is both authoritative and compelling.

Along with biblical and Rabbinic texts, elements of Musar and Chasidic thought, modern philosophers, and well-known cultural icons, the book uses the "language of the heart." This is the language of recovery as it is called in twelve-step circles. Steinberg's use of "we" and "ours" throughout allows the reader to feel they are a part of the process of defining the parallels between Judaism and the twelve steps.

Chapter 1 examines addiction from a scientific approach and explains why medicine isn't enough to solve the problem. For those unaware of the medical view on the subject, this chapter is most poignant.

In Chapter 2, Rabbi Steinberg attempts to define "spirituality." He uses this as a vehicle to beautifully share his own Torah and his understanding of Judaism and God. In particular, he speaks to wrestling with "religion." This is most relevant, as it is often a hinderance to a person new in sobriety. Rabbi Steinberg confronts this topic most capably.

Chapter 3 challenges the reader to consider the complex psychological issues that motivate all of us. Steinberg invites the reader to recognize and honor their own self-worth, which can lead to deep gratitude, a core value in recovery and Judaism.

Chapter 4, "The Evil Inclination," uses timeless parables and scenes from Jewish tradition to make its point about discovering purpose. In one notable example, the author employs the story of Adam and Eve and the Tree of Knowledge as a framework for discussing the ideas of rebirth of consciousness and coming of age. Although this chapter could easily have read like a self-help book, Rabbi Steinberg instead guides the reader into a state of heightened self-awareness, leading to the possibility of spiritual-help, rather than self-help—and encouraging examination of one's own imperfections as an opportunity for growth.

An analysis of the complicated relationship between Jewish institutions and alcohol is the crux of Chapter 5. The reader is given examples of numerous moments in Jewish life when alcohol is present and positive—ranging from rituals of the Temple priesthood to contemporary Jewish preschoolers learning the Friday night blessing over wine—to help the reader understand notions such as "No rejoicing before God is possible except with wine" (BT *P'sachim* 109a). I found the author's use of these positive accounts of alcohol most helpful in understanding the potentially dangerous circumstances for an alcoholic participating in Jewish life. Interestingly, Rabbi Steinberg does not suggest that alcohol be removed entirely from ritual life; rather, he advocates heightened awareness and education, addressing the problematic nature of using alcohol as a marketing tool and the challenges associated with alcohol and Purim. This sensitive discussion affirms the need to attend more fully to the suffering that the disease of alcoholism and addiction can cause.

The next section of the book, "The Covenant of Recovery," is an eye-opener. Walking the reader through the twelve steps in actual practice, he directly connects each step with Jewish values and thought found at the core experiences of the twelve-step process.

The final section of the book, "12 Texts for the 12 Steps," is my favorite. Here, the academic, philosophic, recovering alcoholic, and theological voices of Rabbi Steinberg come together as one—the rabbi speaking from his pulpit. In what reads like a series of short *d'rashot*, Rabbi Steinberg presents each step and associated Jewish text—describing what the twelve steps are like in practice and what Judaism can teach us about the experience. As Jewish professionals who will all encounter people in recovery—whether we realize it or not—we will benefit from this section especially.

I have had the blessing of learning from and meeting Rabbi Steinberg on a few occasions, including at a book release event for this volume. At that event, he signed my copy, "בידידות" (in friendship). After returning to this book, I feel that we have a friend in recovery in Rabbi Steinberg. He has given us a gift—a prolific understanding of the twelve-step process, the world of recovery, and Jewish spirituality.

RABBI MICHAEL SHEFRIN (LA16) serves as associate rabbi at Temple Emanu-El in Sarasota, Florida, where he lives with his wife, Shayna, and son, Jacob. While in the midst of an exciting career in the entertainment industry, Michael experienced a life-changing shift in his goals after volunteering in the Jewish community.

BOOK REVIEWS

Today, he finds fulfillment helping people of all ages and backgrounds connect to their spirituality and elevate their lives and the world through Judaism.

Editors' Note: For more of Paul Steinberg's wisdom, please see his article "Addiction in Body, Mind, and Jewish Spirituality" in the *CCAR Journal* (Summer 2015): 17–35.

The Talmud of Relationships
by Rabbi Amy Scheinerman
(Philadelphia: JPS, 2018)
Vol. 1, *God, Self, and Family*, xxxi + 215 pp.; Vol. 2, *The Jewish Community and Beyond*, xxxi + 253 pp.

Roughly ten years ago, Paul Socken, a Jewish Studies professor at the University of Waterloo, edited an intriguing collection of essays under the title, *Why Study Talmud in the Twenty-First Century?* (Lexington Books, 2009). In aggregate, the contributors sought to answer the question of the book's title along two paths. One was a religious (particularly yeshivah) approach striving to move beyond the standard "Brisker" method, developed in the early nineteenth century by Rabbi Hayyim of Velozhin, that emphasized *minhag v'halachah*, the practical outcome of any *sugya* (Talmudic discussion) exclusively with the tools of the Rabbinic tradition. The second was to explore the value of the Talmud within the context of the disciplines of modern university.

The Summer 2014 edition of the *Reform Jewish Quarterly* was devoted to the same question—why study Talmud in the twenty-first century?—specifically with regard to Reform Judaism; that is, somewhere between the traditional yeshivah and the university. Guest editors Debra Landsberg and Daniel Bronstein collected essays that argued, despite the early Reformers disdain for classic Rabbinic literature, the Talmud is indeed embedded in modern liberal Jewish religious thought and practice. Further, they gathered testimonies of rabbinic colleagues who have engaged in the teaching and/or personal study of Talmud in their professional lives.

So, one can make a compelling argument for a Reform Jew to study Talmud in the twenty-first century. The question to ask now is: how? When it comes to synagogue text study, Scripture is easy. Few Reform congregations do not have courses of study that engage in *parashat hashavuah,* or haftarah, or Tanach. Even seventh graders preparing for the celebration of bar/bat mitzvah can understand the rhetoric, context, narrative flow, and meaning of most of Scripture. Talmud, on the other hand, is many degrees of difficulty more challenging. The work is much much larger, and its style of writing tends to be schematic. Entering the world of Talmud seems to require a level of patience and fortitude far greater than that required for the most obscure passages of Torah.

You cannot learn to swim, the saying goes, until you actually get into the water. If the water is too hot or cold, or the currents are too strong, a beginner might just give up at the start. Further, in Talmud, wherever you start, you are in the middle. Every text, from the first words of the first chapter of the first tractate, assumes knowledge drawn from other parts of the document. The virtue of Talmud study is precisely that one can start anywhere. And the challenge is that the very act of starting presupposes a wealth of knowledge. Continuing the swimming analogy, the text is like a diving pool. You can enter anywhere, but it is all a deep end. Rabbi Amy Scheinerman has put forward a guide for both rabbis and their congregants/students that eases the entry into the "waters."

The Talmud of Relationships has been published in two volumes, each containing seven chapters. There is no specific order either to the volumes (each contains the same introduction) or to the chapters themselves. Each chapter is organized according to a consistent principle. It is given a thematic title ("Approaching Prayer," "Honoring Our Parents," or "Moving to the Land of Israel," for instance), and a text or texts are indicated. Each chapter then begins with "Why Study this Passage?," continues with a reading and explanation of the text, and ends with "Continuing the Conversation." Rabbi Scheinerman notes in her introduction, "My goal is to open Talmud to anyone who is interested" (p. xvii). Access is therefore made as easy as possible. If one of the themes in one of the volumes particularly resonates, then start there!

The Talmudic passages chosen serve, I believe, two purposes. They are relatively free of Rabbinic jargon and thus can be readily understood. Further, they are provocative; that is, they respond to and address concepts and issues that often touch on our own lives, such as faith, anger, suffering, or authority. With the introductory "Why Study This Passage?," Scheinerman reinforces the connection between the Talmudic discussions and the contemporary reader. She not only explicates the relevance, but also does so by drawing on modern resources—social sciences, medicine, and psychology, among them. If one feels daunted by the lack of sufficient knowledge in order to tackle a page of a tractate, Scheinerman subtly reminds a mostly well-educated readership that they do have it. It might not be in Jewish sources, but it is nevertheless a relevant background.

As one's own educational background might inform the Talmudic texts presented, in "Continuing the Conservation," the passages can inform our modern sensibilities. With this section, Scheinerman directs the reader to both Jewish and secular sources for inducing further reflection on the theme of each chapter.

Rabbi Scheinerman has produced a valuable resource. Through fluid writing and with wide-ranging scholarship, she has created an excellent introduction to the study of Talmud. Fourteen "lessons," even in expert hands, is just an initial testing of the waters. Scheinerman scatters all sorts of hints of further inquiry: What is the conceptual move from tannaitic Mishnah to amoraic Gemara? What are the social/cultural distinctions between a Rome-dominated Jerusalem Talmud and the Persian *Bavli*? Just how is the narrative of the text constructed? What is history and what is myth?

In the spirit of the classic Hillel story of the person who insisted on learning Torah while standing on one foot, Rabbi Scheinerman has laid down a starting path and said *Ta ul'mad* (go on and learn).

RABBI PAUL GOLOMB (NY75) is senior scholar of the Vassar Temple, Poughkeepsie, New York, and a past Editor of *The Reform Jewish Quarterly*.

Mourning and Mitzvah: A Guided Journal for Walking the Mourner's Path through Grief to Healing, revised and expanded 25th anniversary edition
by Rabbi Anne Brener, L.C.S.W.
(Nashville: Jewish Lights Publishing, 2017), 313 pp.

Anne Brener has done it again! Or, better put, Anne Brener has done it further. The success of her first edition (1993) and her own development since that time have proven the need for a kind of "update," or supplement to what has already meant so much to so many people. In the interest of full disclosure, I will say that I had been part of her continuing work, having shared devotion in the community of healers that began to emerge in the 1990s and having been invited to guide her through her rabbinic thesis. (On this very subject, with study of Rabbinic sources for support.) I tried to be a "tough" advisor to her wide-open spirit and excellent, wistful mind. So my second disclosure is that I am not a client for her creative and elaborate experience of the grieving process, but I am an advocate for multiple approaches to the grieving experience and a reader of most of the books that are in the popular intellectual culture about death and dying.[1] Brener's book is an essential part of that bibliography, and she herself suggests that the book can be experienced in separate parts according to different people's needs. In that sense the book is both a complete whole and a sequence of modules.

And I have also learned from her as she offers especially the kind of wisdom captured in the simple anecdote that opens her book: She was hiking in southern Oregon, and suddenly got caught in the current of a river that overpowered her. Prospects did not look good. She began to fight the current, but to no avail. (Most of us would fight the current.) Then, as she writes: "I took a deep breath and let the river carry me downstream. This surrender to the swift current brought relaxation. When the river suddenly narrowed, I found the strength to swim to shore" (p. 3).

The analogy is obvious, even if it is not perfectly applicable in every instance, and even if not every river narrows so conveniently. Sometimes people drown in such rivers. But, after the fact, one also realizes how important it is not to fight against every emotional current and to wait until there is some change in the way the river is running. The point is made—even in an "imperfect" metaphor.

And, I could argue, that the advice implied by the anecdote may be the foundation of the most important thing you must learn about grieving. Every book I've read about grieving contains the urgency of letting go as basic to the process of whatever tradition one embraces, whether experienced by someone as classic as C. S. Lewis or someone as contemporary as Leon Wieseltier. And its other great truth is that eventually one yearns for the spring. Brener's book gives permission to live in the incomplete but consecrated dark—and to yearn for that spring. In a sense her "spring" is its own double entendre: the refreshing waters and the brighter spring season.

In fact it is the imperfection in Brener's river metaphor that makes it so helpful. Even this little story will mean different things to different people—at least around its edges. Here it is the water; there it is the season. But Anne Brener has an instinct for those stories that can be used in different ways. Brener's book is loaded with figurative promise—rendering elements of truth in situations where complete and perfect truths are not possible. It seems that part of her wisdom is to teach people to accept partial solutions in imperfect situations.

Teaching Anne is always a thrill—sometimes a challenge, but always a thrill. She comes to her inquiries with some hypotheses that may seem like preconceived notions, but that even she subjects to scrutiny, change, and modification. As a therapist she has been exposed to a variety of "versions" of the mourning-grieving circumstance. She has learned that every mourner will mourn in her own way, and that therefore, exemplary anecdotes, and the urgings that they prompt, will take shape differently for each of us in our inevitable unhappinesses. The metaphors sustain a kind of partial ontological status, and they are partial particularly in the way they apply to every individual. But in a further sense, all personal stories are parables. We can apply them even if they do not match up perfectly with our personal experience.

And the individual is the book's primary concern. Anne Brener is a therapist, and she works day to day on the private and personal level and then discusses that work on a larger—more global—canvas. Thus her book includes many anecdotes about individual situations of mourning—strategies that sometimes did not work for individuals or even for herself. She does NOT provide a "one size fits all" solution and relies instead on traditional mourning practice to address the broader more inclusive and generalized approach to "what one should do" in times of grief. Odds are, she suggests, "this might work," or this helped many people with whom I have worked.

So sometimes the book seems a little "full" because she includes strategies and associations that may be important to different people at different times. The book is too large and cumbersome to be read in bed, and probably shouldn't be anyway, in keeping with its subject. The sukkah material, interesting though it is, reminds me of Rabbi Edgar Magnin's concern about an early siddur of the Reform Movement: "Too heavy for some people to lift," he groused.

I would have wished for a bit more careful editing in this new version of her work. The addition of new material, especially of her exercises recruiting the sukkah as a locus for healing, should have been the occasion to reexamine some stylistic issues, and even an occasional simplification of a complex Jewish principle. There is a suggestion in the book that some of her kabbalistic insights have canonical standing or provenance, when they might not. That doesn't mean that the legendary frameworks can't be helpful in thinking one's way through illness and death; but it does mean that one is recognizing that a particular interpretation or use of the text may be personal and hermeneutical, rather than scholarly. Furthermore, and especially for scholarly purposes, it is not helpful to view the Talmud as "uttering" this or that bit of wisdom. (A lot of people make this mistake, but it grates on me, nonetheless.) Few people are likely to be moved by hearing a rabbi speak of "the Talmud having said" one thing or another; and one hopes that any rabbi knows that the Talmud, as such, doesn't speak. So that is my objection to Anne Brener's epigrams; even one that is appropriately deployed like the line from *Kiddushin* 72b, which may be considered an appropriate application to the chapter on the world of souls, and which gives a false impression of Talmudic discourse (p. 215).

In recent years, we have seen a panoply of good books on death and dying, aging, health and illness, and responses to grief. Something is in the air, and it may be that this "something" is one of the principal reasons that people join synagogues and rely still on rabbis, even though formal affiliation rates seem to be declining. Death is not declining, and tens of thousands continue to rely on systems to respond to grief, while some—or many, in this case—like their system encased in rich experiential ritual possibility.

So here is an objection that has a boomeranged value that my not even have been intended. *Mourning and Mitzvah* is layered with Jewish experiences and ideas that may be foreign to the *"stam"* mourner. I hope that won't distance some readers who may otherwise benefit from the book's wisdom but who don't know the lingo of Jewish life. The "boomerang" I refer to comes around precisely as the book's wisdom may actually be a way of introducing the uninitiated Jew to some traditions and some language that may be of interest and value to the unfamiliar—regardless of their status as a mourner or the stage of life they may be in. There is, in other words, the potential for some of this book to be a Jewish primer. (The phrase these days is "an unintended consequence.")

Anne Brener's book is a valuable contribution to a genre and to a trend; and the help that I know she has brought personally to countless people is also available—especially now—through the printed medium of *Mourning and Mitzvah*, the 25th Anniversary Edition. Congratulations to its author; and strength going forward to its readers!

Note

1. Following is a list of important books that have appeared in the past couple of decades. They fall into several categories: personal experience; philosophical reflection and argument, ethics, pastoral care, theological positioning, sociology, literary representation—prose and poetry: Joan Didion, *The Year of Magical Thinking*; Hillel Halkin, *After One Hundred and Twenty*; Joel H. Baron and Sara Paasche-Orlow, *Deathbed Wisdom of the Hasidic Masters*; Sandra M. Gilbert, *Death's Door*; Lewis Lapham, *Lapham's Quarterly: Death* vol. 6, no. 4); Roz Chast, *Can't We Talk About Something More Pleasant?*; Seneca, *How to Die*, ed. James S. Romm; David R. Dow, *Things I've Learned from Dying*; Andrew Stark, *The Consolations of Mortality*; Leon Wieseltier, *Kaddish*; Eric Weiss, *Mishkan Aveilut: Where Grief Resides*; plus countless handbooks and guidebooks by Kerry Olitzky, William Cutter, Maurice Lamm, and Ron Wolfson. This is not meant to be a research list, but an indication of what has become available in the last twenty-five years. When one adds the latest works from the Hebrew canon, plus the formal Jewish religious resources, one is exhausted keeping up. At least this is true: one's sense of immortality is exhausted by this inventory.

RABBI WILLIAM (BILL) CUTTER (C65) continues to teach part time after fifty-four years on the faculty of HUC-JIR/Los Angeles. Along with some volunteering, he is enjoying private *chevruta* study with some of our colleagues and the pleasure of being father-in-law to a younger rabbi.

Poetry

Ben Zoma Asks, "Who Is a Hero?"

Daniel Polish

The Mother

After stillbirth
and after stillbirth
and after stillbirth
To yet again conceive
This time
    To dwell in her house
    As the joyful mother of children

The Author

After rejection and rejection and rejection
After the boxes of unfinished projects
To yet
set your chair at your desk
And believe
    Of making many books there is no end

We All

Scored still and scarred from
The indignities
Frustrations
And failures
Still each day to essay
A fresh embarkation
    Renewing always the work of creating

RABBI DANIEL POLISH (C68) is the rabbi of Congregation Shir Chadash of the Hudson Valley, LaGrange, New York.

POETRY

On Studying Sacred Texts

Judith Offer

Do not go alone into the Word.
Take someone with you to the place
Where all questions are answered
But all answers are questions.
Travel in a truth-seeking troupe; someone
Is bound to know which verse you're on
And you can reel each other back in
When you slide off the page.

The Book of Endless Light
Is trackless, sometimes steep, verbose, or
Thicketed with metaphor. Each flower
Is the first of its kind, and the last.
You may be frightened at times by
The unspeakable beauty.
Terror can unmake your concentration,
So you do not hear the meanings
Bubble to the surface. You can die of thirst,
With springs everywhere.

It is written, Do not go alone into the Word.
Thus, be a minimum of two of you.
A teacher is the preferred companion,
Or a lover will suffice,
But avoid authorities, and pessimists,
And anyone else who thrives on comparison,
Or who has never studied a dust mote in the sun.

JUDITH OFFER has had two daughters, five books of poetry, and dozens of plays. (Eighteen of the latter, including six musicals, have been produced.) She has read her poetry at scores of poetry venues, but is particularly delighted to have been included in the Library of Congress series and on *All Things Considered,* on NPR. Among her plays are *A Shirtwaist Tale,* a klezmer musical set in Lower East Side New York, and *It Could Always Be Worse,* a children's musical based on the old Yiddish folktale. (The composer for both is Arkadi Serper.)

And take your angels, if they'll go. Also,
Take the memories of those who have gone before,
Yet can form words to speak of it.
When you have gathered all you can;
Teachers, lovers, seekers,
Angels, and memories,
Take a deep breath, take someone's hand,
And take my blessing. And go.

POETRY

Elon Musk, I Trusted You with My Bionic Heart

Matthue Roth

In the moments between asphalt and air
the thought *can cars do this*
as left behind as gravity

A line of unbroken workers
from a factory in Oklahoma to
the Earth's outer atmosphere, one mile
straight up

As a kid I thought I could be bionic
replace my defective muscles
one by one, sweat with steel
what's not to lose

Elon, our dreams are made of ions
the same as anything else in our head
pain is just a hiccup of electricity, like love

I could give you the equation
but I can't tell you how
to add it up

MATTHUE ROTH wrote the novel *Rules of My Best Friend's Body* and the picture book *My First Kafka*. By day, he creates virtual reality experiences at Google. He helps edit Hevria.com, an online creative community about faith, and lives in Brooklyn with his family.

The Day God Destroys Sodom and Gomorrah

Deborah Bacharach

She wears black leather boots, big metal hoops
at the ankles and her tight jeans with the
big metal buckle and silk in sways
of black and gray. She shaves her head.

On this day, as on all days, she commands
all notes. From her open mouth, the dark river
pours out, blood laps the shore.
She does not make mistakes.
She says, *I wish the wars were all over.*

The Ox

But Lot's wife, behind him, looked back, and she became a pillar of salt.
—Gen. 19:26

The ox awakens, ears ringing
from the bellows in his dreams.
He lowers his broken
horns and walks.

The ox comes slowly, swishing
his long pink tongue.
Dust and flies ride
his hooves as he plods.

DEBORAH BACHARACH has a B.A. in English from Swarthmore College and an M.A. in Creative Writing from the University of Minnesota. She is the author of a book of poetry, *After I Stop Lying*, and has published in *Pembroke Magazine, Cimarron Review, The Southampton Review*, and *The Texas Review* among many others. She is a member of Temple Beth Am in Seattle, Washington.

He does not dread. He does
what he must: lick.

From her crown to her tendons,
to the hard ridges
of her toes, Lot's wife is
all ferocious salt. Hard grains
send up small rockets
as she dissolves.

Passed Out under His Daughters' Hands, Lot Dreams of His Wife

> Come, let us make our father drink wine, and we will lie with him, that we may preserve offspring through our father.
> —Gen. 19:32

His wife bends over the well,
the girl she was the day they met.
Warm pomegranates, her breasts.
On generous hips, her skirts
shift like afternoon shadows,
blessings of rest and sanctity.

He settles in those shadows, sips
the sweet water she offers.
Sulfur stabs—sharp, vicious. Fire rends
the tent of peace. She dissolves
in his hands.

He trembles through this dream
twice. He tastes tears.

POETRY

Pregnant with the Dead

Susan Rich

I am a woman swollen with the history of my dead,
great aunts and second cousins murdered

in the old country—bloated with fragments of survivors

who hid months in garbage cans, others in partisan forests;
I'm their bandaged daughters gauzed from toe to forehead

to keep safe from search patrols, from their first rapes.

Yes, I am a body awash in stories of noodle kugel, borscht—
watch the heavy arms of the women waving like sails

as they knead challah each Friday morning,

can't conceive of a few hours free.
What can I do with the women who occupy my vertebrae,

take over my hips and tongue?

They say *coconut bars, mundel bread, hamantaschen*.
They say *that's your problem* as they stride

into my kitchen, toss out the nonfat yogurt, the tofu treats.

It is a rumba move of before and after.
And of course, many *volk* murdered—

SUSAN RICH is the author of five books, most recently *Cloud Pharmacy*, shortlisted for the Julie Suk prize, honoring poetry books from independent presses. She has been awarded a Fulbright Fellowship, PEN USA Award for Poetry, and the Times (of London) Literary Supplement Award. Her poems have appeared in the *Harvard Review, New England Review, O Magazine*, and *World Literature Today*. Her next book is *Blue Atlas*.

abducted our young girls, butchered our sons.

And now, my dead tell me, it's time to enjoy
a brioche—a week in *the Disneyland*.

Don't my dead deserve to mist their skin with *Shalimar*

at the airport perfume cathedrals?
Enough time spent on nightmares!

Instead let us hike up the heat, make selfies.
And later, when it quiets on the hotel balcony,

we vanish like light vessels almost escaped out to sea.

First Graduate School Reception, September

I focused on the pattern of his phrases

his syntactical passion
praising Passover seders, the lyric lift

of the accent on *charoset* and *maror*.

Shrugged it off until someone else
by the bar offered a semiotics of Elijah.

Did everyone in Eugene, Oregon,

celebrate Passover or was this gang
of scholars embarking on new research

for a *We Love Seders* campaign?

Such sweetness in the way he over-poured
our tumblers of nonkosher wine.

What was it that betrayed me?

Later, I scrutinized my body in the mirror,
the six-pointed star dangling by my throat.

This is what I had tasted: small appetizers

of exotic and abused.
My non-Christian skin lit-up

like a lantern or a Russian pogrom.

And then I knew: I was the first,
their first 100 percent full-blooded, *potential* Jewish friend.

No choice but to serve as reluctant guide—

to wash and dress a uniform of humanness—
perhaps tight fitting, perhaps our only one.

A Poem for Mr. Raphael Siv at the Irish Jewish Museum

Portobello, Dublin 8

Write a poem for the museum you demanded
as if you could order a poem the way you
order bread, toasted or with lox and cream cheese.

Or even one line. And this second plea
is what persuades me that you, Mr. Raphael Siv,
are a man who believes in poetry.

And why not? Aren't you Irish *and* Jewish?
a heritage any writer would covet, hurriedly
convert to, if it were that easy. And yet,

this vigil of yours sparks its own
clear artistry. When you set off to work
each morning, traveling down the South Circular

Road, can you sense the museum's
awakening beyond its curtains, prayer
shawls, and scrolls? As you open the interior

doors of the former Walworth Synagogue,
I imagine you welcomed in by the *Shechinah*,
your own bright *avodah*. Upstairs, the bride

will greet you and the pews with brass
plaques removed will recite their humble blessing,
for their tzaddik, their storyteller, for you.

POETRY

Variations on a Horizon (Autumn 2018)

Marc Nieson

Today in Pittsburgh we awaken a little further from the sun. The clocks changed, they say, minutes lost. While outside my third floor bedroom window, I swear, the view's the same. The same slanted rooftops and tip of telephone pole. The same starlings on the wire jockeying for position. The same swathe of sky that fools me into thinking I'm near a seashore.

Still, it feels a little harder getting out of bed this morning. To leave the plaid comforter and puzzling crossword behind. The toothbrush and the floss, a touch heavier today. The mirror's fog a bit more difficult to face.

And yet, blessed is the mint toothpaste and the toilet paper. Blessed the starlings and telephone pole and unseen beaches. Blessed my wife, already up and headed downstairs, and our daughter in a different city. Blessed that same indifferent sun, inching across the windowpane.

Blessed is the stairwell and each step down I must watch now. And blessed the brewed coffee and teaspoon. Blessed the awaiting paper on the front stoop, though its print may prove a little wet with dew and its news will surely stain.

Standing there before the doorframe I'll catch another angle of that slice of sky, now clearly landlocked behind trembling treetops. Certain leaves lost to what is surely autumn now. A new chill in the air, enough so that I'll take pause before going on, and grab myself a jacket. The one with the torn lapel.

MARC NIESON is a graduate of the Iowa Writers' Workshop and NYU Film School. His background includes children's theatre, cattle chores, and a season with a one-ring circus. His memoir, *Schoolhouse: Lessons on Love and Landscape,* came out from Ice Cube Press in 2016. He's won a Raymond Carver Short Story Award, Pushcart Prize nominations, and been noted in Best American Essays. He teaches at Chatham University, edits *The Fourth River*, and is at work on a new novel, *Houdini's Heirs*.

POETRY

Psalm 51: Variations

Ken Seide

Adonai, open my lips, so that I may speak your praise.
Open my heart, so that I may love my neighbor.
Open my hands, so that I may repair our world.
Open my eyes, so that I see the well and save myself.

Poet's note: The well refers to B'reishit/Genesis 21:19.

KEN SEIDE is the pen name of a resident of Newton, Massachusetts. His poems have appeared in journals including *Midstream, Poetica, New Vilna Review, Voices Israel, Soul-Lit, Kerem, The Deronda Review, Napalm and Novocain,* and *Rat's Ass Review/Love & Ensuing Madness*. One of his poems is scheduled to appear in an anthology tentatively titled *101 Jewish Poems for the Third Millennium.*

Tzaddik

Jack M. Freedman

Thirty-six tzaddikim

One of them
is *Mashiach*

I only know
complexity
from those
attempting
to fulfill
a complex

In *G'matria*:

number 35
loh
meaning "nothing"

number 36
ohel
meaning "brightness"

Within this void
shines an *Alef*

One leader emerging
One light emanating
One longing erased

JACK M. FREEDMAN is a poet and spoken word artist from Staten Island, New York. Publications featuring his work span the globe. Countries in which poems found home include the United States, Canada, UK, France, The Netherlands, Ukraine, India, Nigeria, Singapore, and Thailand.

Call for Papers: *Maayanot*

The *CCAR Journal: The Reform Jewish Quarterly* is committed to serving its readers' professional, intellectual, and spiritual needs. In pursuit of that objective, the *Journal* created a new section known as *Maayanot* (Primary Sources), which made its debut in the Spring 2012 issue.

We continue to welcome proposals for *Maayanot* —translations of significant Jewish texts, accompanied by an introduction as well as annotations and/or commentary. *Maayanot* aims to present fresh approaches to materials from any period of Jewish life, including but not confined to the biblical or Rabbinic periods. When appropriate, it is possible to include the original document in the published presentation.

Please submit proposals, inquiries, and questions to *Maayanot* editor Rabbi Daniel Polish, dpolish@optonline.net.

Along with submissions for *Maayanot*, the *Journal* encourages the submission of scholarly articles in fields of Jewish Studies, as well as other articles that fit within our Statement of Purpose.

The *CCAR Journal: The Reform Jewish Quarterly*
Published quarterly by the Central Conference of American Rabbis

Volume LXVI, No. 4. Issue Number: Two hundred sixty-two

Fall 2019

STATEMENT OF PURPOSE

The *CCAR Journal: The Reform Jewish Quarterly* seeks to explore ideas and issues of Judaism and Jewish life, primarily—but not exclusively—from a Reform Jewish perspective. To fulfill this objective, the *Journal* is designed to:

1. provide a forum to reflect the thinking of informed and concerned individuals—especially Reform rabbis—on issues of consequence to the Jewish people and the Reform movement;
2. increase awareness of developments taking place in fields of Jewish scholarship and the practical rabbinate, and to make additional contributions to these areas of study;
3. encourage creative and innovative approaches to Jewish thought and practice, based upon a thorough understanding of the traditional sources.

The views expressed in the *Journal* do not necessarily reflect the position of the Editorial Board or the Central Conference of American Rabbis.

The *CCAR Journal: The Reform Jewish Quarterly* (ISSN 1058-8760) is published quarterly by the Central Conference of American Rabbis, 355 Lexington Avenue, 8th Floor, New York, NY 10017. Application to mail at periodical postage rates is pending at New York, NY and at additional mailing offices.

Subscriptions should be sent to CCAR Executive Offices, 355 Lexington Avenue, 8th Floor, New York, NY 10017. Subscription rate as set by the Conference is $150 for a one-year subscription, $199 for a two-year subscription. Overseas subscribers should add $36 per year for postage. POSTMASTER: Please send address changes to *CCAR Journal: The Reform Jewish Quarterly*, c/o Central Conference of American Rabbis, 355 Lexington Avenue, 8th Floor, New York, NY 10017.

Typesetting and publishing services provided by Publishing Synthesis, Ltd., 39 Crosby Street, New York, NY 10013.

Copyediting services provided by Michael Isralewitz.

The *CCAR Journal: The Reform Jewish Quarterly* is indexed in the *Index to Jewish Periodicals*. Articles appearing in it are listed in the *Index of Articles on Jewish Studies* (of *Kirjath Sepher*) and in *Religious and Theological Abstracts*.

© Copyright 2019 by the Central Conference of American Rabbis
All rights reserved.
ISSN 1058-8760

ISBN: 978-0-88123-338-4

www.ingramcontent.com/pod-product-compliance
Lightning Source LLC
Chambersburg PA
CBHW050441240426
43661CB00055B/2469